FORMAT RECOGNITION PROCESS FOR MARC RECORDS

A LOGICAL DESIGN

Report on a project partially sponsored by the U. S. Office of Education,
conducted by the Information Systems Office,
Library of Congress.

INFORMATION SCIENCE AND AUTOMATION DIVISION

AMERICAN LIBRARY ASSOCIATION

Chicago 1970

International Standard Book Number 0-8389-3122-7 (1970)

Library of Congress Catalog Card Number 70-139250

Published by the
American Library Association
50 East Huron Street
Chicago, Illinois 60611

Printed in the United States of America

FOREWORD

Format recognition is a significant part of the MARC and RECON projects at the Library of Congress. Although much of the work has been completed, much remains to be accomplished. Recognizing, however, that the design work could be useful to automation programs in other institutions, the Library felt that publication of this document would be of value.

Since the American Library Association, through its Information Science and Automation Division, is one of the principal professional organizations concerned with library automation, the Library of Congress is pleased to have its cooperation in the publication of this report.

L. Quincy Mumford
Librarian of Congress

Table of Contents

Table of Contents, Continued

Table of Contents, Continued

Table of Contents, Continued

I.   INTRODUCTION

Format recognition is a technique designed for the computer analysis of bibliographic records. From cues provided by the content and the context of the data, a MARC record will be produced complete with: 1) tags required for the identification of fields, 2) indicators to further define the characteristics of fields, 3) subfield codes for the identification of data elements within fields, and 4) codes representing certain data elements such as language, country of publication, etc.

The algorithms contained in this report concentrate on current English language monographs. Concurrrent with the flowcharting and the program coding for this portion of the project, analysis is continuing for the required modifications and additions to these algorithms to handle other roman alphabet and retrospective records.

Initial efforts assume no human editing. However, the efficiency of automatically determing a condition that rarely occurs in a biblio- graphic record must be measured against the computer time expended to look for that particular condition. This evaluation is now in progress and it is felt that the results will demonstrate the need for records partially edited by humans plus the format recognition process to complete the full editing. The amount of human involvement is not yet known, but whatever it may be, cost savings in terms of manpower should be significant. Statis- tical analysis of current English language monograph records indicates that approximately 67 percent of the records processed by format recognition with no previous human editing should be error free. Regardless of the amount of editing required, proofing of the records will continue.

The source data for the format recognition process is the LC manuscript card, produced during the normal course of cataloging. Procedures have been defined for the transcription of the data into machine-readable form. The resultant machine-readable data becomes the input to the format recognition program which performs the analysis and produces a MARC record.

This report contains the logical design for the format recognition process used by the MARC/RECON staff at the Library for testing records against the algorithms and for the detailed flowcharting for the implementations of the computer programs. In summary, this is a working document and no attempt has been made to produce a finished product from the viewpoint of composition and style. To make the technical content available as rapidly as possible was the most important factor in publication.

This study was conducted under the direction of Lucia J. Rather and the keyword lists appendixes were prepared by James Agenbroad, both members of the Library's Information Systems Office. The logical analysis was performed under contract by Coyle & Stewart, Computer Applications Consultants.

I wish to thank the U. S. Office of Education for its support and also to acknowledge the efforts of all Information Systems Office personnel concerned with this study.

Henriette D. Avram
Project Director, MARC/RECON

II.   MARC RECORD PROCESSING

The MARC record format considered in this report is the Library of Congress MARC II Internal Processing Format. This is a master record format, used internally at the Library of Congress, from which are derived the MARC II Communications Format records used in the MARC Distribution Service.*
The difference between the two formats is primarily one of internal arrangement of the record, rather than content.

For those who are familiar with the MARC II Communications Format, the major differences of the MARC II Internal Processing Format are:

1.   There are additional fixed-length areas at the beginning of the Internal Processing Format record needed for internal processing: the Quality Control Block and the Communications Area. Also, some fields in the various fixed-length areas are carried in binary, rather than as decimal characters.

2.   The LC Card Number and the Variable Fixed Fileds are each carried as a fixed-length area preceding the Record Directory, rather than following it as in the Communications Format.

3.   In the Internal Processing Format, the starting position and length of each variable field are carried in its Record Directory entry in binary, rather than as decimal characters. Each entry may also contain other information needed for internal processing.

4.   In the Internal Processing Format, the subfield codes in a variable field

---

*The Communications Format is described in Books: A MARC Format, 4th ed., issued as v. 1 of The MARC Manuals, 2d ed., Chicago, American Library Association, 1970.

II.   MARC RECORD PROCESSING, Continued

do not immediately precede their subfields, as in the Communications
Format, but are grouped together at the beginning of the field. They
follow the standard delimiter following the indicator(s) and precede
the start of text, separated by another standard delimiter.

II.A.   MARC II Internal Processing Format

A MARC record consists of bibliographic data derived from an LC Manuscript
Card produced during the normal cataloging process. In the MARC II Internal
Processing Format, this data is arranged together with bookkeeping and control
information in four major areas. These are:

1. Bookkeeping Area
2. Fixed Field Bibliographic Information
3. Record Directory of Variable Fields
4. Variable Field Bibliographic Data

A short description of each of these areas follows:

1. Bookkeeping Area

There are four general bookkeeping areas at the beginning of a record.
Together these areas describe the physical attributes of a record,
provide status information about a record, and contain a unique identification number and other sequencing information for file maintenance.
Specifically, these four areas are:

a. Quality Control Block - 6 bytes - contains identification and
sequencing information used for sorting and other file maintenance
(removed from record when transferred to Master Data Base).

b. Record Leader - 12 bytes - contains the record's length, date,
status, and bibliographic category.

c. Communications Area - 12 bytes - contains starting position and size
of the Record Directory and additional record type and status
information.

d. Record Control Block - 14 bytes - contains a unique number identifying
the record, consisting essentially of the LC Card Number.

II.A.   MARC II Internal Processing Format, Continued

2.   Fixed Field Bibliographic Information

This area contains codes and other fixed-length information which are
descriptive of the bibliographic information in the record; this area
is 54 bytes in length.

3.   Record Directory of Variable Fields

This area contains fixed-length (12 bytes) entries, one for each variable
field in the record. Each entry contains a numeric tag which identifies
the variable field, the starting position of the variable field data in the
record, and the variable field's length. In addition, processing codes and
other flags may be stored in a Record Directory entry, for use by MARC
production programs at the Library of Congress. The Record Directory is
maintained in sort order on the variable field's tag number to facilitate
processing.

4.   Variable Field Bibliographic Data

The text input from a Manuscript Card is carried, for the most part, in the
form of variable-field data. Each of these variable fields may be sub-
divided into subfields, with each subfield being described by a subfield
code (alpha character), which is inserted preceding the text. In addition,
one to two indicator codes may be included in the information preceding the
text to further identify the field and describe interrealationships between
fields. The order of these variable fields in the record is not significant
due to the existence of the Record Directory - the starting position and
length of each variable field is contained in its corresponding Record
Directory entry.

The layout on the following page shows the organization of a MARC II Internal
Processing Format record.

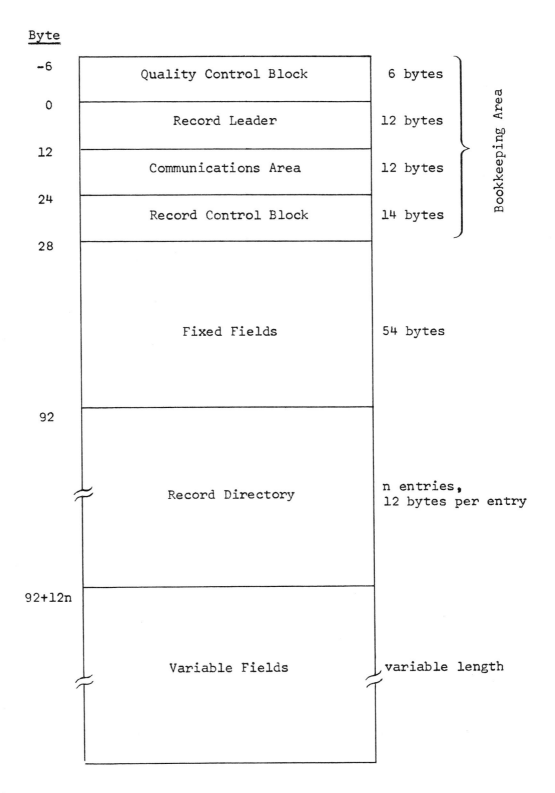

Layout of MARC II Internal Processing Format Record

II.B.   Current MARC Processing

The basic document used to produce a machine-readable MARC record is a
worksheet filled in during cataloging.* It consists of a Xeroxed copy of a
Manuscript Card together with boxes for the filling in of fixed field information. During the course of cataloging, Descriptive Catalogers and Subject
Catalogers provide the appropriate fixed fields. Following this, MARC
Editors delimit the variable fields to complete the worksheet, adding the
variable field tags, subfield codes, etc.** They also make any clarifying
notations necessary to assist the input typist. The tables on the following
pages show the division of resposibility in assigning the fixed fields and
the tags, indicators, and subfield codes for variable fields.

The completely edited Manuscript Card/Worksheet is used by a typist who tran-
scribes it to machine-readable form on magnetic tape, using the IBM MTST.
These machine-readable records are processed by a series of computer programs
which perform a variety of editing, resulting in a MARC formatted record on
magnetic tape. These programs are Pre-Edit, Format Edit, and Content Edit,
run in that order.

The resulting records now enter a verification/correction cycle in which a
printout of the records is made, inspected by MARC Editors, and either
corrected or verified. Both results are converted to machine-readable records,
similar to the above process, and run against their counterpart records retained
in the cycle using an Update program. The verified records are added to a

---

*For an illustration of a MARC Worksheet, see K. D. Guiles, Data Preparation
Manual: MARC Editors, 3d ed., issued as v. 2 of The MARC Manuals, 2d ed.,
Chicago, American Library Association, 1970, p.95.

**This is the current practice. Formerly, Subject Catalogers provided certain of
the Subject Added Entry tags and Descriptive Catalogers provided the tags for
the remainder of the Entries.

II.B.　　Current MARC Production Processing, Continued

permanent data base; the corrected records remain in the cycle for new
inspection by the MARC Editors.

Charts showing the responsibility for assigning fixed fields and tagging
variable fields are given on the following four pages.

Input Box	Filled In By	Field Name
1	-	Gov't Publication Ind. (never used)
2	D	Conference/Meeting Indicator
3	S	Festschrift Indicator
4	D	Index Indicator
5	D	Main Entry in Body Indicator
6	D	Publisher is Main Entry Indicator
10	S	Intellectual Level (Juvenile) Indicator
11	S	Fiction Indicator
12	S	Biography Indicator
13	S	Main Entry is Subject Indicator
20	E	Publication Date Key
21	E	Publication Date 1
22	E	Publication Date 2
23	E	Publication Country Code
24	'C'	Illustration Forms Code(s)
25	E	Micro-Reproduction Code
26	S	Content Code(s)
27	E	Bibliographic Level
28	E	Modified Record Indicator
29	E	Cataloging Source Code

D = Descriptive Cataloger

S = Subject Cataloger

E = MARC Editor

'C' = Generated by Computer Program from contents of Collation Illustration Subfield

Assigning Fixed Fields on the MARC Worksheet

| Tag | Indicators | | Field Name |
	I_1	I_2	

Numbers and Codes

Tag	I_1	I_2	Field Name
P	-	-	CRD - LC Catalog Card Number
P	E	-	CAL - LC Call Number
E	-	-	NLM - NLM Call Number
E	-	-	NAL - NAL Call Number
P	-	-	DDC - Dewey Decimal Number
E	-	-	NBN - National Bibliography Number
E	-	-	SBN - Standard Book Number
E	-	-	OAN - Overseas Acquisition Number
E	-	-	COP - Copy Statement
E	-	-	CAS - Cataloging Source
P	-	-	GAC - Geographic Area Code(s)
P	D	-	LAN - Language Code(s)

(Note - GAC and LAN codes proper are entered in fixed field area by Subject and Descriptive Cataloger, respectively.)

Titles, etc.

Tag	I_1	I_2	Field Name
E	E	-	TIL - Title Statement
E	E	-	ROM - Romanized Title
E	E	-	UTI - Uniform Title
E	-	-	EDN - Edition Statement
E	D*	-	IMP - Imprint
E	-	-	COL - Collation Statement
E	-	-	PRI - Bibliographic Price

P = Preprinted Tag

D = Entered by Descriptive Cataloger

D* = Entered by Descriptive Cataloger in Fixed Field 6

S = Entered by Subject Cataloger

E = Entered by MARC Editor

- = Does not occur

Assigning Variable Field Tags and Indicators on the MARC Worksheet

Tag	Indicators I_1	I_2	Field Name

Main Entry

E	E	S*	MEP - Main Entry Personal Name
E	E	S*	MEC - Main Entry Corporate Name
E	E	S*	MEM - Main Entry Meeting
E	-	S*	MEU - Main Entry Uniform Heading

Notes

E	-	-	NOA - Annotation or Abstract Note
E	-	-	NOB - Bibliography Note
E	E	-	NOC - Contents Note
E	-	-	NOD - Dissertation (Thesis) Note
E	-	-	NOG - General Note
E	-	-	NOW - "Bound With" Note

Series Entries

E	E	'C'	SEP - Series Statement Personal Name
E	E	'C'	SEC - Series Statement Corporate Name
E	E	'C'	SEM - Series Statement Meeting
E	-	-	SET - Series Statement Title
E	E	-	SER - Series Untraced or Traced Differently

S* = Entered by Subject Cataloger in Fixed Field 13

E = Entered by MARC Editor

'C' = Generated by Computer Program from 'His', 'Her', 'Their', or 'Its' at start of field text

- = Does not occur

Assigning Variable Field Tags and Indicators on the MARC Worksheet, Continued

Tag	Indicators I₁	I₂	Field Name

Subject Added Entries

Tag	I₁	I₂	Field Name
E	E	E*	SUP – Subject Added Entry Personal Name
E	E	E*	SUC – Subject Added Entry Corporate Name
E	E	E*	SUM – Subject Added Entry Meeting
E	–	E*	SUU – Subject Added Entry Uniform Heading
E	–	E*	SUG – Subject Added Entry Geographic Name
E	–	E*	SUT – Subject Added Entry Topical

(Other) Added Entries

Tag	I₁	I₂	Field Name
E	E	E	AEP – (Other) Added Entry Personal Name
E	E	E	AEC – (Other) Added Entry Corporate Name
E	E	E	AEM – (Other) Added Entry Meeting
E	–	E	AEU – (Other) Added Entry Uniform Heading
E	–	E	AED – (Other) Added Entry Title Traced Differently

Series Added Entries

Tag	I₁	I₂	Field Name
E	E	–	SAP – Series Added Entry Personal Name
E	E	–	SAC – Series Added Entry Corporate Name
E	E	–	SAM – Series Added Entry Meeting
E	–	–	SAT – Series Added Entry Title

E   = Entered by MARC Editor

E* = Set by default to 'L' by Computer Program
      if not entered by MARC Editor

–   = Does not occur

Assigning Variable Field Tags and Indicators on the MARC Worksheet, Continued

II.C.   Current Processing Augmented by Format Recognition

The purpose of a Format Recognition program is to eliminate the need for tagging and other descriptive annotation being provided by Catalogers and Editors. In such a process, the transcription typist would type directly from a Manuscript Card, essentially typing exactly what she sees. The resulting machine-readable record would then be converted to a magnetic tape record similar to that now produced by the Pre-Edit program. This record is processed by the Format Recognition program which analyzes the content and context of the record and produces a fully-formatted MARC II Internal Processing Format record. The correction/verification cycle, described in the previous section, remains the same.

The Format Recognition program provides the tagging and other descriptive annotations now supplied by Catalogers, Editors, and the Content Edit program. It also formats and assembles the MARC record, which is currently done by the Format Edit program. Therefore, it can be seen that a Format Recognition program would relieve the Catalogers and Editors of this work and would also replace two of the processing programs for new records: Format Edit and Content Edit.

The block diagram on the following page illustrates the record processing with and without a Format Recognition program.

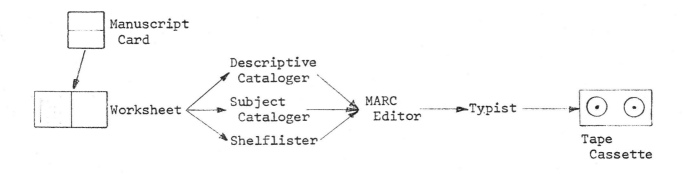

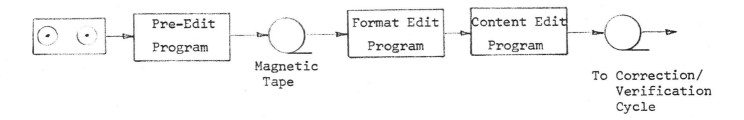

Current Input Process

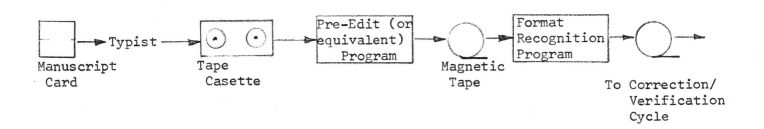

Input Process using Format Recognition

II.D.   Input Specifications for Format Recognition

In the preparation of machine-readable records directly from Manuscript Cards, the basic rule for the transcription typist would be to type exactly what she sees, from top to bottom and from left to right, with a few exceptions, as noted in the individual input field descriptions which follow. Each logical part of the Manuscript Card text is input separately, using the convention of a double carriage return at the end of each of these logical parts to signal the end of a field and four carriage returns at the end of a record. Unlike the current typing from MARC Worksheets, no tabbing is necessary, since the variable field tags are not provided to the typist, nor are they required for the Format Recognition program. Where arrows have been used by Catalogers to indicate a change of field order (actually a note to the Government Printing Office Linotypist who sets up the printed Catalog Card), these should be followed by the transcription typist as well. (See Fig. 1)

The following are exceptions to the 'type what she sees' rule for the transcription typist:

1.   In the middle of the Manuscript Card is a box which extends the full width of the card, and contains the phrase 'DO NOT SET' in its center. The typist should ignore anything in this box.

2.   The typist should not type the word 'Stamp' or 'Exclude' or accompanying braces.

3.   Formulas, legends, or priority symbols which appear at the top of a Manuscript Card should not be typed.

4.   The edition number and the number of cards to be printed information appearing in the bottom center of the Manuscript Card should not be typed.

Z 2019
M34
1970

Madden, Lionel.
       How to find out about the Victorian
Period; a guide to sources of information
by Lionel Madden. [1st ed.] Oxford,
New York, Pergamon Press [1970]

       xiv, 173 p.

       20 cm. (The Commonwealth and internatio-
nal library. Libraries and technical information division)
       SBN 08-015833-1 (pbk)

a ad   22ap70 ab2   DO NOT SET   unb 74-116777

1. Gt. Brit. — Civilization —
   19th century — Bibliography.

I. Title.

	DDC	CRD
Library of Congress	016.9142/038	74-116777
		MARC

Z2019.M34 1970

Madden, Lionel.

How to find out about the Victorian period; a guide to sources of
information.‡[1st ed.]‡Oxford, New York, Pergamon Press [1970]

xiv, 173 p. 20 cm. (The Commonwealth and international library. Libraries
and technical information division)

SBN 08-015833-1 (pbk)

1. Gt.Brit.--Civilization--19th century--Bibliography.

I. Title.

016.9142/038

74-116777

II.D.   Input Specifications for Format Recognition, Continued

5.   The word 'MARC' appearing at the top or bottom of a Manuscript Card
     should not be typed.

6.   The Cataloger's initials appearing in the lower left-hand corner of the
     Manuscript Card should not be typed.

7.   All underlining should be ignored.

8.   Information in red or blue parentheses should be ignored, except:

     a.   Type the 'thru' phrase in a Title Added Entry.

     b.   Type any other information in parentheses at the end of an
          Added Entry.

     c.   Type an entire Added Entry in blue parentheses as a separate input
          field.

     d.   Where red or blue parentheses appear in the middle of any other
          field, they should be ignored but replaced by 3 spaces.

9.   Spaces between multiple initials, other than initials in personal
     names, should be ignored by the typist and the data 'closed up'
     [e.g. 'I.B.M.' or 'U.S.'].

10. Add periods (and commas if necessary) to initials in personal names and
     close up. Close up open dates leaving one space if open date is followed
     by data.

     Examples:
         Bond, C   J   - type -   Bond, C. J.
         Smith, John C   1924-   - type -   Smith, John C., 1924-
         Smith, John C   1924-   ed. - type -   Smith, John C., 1924- ed.

II.D.   Input Specifications for Format Recognition, Continued

The general ordering of the input text of the logical parts of a Manuscript
Card, to be called input fields by the Format Recognition program, is given
in the table on the following page. This order cannot be guaranteed,
however, although it is quite regular down into the Added Entries. Due to
the fact that the Manuscript Cards also originate at institutions other than
the Library of Congress, through shared cataloging, the precise ordering of
the input fields occurring near the bottom of the Manuscript Card may vary.
Beyond the input of the Collation Statement, however, the Format Recognition
program is not dependent on input field order for the identification of
these fields. Therefore, the variations in expected input order is not
crucial.

II.D.   <u>Input Specifications for Format Recognition, Continued</u>

	Input Order	Always Present?	Tag	Name
(On front of card)	1	N*	CAL	Call Number
	2	N	ME-	Main Entry
	3	N	UTI	Uniform Title - Type 1
	4	Y	-	Title Paragraph
	a	Y	TIL	Title Statement
	b	N	EDN	Edition Statement
	c	Y	IMP	Imprint
	5	Y	-	Collation Paragraph
	a	Y	COL	Collation Statement
	b	N	SE-	Series Statement
	c	N	PRI	Bibliographic Price
	6	N	-	Numbers
	a	N	NBN	National Bibliography No.
	b	N	SBN	Standard Book No.
	c	N	OAN	Overseas Acquisition No.
	7	N	NO-	Series Notes and other Notes
	8	N	SU-	Subject Added Entries
	9	N	AE-	(Other) Added Entries
	10	N	SA-	Series Added Entries
	11	N	UTI	Uniform Title - Type 3
	12	N	COP	Copy Statement
	13	N	ROM	Romanized Title
	14	N	CAL	Bracketed LC Call Number
	15	N	'NLC'**	Non-LC Call Number
	16	N	'CAL+'**	Second Class Number
	17	N	DDC	Dewey Decimal Number
	18	Y	CRD	LC Card Number
	19	Y	CAS	Cataloging Source
(On back of card)	20	N	UTI	Uniform Title - Type 2
	21	N	SU-	Non-LC Subject Added Entries
	22	N	'NLC'**	Non-LC Call Number

<u>General Order of Input Fields from Manuscript Card</u>

*Always present except in some cases of Shared or Cooperative Cataloging.
**Pseudo-tag assignment recognized in Step 3 for special processing.

II.D.   Input Specifications for Format Recognition, Continued

Comments on each of the expected input fields follow:

1.   Call Number

The Call Number should appear in the upper left margin of the Manuscript
Card, broken into two or more short lines. This is typed as a single
continuous field. If the number includes a date, a space should be typed
before the date to separate it from the rest of the Call Number.

2.   Main Entry

The Main Entry is **typed** as a single input field. Add periods or commas
to personal name initials (where necessary) and close up spaces. If an
open date [e.g. 1924-] follows a name, follow the name with a comma and
a space, and then the date. If the open date is followed by more data,
type a space between the hyphen and the remaining data.

3.   Uniform Title - Type 1

The Uniform Title which may follow the Main Entry is typed as a single
input field, including the enclosing brackets.

4.   Title Paragraph

The entire Title Paragraph is typed as a single input field. However,
the typist will type the standard delimiter character, '‡', between the
three possible components of this paragraph: Title Statement, Edition
Statement (when present), and Imprint. (It is felt that the typist can
accomplish this delimiting through inspection of the paragraph with a
high degree of accuracy.) If two full Imprints (Place, Publisher, and
Date) occur within the Title Paragraph, only the last one is delimited
as the start of the Imprint proper.

II.D.   Input Specifications for Format Recognition, Continued

5. Collation Paragraph

The entire Collation Paragraph is typed as a single input field,
including the Series Statement (in parentheses) and the Bibliographic
Price, if either or both are present.

6. Numbers

The possible numbers which may follow the Collation Paragraph are:
National Bibliography Number, Standard Book Number, and Overseas
Acquisition Number. Each is typed as a separate field, when it occurs.

7. Series Notes and other Notes

Each Note, whether a Series Note or other type, is typed as a separate
input field. It is not necessary for the typist to distinguish among
the various types of Notes.

8. Subject Added Entries

Each Subject Added Entry, designated by an Arabic Numeral*, is typed as
a separate input field, including the full Numeral. The long dash, used
to point off Subject Subdivisions, is typed as two hyphens when it occurs.

The Subject Added Entries may be followed by, or replaced by, a set of
Subject Added Entries enclosed in a single pair of brackets. An identification code may precede the first Subject Entry, usually followed by a
colon and space. Each Subject Entry, designated as above by an Arabic
Numeral, is typed as a single input field, including the Numeral. The
initial bracket and the identification code (when present) is included
with the first Subject Entry of the set. The terminating bracket is
included with the last Subject Entry of the set.

---

*An Arabic Numeral is defined as: numbers, followed by a period, followed by
a space.

II.D.   Input Specifications for Format Recognition, Continued

9.   (Other) Added Entries

Each (Other) Added Entry, designated by a Roman Numeral, is typed as a
separate input field, including the Numeral, period, and space preceding
the text.

10.   Series Added Entries

The entire Series Added Entry paragraph is typed as a single input
field, exactly as expressed on the Manuscript Card, including the
enclosing parentheses.

11.   Uniform Title - Type 3

This Uniform Title is typed as a single input field, including the
enclosing parentheses.

12.   Copy Statement

The entire Copy Statement is typed as a single input field. Where a
Call Number exists in this area, broken up into several short lines in
the left margin of the Manuscript Card, it should be input as a single
continuous field, as in the Call Number instructions. The Copy Statement
itself will follow one or two long dashes. If there are two long dashes,
the first long dash should be typed as two hyphens, and the second should
be typed as three hyphens, following a separating space. If there is only
one long dash, it should be typed as three hyphens.

13.   Romanized Title

The Romanized Title is typed as a single input field preceded by the
phrase 'Title romanized: ' or 'Title transliterated: ', whichever is
present on the Manuscript Card.

II.D.   <u>Input Specifications for Format Recognition, Continued</u>

14.   <u>Bracketed LC Call Number</u>

The bracketed LC Call Number is expressed on the Manuscript Card as a
single line, unlike the other Call Numbers in the left margin, which are
broken into several short lines. It is input as a single input field,
including the enclosing brackets.

15.   <u>Non-LC Call Number</u>

Like the bracketed LC Call Number, the Non-LC Call Number is expressed
on the Manuscript Card as a single line; however, with no enclosing
brackets. It is typed as a single input field.

16.   <u>Second Class Number</u>

This number occurs in the left-most of the three horizontal boxes near
the bottom of the Manuscript Card and is typed as a single input field,
including the enclosing brackets, if present.

17.   <u>Dewey Decimal Number</u>

This number occurs in the center of the three horizontal boxes near the
bottom of the Maunscript Card and is typed as a single input field.

18.   <u>LC Card Number</u>

This number occurs in the right-most of the three horizontal boxes near
the bottom of the Manuscript Card and is typed as a separate input field.
If an alphabetic identifier, such as 'AC' or 'MN', is found in the box
below the number, type a slash after the card number and then the characters in the box. If 'Rev.' is found with the alphabetic identifier,
type another slash and 'Rev.'. If 'Rev.' occurs without an alphabetic
identifier, type two slashes and 'Rev.'.

II.D.   Input Specifications for Format Recognition, Continued

19.   Cataloging Source

The notation 'Library of Congress' is printed at the bottom left-hand corner of the Manuscript Card and is typed, together with any additional statements which may occur in this area, as a separate input field.

Alternatively, it is possible that the left-most of the three horizontal boxes near the bottom of the Manuscript Card may contain a Non-LC Cataloging Source statement. It should be typed, if found in this area of the card, as a single input field. It is not necessary then to repeat or restate the Cataloging Source statement which may be encountered again (printed) at the bottom of the Manuscript Card.

20.   Uniform Title - Type 2

This Uniform Title appears on the reverse side of the Manuscript Card and is typed as a single field preceded by the phrase 'Filing Title: ' or 'Uniform Title: ', whichever is printed on the Manuscript Card.

21.   Non-LC Subject Added Entries

The Non-LC Subject Added Entries may occur on the bottom of the reverese side of a Manuscript Card. The entire set will be enclosed in brackets. An identification code may precede the first Subject Entry, usually followed by a colon and space. Since most of the data here are Subject Added Entries, each is preceded by an Arabic Numeral, with a possible Call Number, when present, appearing as the last statement within the brackets. Each Subject Entry is typed as a separate input field, together with any identification code and/or Numeral which may precede it; the Call Number is also typed as a separate field. The initial bracket is included with the first field; the terminating bracket is included with the last field. The long dash used to point off Subject Subdivisions is typed as two hyphens, when it occurs.

II.D.   Input Specifications for Format Recognition, Continued

22. Non-LC Call Number

The Non-LC Call Number, occurring at the bottom of the reverse side of
the Manuscript Card, is included following the Non-LC Subject Added
Entries, enclosed within their brackets. As is described in 22. on
the preceding page, this number is typed as a single input field,
including the terminating bracket.

III.   GENERAL APPROACH OF THE FORMAT RECOGNITION PROCESS

A.   Overall Flow

The production of a MARC record, from the input fields transcribed from a
Manuscript Card through a Format Recognition Program, consists of a five step
process, as follows:

1.   Setting up the Record
2.   Identifying Input Fields
3.   Processing Variable Fields
4.   Completing the Processing of Variable Fields
5.   Final Record Assembly

Step 1 - Sets up the framework for the MARC II Internal Processing Format
          record, initializes the fixed length areas, and builds those
          areas which are not dependent on the contents of the input
          fields.

Step 2 - Identifies all of the input fields, breaking up those which
          represent a cluster of MARC record variable fields, such as the
          Title Paragraph, the Collation Paragraph, and the Series Added
          Entries Paragraph. It also builds the Preliminary Record
          Directory with an entry for each variable field identified.

Step 3 - Processes the variable fields, one at a time, utilizing the
          information in the Preliminary Directory sequentially. As each
          variable field is processed, all information which can be
          extracted from it is determined, to include the remainder of its
          Record Directory entry, any fixed field codes and indicators
          which can be derived, and any other variable field's indicators
          which can be generated. The processing must complete the third
          tag letter (where necessary), delimit and assign subfield codes,
          and build those of its variable field indicator(s) which can be
          derived from the field's contents.

III.A.   Overall Flow, Continued

Step 4 - Performs those functions necessary to complete the processing
of the variable fields in a record. This includes building
two additional variable fields and correlating certain
variable fields, when present.

Step 5 - Performs the sorting of the Record Directory and the final
assembly of the parts of the record, including making some
final entries in the record's Bookkeeping Areas. The record
is then output.

The overall flow of processing is shown in the block diagram on the following
page. Note that Step 3 is further expanded in an additional diagram following
the overall flow diagram.

START

```
┌─────────────────────────────────────────────────┐
│ Set up framework for Bookkeeping Areas and Fixed │    Step 1
│ Fields and make standard initializations.        │
└─────────────────────────────────────────────────┘
```

```
┌─────────────────────────────────────────────────┐
│ Input fields through Collation to determine      │
│ existence of LC Call Number, Main Entry, and     │
│ Type 1 Uniform Title.  Break up, where           │
│ necessary, Title Paragraph into Title Statement, │
│ Edition Statement, and Imprint; Collation        │
│ Paragraph into Collation Statement, Series       │
│ Statement, and Price.  Assign tags to each       │    Step 2
│ variable field in the Preliminary Record         │
│ Directory.                                        │
└─────────────────────────────────────────────────┘
```

```
┌─────────────────────────────────────────────────┐
│ Input and identify remaining fields, assigning   │
│ tag for each variable field (first part of tag   │
│ for Entries), and complete Preliminary Record    │
│ Directory. (Series Added Entries, which are      │
│ clustered in a paragraph, are broken into        │
│ separate variable fields.)                        │
└─────────────────────────────────────────────────┘
```

```
┌─────────────────────────────────────────────────┐
│ Process each variable field in turn:             │
│   1. Complete tag, where necessary.              │
│   2. Delimit field into subfields and assign     │
│      subfield codes.                              │    Step 3
│   3. Assign indicators to field and perform      │
│      special tests to determine fixed fields     │
│      or indicators for other variable fields.    │
└─────────────────────────────────────────────────┘
```

```
┌─────────────────────────────────────────────────┐
│ Complete variable field processing:              │
│   1. Correlate any Series Added Entries with     │
│      any Series Statement/Notes.                  │
│   2. Set indicator in TIL and/or ROM fields      │    Step 4
│      based on presence of 'Title.' Added Entry.  │
│   3. Build LAN and GAC fields, using data        │
│      accumulated in Step 3.                       │
└─────────────────────────────────────────────────┘
```

```
┌─────────────────────────────────────────────────┐
│ Assemble record:                                 │
│   1. Sort Record Directory and remove any        │
│      entries flagged as deleted.                  │    Step 5
│   2. Assemble record and output.                  │
└─────────────────────────────────────────────────┘
```

FINISH

Format Recognition Overall Flow of Processing

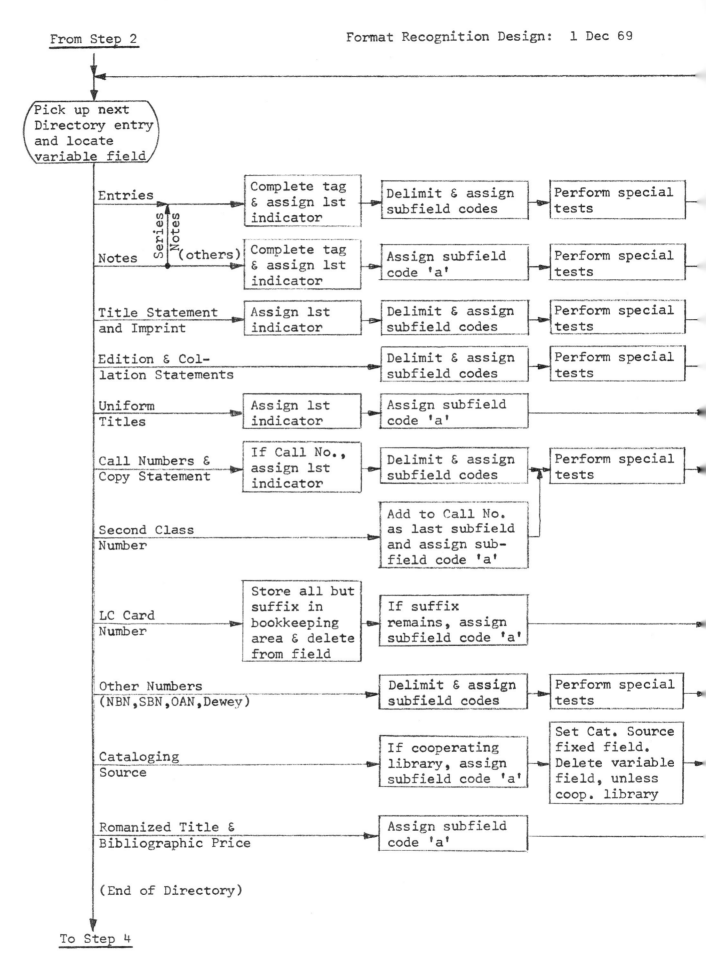

III.B.   Step 1 - Setting Up the Record

This step involves setting up the framework for a MARC II Internal Processing
Format record which consists of five fixed length areas, all of which occur
at the beginning of the record. These are: the Quality Control Block, the
Record Leader, the Communications Area, the Record Control Area, and the
Fixed Fields Area. Before the fields in these areas are built, all five
areas are initialized to binary zero.

Most of the contents of the first three areas is canned information which can
be inserted directly. The only exceptions are: the Record Date in the Record
Leader (which is obtainable through programming via the Computer's operating
system), the Record Length in the Record Leader, and the Record Directory
Entry Count in the Communications Area. These latter two are computed during
the course of processing the input data for the record and are stored in
their respective areas in Step 5.

The Record Control Area is determined from the LC Card Number input field in
Step 3. It also includes a Check Digit which is currently not used, and a
Segment Number byte which is stored in Step 4.

All of the fixed fields in the Fixed Field Area are determined during the
course of processing the input fields in Step 3, with the exception of the
File Date, which is set equal to the Record Date in the Record Leader in this
Step.

In addition to setting up the record, working areas are set up to accumulate
data generated during the course of processing the input fields in Step 3,
which are subsequently used in building the Language Codes field (LAN)
and the Geographic Area Codes field (GAC) in Step 4. These are, for LAN,
a Language Code Subfield A Working Buffer, a Language Code Subfield B
Working Buffer, a Count byte for each buffer, and a Translation Indicator
Byte. For GAC there is set up a Geographic Area Code Working Buffer and
a Count byte.

III.C.   Step 2 - Input Field Identification

This step performs the preliminary identification of the input fields. It
includes the breaking up of cluster of input fields, such as the Title
Paragraph, the Collation Paragraph, and the Series Added Entries Paragraph,
and the building of a Preliminary Record Directory entry for each variable
field encountered. It can be seen from the Input Specifications Table in
Section II.D. that not all of the fields which may possibly be present on a
Manuscript Card necessarily do occur there. Therefore, in order to get a
foothold on the input fields which are present, it is necessary to distinguish
between the first five possible fields of text. The Collation Statement,
which is always present, is initially located using the following procedure:
The first five input fields of a record are read in from magnetic tape.
Since the Call Number is not always present, the only input fields which must
be present are the Title Paragraph and the Collation Paragraph. However,
only the Collation Statement portion of the Collation Paragraph is easily
recognized. Therefore, based on the following chart, an attempt is made to
identify the second field, then the third field, and so on through the fifth
input field, as a Collation Statement.

Case	1st Field	2nd Field	3rd Field	4th Field	5th Field
1	TP	CP	-	-	-
2	CN	TP	CP	-	-
3	ME	TP	CP	-	-
4	CN	ME	TP	CP	-
5	ME	UT	TP	CP	-
6	CN	ME	UT	TP	CP

where: CN = Call Number

ME = Main Entry

TP = Title Paragraph

UT = Uniform Title - Type 1

CP = Collation Paragraph

III.C.   Step 2 - Input Field Identification, Continued

When the Collation is found to be the 3rd input field, then it is necessary to distinguish between Cases 2 and 3, and the first input field is inspected to determine if it is a Call Number. If it is, Case 2 exists; otherwise, Case 3. Similarly, when the Collation is found to be the 4th input field, Cases 4 and 5 can be distinguished by inspecting the first input field to determine if it is a Call Number. Again, if it is a Call Number, Case 4 exists; otherwise, Case 5. A further distinguishing factor is that if it is Case 5 then the Uniform Title in the 2nd input field should start with an open bracket.

The Preliminary Directory is now started with the tag and starting position of the identified input fields. The Title Paragraph is broken into its possible component parts (Title Statement, Edition Statement, and Imprint), based on the standard delimiters inserted in this input field by the typist, and separate Directory entries are set up for each. The Collation Paragraph is inspected for the existence of parentheses following the Size Subfield of the Collation Statement proper. If present, the enclosed phrase is broken out as the Series Statement and given a separate Directory entry. Any data following the Series Statement (or following the Collation if no Series Statement) is given a separate Directory entry and assigned the variable field tag for Bibliographic Price

Once the preliminary work has been done, the remaining input fields past Collation which have already been read are identified with their respective Directory entries being built. Following this, the remaining input fields are read one at a time and identified in the same manner. The Series Added Entries Paragraph is broken into separate variable fields when encountered, and a separate Directory entry given to each.

The result of this process is that the MARC record variable fields have been located and partially identified from the input fields for this record. For many of the variable fields the complete three-letter tag has been established. For the Notes and the five kinds of Entries (Main, Series, Subject Added, (Other) Added, and Series Added), only the first two letters of the tag have

III.C.   <u>Step 2 - Input Field Identification, Continued</u>

been established. Also, at this point, both Series Notes and other Notes are
all simply identified as 'Notes'. (It should be noted that the Record Directory
at this time is only a preliminary one, since certain of the variable fields
may disappear when fully processed in Step 3 and 5, and two other variable
fields may be constructed and added in Step 4.)

The characteristics of the **possible** input fields are given beginning on the
following page.

III.C.   Step 2 - Input Field Recognition, Continued

Each of the possible input fields are described below as to their individual identifiable characteristics and not from the point of view of their interrelationship with other possible input fields. This latter is detailed in the Step 2 procedure proper, given in Section VI., which is not dependent on input field order, once past the Collation Paragraph.

1.   LC Call Number

   This field is usually present as the first input field of a record. The general form of this number is: 1-3 capital letters, followed by 1-4 numbers (optionally followed by a period and more numbers), followed by a period or space, followed by a capital letter and additional numbers and letters. There are several recognizable variants of the latter portion of a Call Number, including the addition of a date, separated by a blank.

2.   Main Entry

   Since this field is not always present in a record, it must be identified from its relative position preceding the Collation Statement, which is the first easily identifiable field in the record and which is always present. As the contents of the Main Entry field can be any sort of text, there is no way to positively identify it from its contents.

3.   Uniform Title - Type 1

   This field is not always present; however, when it is present, it must follow a Main Entry field. It can be recognized by the fact that it is enclosed in brackets and precedes the Collation Statement.

III.C.   Step 2 - Input Field Recognition, Continued

4. Title Paragraph

This field is always present in a record and immediately precedes the
Collation Paragraph. It is a cluster of three possible fields, the
first and third of which should always be present. These are: Title
Statement, Edition Statement, and Imprint. Since for the most part,
the Title Paragraph contains text and therefore it would be difficult
to break out the various fields with a high degree of success, the
transcription typist indicates the start of each of the variable fields
in this input field by inserting the standard delimiter character. It
is possible, therefore, to break up this field cluster quite easily
by inspecting for the delimiter(s).

5. Collation Paragraph

This field may contain a cluster of three possible fields, the first of
which is always present. These are: Collation Statement, Series
Statement, and Bibliographic Price. It is the Pagination and Size Subfields (first and third) of the Collation Statement which are uniquely
recognizable due to their format and abbreviations in relation to the
other possible input fields which precede it in a record. Following the
end of the Collation Statement, there may appear a Series Statement,
which is identified by the fact that it is text enclosed in parentheses.
Also, there may appear, following either of the previous fields, a
numeric statement which is the Bibliographic Price variable field.

6. Numbers (NBN, SBN, and OAN)

These number fields are not always present, but when they occur they are
self-identifying. The National Bibliography Number (NBN) begins with
an alphabetic country code, the Standard Book Number (SBN) is a 9-digit
number preceded by 'SBN', and the Overseas Acquisition Number (OAN) is
usually preceded by a specific code, such as 'PL480' or 'LACAP', which
refers to the acquisition program involved. These numbers may also be
enclosed in parentheses.

III.C.   Step 2 - Input Field Recognition, Continued

7. Notes

These input fields are not always present. There are several different
kinds of Notes fields, at this point including the Series Notes as well.
In general, Notes are fields beginning with text which are not identifiable
as anything else. The distinction between Series Notes and the other Notes
is made in Step 3.

8. Subject Added Entries

Each Subject Added Entry, when it occurs, can be recognized by the fact
that it is preceded by an Arabic Numeral. In some cases, the set of
Subject Added Entry fields may be enclosed in brackets and the Arabic
Numeral may be preceded by an identification code as well.

9. (Other) Added Entries

Each (Other) Added Entry field, when it occurs, can be recognized by the
fact that it is preceded by a Roman Numeral.

10. Series Added Entry Paragraph

This field is not always present. It may consist of more than one Series
Added Entry statement and is input as one continuous paragraph enclosed
in parentheses. The separate entries in this input field can be easily
recognized since each is preceded by the word 'Series: '. In some
instances, the first Series Added Entry field will consist simply of the
word 'Series.'.

11. Uniform Title - Type 3

This input field, when present, occurs following all of the Tracings.
It can be recognized by the fact that the text is enclosed in parentheses
and begins with the word 'Title: '.

III.C. <u>Step 2 - Input Field Recognition</u>, Continued

12. <u>Copy Statement</u>

This input field is not always present. However, when it is, it is either directly preceded by multiple hyphens, or a Call Number and multiple hyphens.

13. <u>Romanized Title</u>

This input field is not always present. However, when it is, it can be recognized by the words 'Title romanized: ' or Title transliterated: ' which precede it.

14. <u>Bracketed LC Call Number</u>

This input field, when it occurs, looks exactly like the LC Call Number with the exception that it appears enclosed in brackets and follows the Tracings.

15. <u>Non-LC Call Number</u>

This input field, when it occurs, looks exactly like the LC Call Number. It can be identified as the Non-LC Call Number by its position in the record following the Tracings. In some cases, this field directly follows the Bracketed Subject Added Entries and is enclosed within the latter's brackets.

16. <u>Second Class Number</u>

This number is not always present. It has the form of the initial part of a Call Number, that is - it contains 1-3 capital letters, followed by 1-4 numbers, optionally followed by a period and more numbers. This input field is enclosed in brackets, when it occurs.

III.C.   Input Field Recognition, Continued

17. Dewey Decimal Number

This field is not always present. It consists of a decimal number containing at most a single decimal point; it may also contain slashes ('/'), may be preceded by 'j', and may be followed by '(B)', '92', or '920', or combinations thereof. In place of or in addition to a number, this field may contain the term: 'Fic', 'E', or 'B'. Any portion of this field may be in brackets.

18. LC Card Number

This field is always present and is easiliy identified by the fact that it consists of a two-digit number followed by a hyphen and then followed by 1-6 digits. In addition, there are certain standard prefixes and suffixes which may occur with this number.

19. Cataloging Source

This field is always present. If the cataloging source is the Library of Congress, this field consists of the statement 'Library of Congress'. Otherwise, the field may be identified by two distinctive phrases: 'Shared Cataloging with DNLM' or 'Shared Cataloging for DNAL'. Also, the text may end with the phrase '... for Library of Congress'.

20. Uniform Title - Type 2

This field is not always present. It can be recognized by the fact that it begins with the phrase 'Filing Title: ' or 'Uniform Title: '.

III.D. Step 3 - Variable Field Processing

This third step processes the variable fields, one at a time, utilizing the information in the Preliminary Directory sequentially. As each variable field is processed, all information which can be extracted from it is determined to complete its corresponding Record Directory entry. Also, through a series of special tests, other information is extracted from the field, to include any fixed field indicators and codes which can be derived, and any other variable field's indicators which can be generated. The processing of each field in Step 3 must complete the third-letter tag, where necessary, delimit the field and assign subfield codes, and build those indicator(s) which can be determined from the field's contents.

All of the special tests in this step have been selected so as to interrogate previously-processed fields in a lookback approach. This has the obvious advantage of only referencing fields which have been reduced to a well-defined form. Where there is an exception to this, it involves the lookahead for the existence or non-existence of a possible subsequent field; this does not involve inspecting the contents of a field, but rather interrogating the Preliminary Record Directory only.

A summary of Step 3, giving the substeps appropriate to each variable field type, is presented in table form on the following page.

Variable Field	Complete Tag	Assign 1st Indicator	Assign Subfield 'a' Only	Delimit & Assign Subfield Codes	Perform Related Special Tests	Not Kept as a Variable Field
Call Number		X		X	X	
Main Entry	X	X		X	X	
Uniform Title - Type 1		X	X			
Title Statement		X^1		X	X	
Edition Statement				X	X	
Imprint		X		X	X	
Collation Statement				X	X	
Series Statement	X	X		X	X	
Bibliographic Price				X		
Numbers (NBN, SBN, OAN)				X	X	
Notes	X^2	X	X^2	X^2	X	
Subject Added Entries	X	X		X	X	
(Other) Added Entries	X	X		X	X	
Series Added Entries	X	X		X	X	
Uniform Title - Type 3		X	X			
Copy Statement				X	X	
Bracketed LC Call Number		X		X	X	
Non-LC Call Number	X^3			X	X	
Romanized Title		X^1	X			
Second Class Number				X	X	X
Dewey Decimal Number				X	X	
LC Card Number			X^4		X	X^4
Cataloging Source			X^5			X^5
Uniform Title - Type 2		X	X			

1 - May also be assigned in Step 4.
2 - Series Notes are distinguished from other Notes. Only Series Notes are delimited
3 - Appropriate tag (NAL or NLM) is assigned.
4 - Only suffix, if present, is retained as a variable field.
5 - Kept as variable field if cooperating library, other than NAL or NLM.

Summary of Step 3 Processing

III.E.   Step 4 - Completing the Processing of the Variable Fields

This fourth step performs those functions which can only be done after the variable fields have been individually processed. Since the processing concerned here involves relationships between fields which may or may not be present, it is necessary to set them up as a separate step from Step 3, in order to guarantee that they be accomplished. There are three substeps to this step, as follows:

1.   Correlate Series Added Entries with Series Statement/Notes

This involves changing the third tag letter and indicators of Series Statement/Notes, where necessary, based on their correlation with Series Added Entries. In addition, some of the Series Added Entry fields may be discarded.

2.   Set First Indicator of Title Statement and Romanized Title

Based on the existence of an (Other) Added Entry consisting of the word 'Title.', the 1st indicator of the Title Statement and of the Romanized Title, if present, is set. Also, if this Entry is of the form 'Title (thru "word")', the "word" is correlated with the delimitation of Subfield b of the Title Statement. In either case, the (Other) Added Entry variable field is discarded.

3.   Assemble Two Additional Variable Fields, LAN and GAC

If any codes have been generated in the working buffers in Step 3, the Language Codes (LAN) and Geographic Area Codes (GAC) variable fields are assembled using the following rules:

a]   For Language Codes, if the work is not a translation and only one language code ('ENG') has been determined, the language code is stored in the field provided for it in the record's Fixed Field Area. Otherwise, a variable field is created from the two language code working buffers, the data is added to the variable field data, and a new Directory entry is formed referencing the new varaiable field.

III.E.   Step 4 - Completing the Processing of the Variable Fields, Continued

    b]   For Geographic Area Codes, if any codes have been generated they
are added to the variable field data and a new Directory entry is
formed referencing the new variable field. If there are more than
three area codes, they are 'collapsed' together until three or
fewer remain.

III.F.   Step 5 - Final Record Assembly

This fifth and final step performs the record assembly from the various parts
of the record built during the previous processing: the four initial Bookkeeping Areas, the Fixed Field Area, the Record Directory, and the Variable
Fields. Just prior to the record assembly, the Record Directory is sorted on
numeric tag and site number.* Also, the Record Control Area is inspected to
ensure that a record identification (the LC Card Number) has been stored in
that area. If not, a pseudo-card number is generated for subsequent accessing
and retrieval. Where the assembled record does not exceed the maximum record
size, this assembly of the record is quite straightforward. Where the record
size exceeds the maximum, continuation record segments are constructed.

1.   Sort the Record Directory

The Record Directory entries are sorted on tag and site number.* The
entries which are flagged for deletion (sorted to the bottom by the use
of a special flag in their Directory entries) are removed from the Record
Directory and the Directory Entry Count is stored in the Communications
Area of the record.

2.   Assemble and Output the Record

The record is assembled from the Bookkeeping Areas, the Fixed Field Area,
the Record Directory, and the Variable Fields. The Record Length is
stored in the Record Leader and the record is output, numbering segments
in the Segment Number field in the Record Control Area, as necessary.

---

*A site number is assigned in the Record Directory entry of each variable field
of a given type, in order of input. For example, if there are five Subject
Added Entries, their Directory entries will be assigned the site numbers 1-5.
Site numbers are included in the Record Directory entries because sorting on
tags generally changes the input order; the site numbers can subsequently be
used to restore this order when desired.

III.G.   Considerations of Future Changes to Input Order

Two possible new sources of input records can be anticipated in the future:
a new Worksheet not utilizing the Manuscript Card, and the direct reading of
a printed LC Catalog Card using an Optical Character Reader (OCR). It can
be anticipated that the order of input fields from these new sources will
not be the same as that from the Manuscript Card. In order to accommodate
this eventuality, Step 3 will actually begin with a sort of the Record
Directory into numeric tag and site number order. This will require some
slight readjustment of the Special Tests in Step 3, since they are based on
a lookback procedure of interrogating previous variable fields of data which
have already been processed. However, once this readjustment has been done,
any new input order can be handled by simply providing an alternate to
Step 2 for each new input order anticipated. This Alternate Step 2 will
perform the same function as the Step 2 in this report, inputting and
identifying the input fields, using methods appropriate to that particular
input order.

It should be noted that the Manuscript Card input order is virtually in
numeric tag order already. In general, the fields whose entries would change
position in the Record Directory would be most of the Numbers, some of the
Uniform Titles, the Romanized Title, the Copy Statement, and the Cataloging
Source. Therefore, the sorting technique used in Step 3 would be one which
takes advantage of some data being already in sort order.

Since the primary purpose of this report is to provide the logical
specifications for hand processing a sample of Manuscript Cards in order to
test the correctness and completeness of the Format Recognition algorithms,
keyword lists, etc., the broader base for handling the various other possible
input orders has not been included in this report.

IV.   STATISTICS

A.   Occurrence Statistics

These statistics result from the making of counts on samples of MARC II
Internal Processing Format records for English-language monographs. The
samples were drawn from the current MARC processing of the time and cannot
be guaranteed to be fair random samples in the statistical sense. However,
close examination of the records involved suggests that they are quite typical
of English monograph records in general.

Sample sizes ranged from 1000 to nearly 4000 records, except when fewer than
1000 were available, which was the case in a few instances involving very
infrequently-occurring fields.

IV.A.1. Occurrence of Major Variable Fields per Record

These statistics represent counts of variable field occurrences divided by the number of records involved. For Main Entry through Collation Statement (since these fields can occur at most once in a record), the statistic gives the percentage of records containing them. For the remaining fields, the statistic gives the percentage of occurrence of each type of field per record

Field Name	%
Main Entry	98.6
Title Statement	100.0
Edition Statement	4.1
Imprint	100.0
Collation Statement	100.0
Series Statement/Notes	8.5
Notes	83.2
Subject Added Entries	131.6
(Other) Added Entries	34.6
Series Added Entries	5.1

IV.A.2. Occurrence of Entries by Type of Entry

These statistics reflect the occurrence of the five Entries, broken down by type. This is expressed both as percent of Entry and percent of record. Thus, for example, the table expresses the percentage of all Series Added Entries (SA) which are Corporate Names (C), which is 89.6%. However, since the total occurrence of Series Added Entries per record is only 5.2%, then the occurrence of Series Added Entry Corporate Names (SAC) per record is 89.6 x 5.2 = 4.6%. In the notation used in this table, 0 = no observed occurrence, - = occurrence is not possible.

		(P) Personal Name	(C) Corporate Name	(M) Meeting	(U) Uniform Heading	(T) Title	(T) Topical	(G) Geographic	Total % per Entry	Total % per Record
Main (ME)	% of Entry	86.3	12.0	1.5	0.2	-	-	-	100.0	
	% per Record	84.7	11.7	1.5	0.2	-	-	-		98.1
Series (SE)	% of Entry	0.8	28.8	0.2	-	70.2	-	-	100.0	
	% per Record	<0.1	2.4	<0.1	-	6.0	-	-		8.5
Subject Added (SU)	% of Entry	9.2	3.6	<0.1	0.7	-	73.1	13.4	100.0	
	% per Record	12.1	4.8	0.1	0.9	-	95.9	17.5		131.3
(Other) Added (AE)	% of Entry	64.9	32.0	0.6	2.5	-	-	-	100.0	
	% per Record	22.4	11.1	0.2	0.8	-	-	-		34.5
Series Added (SA)	% of Entry	0	89.6	0.2	-	10.2	-	-	100.0	
	% per Record	0	4.6	<0.1	-	0.5	-	-		5.2

Total % of Entries per Record   277.5

IV.A.3. Occurrence of Types of Entries by Entry

These statistics reflect the occurrence of the types of Entries, broken down by Entry. This is expressed both as percent of type and precent of record. Thus, for example, the table expresses the percentage of all Corporate Names (C) which are Series Added Entries (SA), which is 13.2%. However, since the total occurrence of Corporate Names per record is only 34.6%, then the occurrence of Series Added Entry Corporate Names (SAC) per record is 13.2 x 34.6 = 4.6%. In the notation used in this table, 0 = no observed occurrence, - = occurrence is not possible.

		(ME) Main	(SE) Series	(SU) Subject Added	(AE) (Other) Added	(SA) Series Added	Total % per Type	Total % per Record
Personal Name (P)	% of Type	71.0	0.1	10.1	18.8	0	100.0	
	% per Record	84.7	<0.1	12.1	22.4	0		119.3
Corporate Name (C)	% of Type	33.9	7.1	13.8	32.0	13.2	100.0	
	% per Record	11.7	2.4	4.8	11.1	4.6		34.6
Meeting (M)	% of Type	81.8	0.6	6.1	11.2	0.3	100.0	
	% per Record	1.5	<0.1	0.1	0.2	0.1		1.8
Uniform Heading (U)	% of Type	8.6	-	46.6	44.8	-	100.0	
	% per Record	0.2	-	0.9	0.8	-		1.9
Title (T)	% of Type	-	92.0	-	-	8.0	100.0	
	% per Record	-	6.0	-	-	0.5		6.5
Topical (T)	% of Type	-	-	100.0	-	-	100.0	
	% per Record	-	-	95.9	-	-		95.9
Geographic (G)	% of Type	-	-	100.0	-	-	100.0	
	% per Record	-	-	17.5	-	-		17.5

Total % of Types per Record   277.5

IV.A.4.   Occurrence of Notes

The total occurrence per record of the 7 types of Notes is 83.2%. This
breaks down as follows, with 0 = no observed occurrence in the sample
used:

	% of Notes	% per Record
NOA - Abstract or Annotation Notes	0.7	0.6
NOB - Bibliography Notes	54.8	45.6
NOC - Content Notes	3.5	2.9
NOD - Dissertation (Thesis) Notes	1.1	0.9
NOG - General Notes	39.9	33.2
NOL - "Limited Use" Notes	0	0
NOW - "Bound With" Notes	0	0
Totals	100.0	83.2

The General Notes (NOG) in the above include the former category of History
Notes (NOH), which is no longer used. The breakout of History Notes from
General Notes is as follows:

	% of Notes	% per Record
NOG - without NOH	26.2	21.8
NOH - History Notes	13.7	11.4
Current NOG Totals	39.9	33.2

For a breakdown of the occurrence of number of Notes per record, see the
following page.

IV.A.4.   Occurrence of Notes, Continued

The number of Note fields per record varies considerably. The breakdown is
shown in the following, with 0 = no occurrence observed in the sample used:

Number of Notes in Record	% of All Records
0	39.1
1	48.9
2	14.0
3	1.7
4	0.2
5	0.1
over 5	0
Total	100.0

IV.A.5. Occurrence of Subfields by Type of Entry

The following gives the percentage of occurrence of each subfield within each type of Entry, with 0 = no observed occurrence, - = occurrence is not possible:

Subfield	(--P) Personal Name	(--C) Corporate Name	(--M) Meeting	(--U) Uniform Heading	(SET)(SAT) Title	(SUT) Topical	(SUG) Geographic
a	100.0	100.0	100.0	100.0	100.0	100.0	100.0
b	0.2	51.5	33.1	-	-	0.4	0
c	3.6	-	90.6	-	-	-	-
d	42.2	-	96.1	-	-	-	-
e	18.3	0.1	0	-	-	-	-
g	-	-	0	-	-	-	-
k	0	2.6	0	-	-	-	-
t	1.4	21.3	2.4	1.7	-	-	-
u	0.3	0	0.9	0	-	-	-
v	0.1	19.0	0.3	-	76.9	-	-
x	1.7	3.4	0.3	39.6	-	39.1	88.3
y	0.1	0	0	0	-	3.7	27.5
z	0	0	0	0	-	25.6	4.5

IV.A.6.   Occurrence of Subfields for Other Fields

Title Statement

The percentage of occurrence of the three subfields within the Title
Statement is as follows:

		%
a =	Short Title	100.0
b =	Remainder of Title	32.1
c =	Remainder of Statement	64.5

Edition Statement

The percentage of occurrence of the two subfields within the Edition
Statement is as follows:

		%
a =	Edition Statement Proper	100.0
b =	Remainder of Statement	4.6

IV.A.6. <u>Occurrence of Subfields for Other Fields, Continued</u>

<u>Imprint</u>

The three possible subfields of the Imprint are:

      a = Place of Publication

      b = Publisher

      c = Date of Publication

Of these, Subfield a and b may occur more than once, so it is more meaningful
to express the percentage of occurrence of <u>patterns</u> of subfields in the
Imprint. This is somewhat complicated by the fact that, 3.4% of the time, the
Publisher is the Main Entry so that a Subfield b which would normally be
present is missing in the Imprint; for example - an 'abc' would appear as an
'ac'. Therefore, the statistics are presented twice, as follows:

Subfield Pattern	% of Occurrence as noted in record sample	% of Occurrence as it would have been if Publisher were not Main Entry
ac	5.5	2.2
abc	93.5	96.6
aabc	0.8	0.8
aabbc	< 0.1	< 0.1
ababc	< 0.1	< 0.1
abaabc	< 0.1	< 0.1
abbc	0	0.2
Totals	100.0	100.0

IV.A.6.   Occurrence of Subfields for Other Fields, Continued

Imprint, Continued

Expressing the percentage of occurrence of the number of Places and Publishers in the Imprint yields the following:

Number of Places	% of Imprints	Number of Publishers	% of Imprints
1	99.0	0	2.2
2	1.0	1	97.4
3	<0.1	2	0.4
Totals	100.0		100.0

Collation Statement

The three possible subfields of the Collation Statement are:

    a = Pagination
    b = Illustrative Matter
    c = Size

In a similar manner as with the Imprint, it seems more meaningful to express the percentage of occurrence of patterns of subfields in the Collation Statement, as follows:

Subfield Pattern	% of Collations
ac	39.2
abc	60.7
bc	<0.1
abcabc	<0.1
Total	100.0

IV.A.7.   Occurrence of 1st Indicator by Type of Entry

These statistics reflect the occurrence of the 1st indicator, broken down
by the five Entries. They are arranged by the three major types of Entries:
Personal Names, Corporate Names, and Meetings. This is expressed both as
percent of indicator and as percent of type. Thus, the percentage of all
Personal Forenames which are Main Entries is 25.0%, while the percentage of
all Personal Names which are both Forenames and Main Entries is 0.4%.
In the notation used in this table, 0 = no observed occurrence.

Personal Name		(ME) Main	(SE) Series	(SU) Subject Added	(AE) (Other) Added	(SA) Series Added	Total % per Indicator	Total % per Type
Forename (--PF)	% of Indicator	25.0	0	67.8	7.2	0	100.0	
	% per Type	0.4	0	1.0	0.1	0		1.5
Surname (--PS)	% of Indicator	72.1	0.1	8.6	19.2	0	100.0	
	% per Type	69.7	0.1	8.2	18.6	0		96.6
Multiple Surname (--PM)	% of Indicator	70.6	0	23.5	5.9	0	100.0	
	% per Type	1.0	0	0.3	0.1	0		1.4
Family Name (--PN)	% of Indicator	0	0	100.0	0	0	100.0	
	% per Type	0	0	0.5	0	0		0.5

Total   100.0

Corporate Name		(ME) Main	(SE) Series	(SU) Subject Added	(AE) (Other) Added	(SA) Series Added	Total % per Indicator	Total % per Type
Direct Order (--CN)	% of Indicator	28.8	7.3	16.0	37.1	10.8	100.0	
	% per Type	15.5	4.0	8.6	20.1	5.8		54.0
Inverted Order (--CS)	% of Indicator	0	0	100.0	0	0	100.0	
	% per Type	0	0	0.5	0	0		0.5
Place (--CP)	% of Indicator	40.4	6.8	10.1	26.3	16.4	100.0	
	% per Type	18.4	3.1	4.6	12.0	7.4		45.5

Total   100.0

IV.A.7. Occurrence of 1st Indicator by Type of Entry

Meeting			(ME) Main	(SE) Series	(SU) Subject Added	(AE) (Other) Added	(SA) Series Added	Total % per Indicator	Total % per Type
Direct Order	(--MN)	% of Indicator	83.6	0.6	4.8	10.7	0.3	100.0	
		% per Type	80.6	0.6	4.6	10.3	0.3		96.4
Inverted Order	(--MS)	% of Indicator	100.0	0	0	0	0	100.0	
		% per Type	0.9	0	0	0	0		0.9
Place	(--MP)	% of Indicator	11.1	0	55.6	33.3	0	100.0	
		% per Type	0.3	0	1.5	0.9	0		2.7

Total   100.0

IV.A.8.   Occurrence of Fixed Fields

The following gives the percentage of records containing the various fixed
fields in the record's Fixed Field Area. The 'Worksheet Box' refers to the
numbered box on the MARC Worksheet into which the fixed field information
is currently entered by Catalogers and MARC Editors.

Worksheet Box	Byte Position(s) in Record	Name of Fixed Field	% of Occurrence
2	74	Conference/Meeting Indicator	1.8
3	75	Festschrift Indicator	0.3
4	76	Index Indicator	42.8
5	77	Main Entry in Body Indicator	47.9
6	88	Publisher is Main Entry Indicator	3.4
10	67	Intellectual Level (Juvenile) Indicator	10.4
11	78	Fiction Indicator	9.4
12	79	Biography Indicator	7.4
13	87	Main Entry is Subject Indicator	1.6
20	51	Publication Date Key	100.0
21	52-55	Date 1	100.0*
22	56-59	Date 2	21.0
23	60-62	Country of Publication Code	100.0
24	63-66	Illustration Forms Code	54.7
25	68	Form of Reproduction Code	near zero
26	69-72	Form of Contents Code	49.5
27	8**	Bibliographic Level Code	100.0
28	89	Modified Record Indicator	0.7

---

*Including the notation '[n.d.]' as a date.

**In the Record Leader rather than the Fixed Field Area, which occupies bytes 38-91.

IV.B.   Correctness of Processing Statistics

Of the five Format Recognition steps required to produce a MARC II Internal Processing Format Record, virtually all of the potential for processing error lies in Step 3.

Step 1 is quite cut-and-dried, since it merely initializes and sets up fixed portions of the record and inserts 'canned' data.

Step 2 can identify fields through Collation quite easily, and all fields following are essentially self-identifying. The only possible area of confusion lies in distinguishing between Series Notes and (other) Notes. However, in Step 2 these are all tagged as 'NO-' (Notes), and it is left to Step 3 to determine which, if any, of them should actually be retagged 'SE-' (Series Notes).

Step 4 performs correlations between variable fields, which is assumed to be a relatively error-free process. It also assembles the Language Codes (LAN) and Geographic Area Codes (GAC) variable fields; however, the data used is accumulated in Step 3 and therefore any error involved is given to this prior step.

Step 5, like Step 1, is quite cut-and-dried, since it consists of sorting the Record Directory and assembling and outputting the record.

Therefore, it can be reasonably estimated that the error in processing resulting from Steps 1, 2, 4, and 5 will be near zero.

The cumulative error in processing resulting from all Step 3 processing is 32.8%; therefore, 67.2% of all records produced by the Format Recognition process, as described in this report, should be completely free of error. This would seem to substantiate the feasibility of the Format Recignition approach.

The method of determining the estimated error in Step 3 processing, and a table giving an error breakdown is given on the following pages.

IV.B.   Correctness of Processing Statistics, Continued

Determining Estimated Error in Step 3 Processing

The general approach used in arriving at these estimates has been to determine the percentage of occurrence of a data element in a record and to then determine the error in processing the element. The product of these two percentages is then assumed to be the percentage of all records which would be in error due to the processing of that particular data element. These percentages of records in error are then summed to give a total estimate of the percentage of all records which will be in error. This is of course a highly-pessimistic, worst-case approach, since it implicitly assumes that the errors are evenly distributed, with no more than one to a record. This will certainly not be the case, but is probably the best assumption to make from the point of view of feasibility.

The rough determination of occurrences of data elements can be made by running counts on record samples, and the results of such counts are given in Section IV.A. In most cases, the error rates have also been determined by running samples of fields through the processing algorithms and tabulating the percentages which were handled incorrectly. In a few cases, where the determination of the data element is particularly secure, the a priori error rate of 'near zero' was assumed.

In the case of determining subfield codes for Entries, each subfield was analyzed and assigned a correctness of processing estimate of 'Yes'=100%, 'Mostly'=80%, and 'No'=0%. The 'Yes' cases are cut-and-dried and near-zero error can be assumed. The 'Mostly' cases stem from the use of keyword lists which are assumed worst-case to cover all cases 80% of the time, and therefore 20% error rate is assumed. The few 'No' cases assume 100% error and arise in cases where the algorithm is faced with a blind choice between two alternatives and therefore picks the more frequently-occurring one.

IV.B.   Correctness of Processing Statistics, Continued

Breakdown of Step 3 Error in Processing Statistics

Description of Processing	% Records in Error
Completion of Tag and 1st Indicator	
Entries	3.3
Notes	0.5
Determining Series Notes	0.7
Delimiting and Assigning Subfield Codes	
Entries: Main Entry	1.4
Series Statement/Notes	0.0
Subject Added Entries	7.3
(Other) Added Entries	0.7
Series Added Entries	0.0
Title Statement	9.3
Edition Statement	0.0
Imprint	1.0
Collation Statement	0.0
Call Number	1.8
Assigning all other 1st Indicators (CAL, TIL, ROM, UTI, & IMP)	0.2
Assigning 2nd Indicator for Entries (ME-, SE-, SU-, & AE-)	0.8
Accumulating Data for Additional Variable Fields	
Language Codes Field	2.9
Geographic Area Codes Field	0*
Building Fixed Fields	2.9**
Total	32.8%

---

*Estimated. The Geographic Area Codes are not yet in use and data is unavailable.

**Excludes the Index Indicator, which cannot be determined and which occurs in 42.8% of all records.

V.   STEP 1 - SETTING UP THE RECORD

This step initializes the Bookkeeping and Fixed Field Areas of the record and
also clears the buffers used in Steps 3 and 4. It first sets to binary zeros
a contiguous 98-byte area of memory to be used as follows:

Record Area	Length	Byte Positions
Quality Control Block	6 bytes	minus 6 - minus 1
Record Leader	12 bytes	0 - 11
Communications Area	12 bytes	12 - 23
Record Control Area	14 bytes	24 - 37
Fixed Fields Area	54 bytes	38 - 91

It then sets to binary zeros the buffers used for accumulating data for the
Language Codes Field (tag LAN) and the Geographic Area Codes Field (tag GAC),
as follows:

    LAN -   Language Code Subfield A Working Buffer, plus its count byte
             Language Code Subfield B Working Buffer, plus its count byte
             Translation Indicator Byte

    GAC -   Geographic Area Code Working Buffer, plus its count byte

Finally, the following steps are taken to insert 'canned' data in the
appropriate portions of the bookkeeping and Fixed Field Areas. Those
portions not referenced are either already initialized as binary zeros,
are currently not used, or are completed in Steps 3, 4, or 5.

V.   STEP 1 - SETTING UP THE RECORD, Continued

Quality Control Block

a. Set the Record Process Code (byte minus 6) to 01_{16}, indicating that record is a Transaction Record.

Record Leader

b. Obtain the current date from the computer operating system and save it. Store it in the Date Field of the Record Leader in the following form:

> Year   (byte 2)   store as packed decimal (00-99)
>
> Month (byte 3)   store as packed decimal (01-12)
>
> Day   (byte 4)   store as packed decimal (01-31)

c. Set the Status (byte 5) to $0A_{16}$, indicating that the record is a New Record.

d. Set the Record Type (byte 7) to 'A', indicating that the record is "Language, Printed".

e. Set the Bibliographic Level (byte 8) to 'm', indicating that the record is a Monograph.

Communications Area

f. Set the Record Directory Location (bytes 12-13) to $005C_{16}$ (i.e. 92_{10}), indicating Directory starts in the position following the Fixed Field Area.

g. Set the Record Source (byte 16) to 'P', indicating source is Processing Department.

h. Set the Record Destination (byte 17) to 'M', indicating destination is MARC Data Base.

V.   STEP 1 - SETTING UP THE RECORD, Continued

    i.   Set the In Process Type (byte 18) to $0A_{16}$, indicating entire record
          is to be added.

    j.   Set the In Process Status (byte 19) to 46_{16}, indicating record is
          unverified.

Record Control Area

    (This is built from the LC Card Number in Step 3.)

Fixed Field Area

    k.   Using the current date obtained in Step b. on the previous page,
          store it in the File Date field of the Fixed Field Area in the
          following form:

              Year   (bytes 41-42)   store as decimal characters (00-99)
              Month (bytes 43-44)   store as decimal characters (01-12)
              Day   (bytes 45-46)   store as decimal characters (01-31)

VI.   STEP 2 - IDENTIFY INPUT FIELDS

The processing in this step is the first related to the input data itself. Its primary purpose is to read the input data for a given record and identify each input field which is present. When necessary, it must break up clusters of input fields into their respective individual input fields. Most of the input fields can be identified completely; others, like the Entries, are only identified as to their general type, with their more detailed identification left to Step 3 to complete. For each input field identified, a corresponding Record Directory entry is built in the Preliminary Directory area. Each entry will include a numeric code corresponding to the identified field's mnemonic tag, the starting position of the data and its length, its site number, and possibly other pertinent information, such as the 'data occurred within brackets' flag. Throughout the processing of Step 2, an incremented count is kept of the number of entries in the Record Directory. Also, when the last input field has been processed, an end-of-field character is inserted following its Record Directory entry.

The Identify Input Fields process requires two separate substeps: one to identify the Collation Statement within the first five input fields, the other to make the identification of the remaining input fields. The reason that two substeps are required is that of the first five possible input fields, only two always occur: the Title Paragraph and the Collation Paragraph. Of these two, the Collation Statement portion of the Collation Paragraph is the most readily identifiable. From this foothold, the input fields which precede the collation can be identified. The remaining input fields following the Collation, when present, are for the most part self-identifying and can be processed on a one-at-a-time basis in a straight-forward manner to complete the input field identification for this record.

VI.A.   Substep 1 - Input Field Identification through Collation

The initial input field identification provides the necessary foothold to
establish among the first five input fields a positive identification of
one of them. The one most readily identifiable is the Collation Statement,
as follows:

The first five input fields are examined successively with each of the
following tests. The first success determines that field to be the
Collation:

1.   Ignoring any leading open bracket, test if the field begins with an
     Arabic Numeral, followed by a space and either 'p.', 'v.', or
     'l.' (lower-case 'L').

2.   Ignoring any leading open bracket, test if field begins with a
     Roman Numeral, 'v.', or 'p.'.

3.   Test if field contains 'cm.' or 'mm.'.

There are six Collation identification cases which can result from the above
tests:

Case 1 - Collation occurs as first input field - See Procedure 1.

Case 2 - Collation occurs as second input field - See Procedure 2.

Case 3 - Collation occurs as third input field - See Procedure 3.

Case 4 - Collation occurs as fourth input field - See Procedure 4.

Case 5 - Collation occurs as fifth input field - See Procedure 5.

Case 6 - Collation cannot be recognized among
          first five input fields   - See Procedure 6.

VI.A.1.   Procedure 1 - Collation Statement Occurs as First Input Field

This is not a valid case; however, an attempt will be made to identify the remaining input fields. This is feasible since most of the fields following the Collation are self-identifying. This procedure in Substep 1 merely attempts to break up the possible clustered fields of the Collation Paragraph. When completed, the processing should be continued at Substep 2 of this Step.

a]   A Record Directory entry is created with the tag 'COL' for the Collation Statement and its starting position and site number are stored in the entry.

b]   The Collation Paragraph is now inspected for the ending of the Size Subfield of the Collation Statement (Subfield c - which should always be present) or the end-of-field indication. One of the following is now completed:

1]   End-of-Subfield found - The length of this field is computed through the blank following the 'cm.' or 'mm.' not followed by 'and' in the Size Subfields and stored in the Record Directory entry; the last blank character is replaced by the end-of-field character.

2]   End-of-Field found - The length of this field is computed through the end-of-field character and stored in the Record Directory entry. The processing of this First Substep of Step 2 is now complete.

c]   The Collation Paragraph is now inspected forward from the current position, at the end of the Collation Statement proper, for the occurrence of one or both of the following:

1]   A text statement enclosed in parentheses or brackets - A Record Directory entry is created with the tag 'SE-' for Series Statement and its starting position (at the open parenthesis or bracket), its length (through space or end-of-field character following the close parenthesis or bracket), and its site number are stored in the entry. If the last character of the field is a blank, it is replaced by the end-of-field character.

VI.A.1.   <u>Procedure 1 - Collation Statement Occurs as 1st Input Field, Continued</u>

2]   <u>Any other statement</u> - A Record Directory entry is created with the tag 'PRI' for Bibliographic Price and its starting position (first non-blank character following the Collation or Series Statement), its length, and its site number are stored in the entry. The processing of the First Substep of Step 2 is now complete.

VI.A.2.   Procedure 2 - Collation Statement Occurs as the Second Input Field

When the Collation Statement is the second input field, the first input field must be the Title Paragraph. This procedure includes the following tests. When completed, the processing should continue at Substep 2 of this Step.

a]   A Record Directory entry is created with the tag 'TIL' for the Title Statement and its starting position (the beginning of the first input field) and its site number are stored in the entry.

b]   The Title Paragraph (first input field) is inspected for the first occurrence of the standard delimiter, '$\neq$', (which sets off the Title Statement from the rest of the Title Paragraph) or the occurrence of the end-of-field indication. One of the following is now completed:

    1]   Delimiter found - The length of the Title Statement is computed through the delimiter character and stored in the Record Directory entry. The delimiter is replaced with the end-of-field character.

    2]   Delimiter not found - The length of the Title Statement is computed through the end-of-field character and stored in the Record Directory entry. The processing is continued at d].

c]   The Title Paragraph is now inspected forward from the current position, at the end of the Title Statement, for the occurrence of another standard delimiter or the end-of-field indication. One of the following is now completed:

    1]   Delimiter found - A Record Directory entry is created with the tag 'EDN' for the Edition Statement and its starting position (the first non-blank character following the Title Statement) and its site number are stored in the entry. The length of this field is computed through the second delimiter and also stored in the entry. The delimiter is replaced with an end-of-field character. Processing continues at c]2c, immediately following.

VI.A.2. **Procedure 2 - Collation Statement Occurs as 2nd Input Field, Continued**

2] <u>Delimiter not found</u> - A Record Directory entry is created with the tag 'IMP' for Imprint and its starting position (the first non-blank character after the last field encountered) and its site number are stored in the entry. The length of this field is computed through the end-of-field character and also stored in the entry.

d] A Record Directory entry is created with the tag 'COL' for the Collation Statement and its starting position (the beginning of the second input field) and its site number are stored in the entry.

e] The Collation Paragraph (second input field) is now inspected for the ending of the Size Subfield of the Collation Statement (Subfield c - which should always be present) or the end-of-field indication. One of the following is now completed:

1] <u>End-of-Subfield found</u> - The length of this field is computed through the blank following the 'cm.' or 'mm.' not followed by 'and' in the Size Subfield and is stored in the Record Directory entry; the last blank character is replaced by the end-of-field character.

2] <u>End-of-Field found</u> - The length of this field is computed through the end-of-field character and stored in the Record Directory entry. The processing of this First Substep of Step 2 is now complete.

(Continued on following page.)

VI.A.2. Procedure 2 - Collation Statement Occurs as 2nd Input Field, Continued

f] The Collation Paragraph is now inspected forward from the current
position, at the end of the Collation Statement proper, for the
occurrence of one or both of the following:

1] A text statement enclosed in parentheses or brackets - A Record
Directory entry is created with the tag 'SE-' for Series Statement
and its starting position (at the open parenthesis or bracket), its
length (through space or end-of-field character following the
close parenthesis or bracket), and its site number are stored
in the entry. If the last character of this field is a blank,
it is replaced by the end-of-field character.

2] Any other statement - A Record Directory entry is created with
the tag 'PRI' for Bibliographic Price and its starting position
(first non-blank character following the Collation or Series
Statement), its length, and its site number are stored in the
entry. The processing of the First Substep of Step 2 is now
complete.

VI.A.3.   <u>Procedure 3 - Collation Statement Occurs as the Third Input Field</u>

When the Collation Statement is the third input field, two possibilities may occur; these are:

1.   Call Number   Title Paragraph   Collation Paragraph

2.   Main Entry   Title Paragraph   Collation Paragraph

The following tests handle this procedure. When completed, the processing should continue at Substep 2 of this Step.

a]   A Record Directory entry is created and the starting position, length, and site number of the first input field are stored in the entry. A test is made on the contents of this field to establish if it is a Call Number. The form of a Call Number is: 1-3 capital letters, followed by 1-4 numbers (optionally followed by a period and more numbers), followed by a space or period, and finally followed by a capital letter and more numbers and letters. (It may also equal the word 'LAW'.) If this field has the appearance of a Call Number, the tag 'CAL' for Call Number is stored in the Record Directory entry. Otherwise, the tag 'ME-' for Main Entry is stored in the entry. In addition, for the Call Number case, the first character of the input field is tested for being an open bracket. If so, the bracket is removed from the data and the starting position and length are adjusted accordingly in the Record Directory entry. A flag is set in the entry as well, to indicate that the field was in brackets. Similarly, the last character preceding the end-of-field character is tested for being a close bracket. If so, it is removed from the data and the length of the field is again adjusted in the entry.

b]   A Record Directory entry is created with the tag 'TIL' for the Title Statement and its starting position (the beginning of the second input field) and its site number are stored in the entry.

VI.A.3.   <u>Procedure 3 - Collation Statement Occurs as 3rd Input Field, Continued</u>

c]   The Title Paragraph (second input field) is inspected for the first occurrence of the standard delimiter, '‡', (which sets off the Title Statement from the rest of the Title Paragraph) or the occurrence of the end-of-field indication. One of the following is now completed:

1]   <u>Delimiter found</u> - The length of the Title Statement is computed through the delimiter character and stored in the Record Directory entry. The delimiter is replaced with an end-of-field character.

2]   <u>Delimiter not found</u> - The length of the Title Statement is computed through the end-of-field character and stored in the Record Directory entry. The processing is continued ar e].

d]   The Title Paragraph is now inspected forward from the current position at the end of the Title Statement, for the occurrence of another standard delimiter or the end-of-field indication. One of the following is now completed:

1]   <u>Delimiter found</u> - A Record Directory entry is created with the tag 'EDN' for the Edition Statement and its starting position (the first non-blank character following the Title Statement) and its site number are stored in the entry. The length of this field is computed through the second delimiter and is also stored in the entry. The delimiter is replaced with an end-of-field character. Processing continues at d]d2, immediately following.

2]   <u>Delimiter not found</u> - A Record Directory entry is created with the tag 'IMP' for Imprint and its starting position (the first non-blank character after the last field encountered) and its site number are stored in the entry. The length of this field is computed through the end-of-field character and also stored in the entry.

VI.A.3. <u>Procedure 3 - Collation Statement Occurs as 3rd Input Field, Continued</u>

e] A Record Directory entry is created with the tag 'COL' for the Collation Statement and its starting position (the beginning of the third input field) and its site number are stored in the entry.

f] The Collation Paragraph (third input field) is now inspected for the ending of the Size Subfield of the Collation Statement (Subfield c - which should always be present) or the end-of-field indication. One of the following is now completed:

    1] <u>End-of-subfield found</u> - The length of this field is computed through the blank following the 'cm.' or 'mm.' not followed by 'and' in the Size Subfield and is stored in the Record Directory entry; the last blank character is replaced by the end-of-field character.

    2] <u>End-of-Field found</u> - The length of this field is computed through the end-of-field character and stored in the Record Directory entry. The processing of this First Substep of Step 2 is now complete.

g] The Collation Paragraph is now inspected forward from the current position, at the end of the Collation Statement proper, for the occurrence of one or both of the following:

    1] <u>A text statement enclosed in parentheses or brackets</u> - A Record Directory entry is created with the tag 'SE-' for Series Statement and its starting position (at open parenthesis or bracket), its length (through the space or end-of-field character following the close parenthesis or bracket), and its site number are stored in the entry. If the last character of the field is a blank, it is replaced by the end-of-field character.

    2] <u>Any other statement</u> - A Record Directory entry is created with the tag 'PRI' for Bibliographic Price and its starting position (first non-blank character following the Collation or Series Statement, its length, and its site number are stored in the entry. The processing of the First Substep of Step 2 is now complete.

VI.A.4.   Procedure 4 - Collation Statement Occurs as the Fourth Input Field

When the Collation Statement is the fourth input field, two possibilities may occur; these are:

1.   Call Number   Main Entry   Title Paragraph   Collation Paragraph

2.   Main Entry   Uniform Title   Title Paragraph   Collation Paragraph

The following tests handle this procedure. When completed, the processing should continue at Substep 2 of this Step.

a]   A Record Directory entry is created and the starting position, length, and site number of the first input field are stored in the entry. A test is made on the contents of this field to establish if it is a Call Number. The form of a Call Number is: 1-3 capital letters, followed by 1-4 numbers (optionally followed by a period and more numbers, followed by a space or period, and finally followed by a capital letter and more numbers and letters (It may also equal the word 'LAW'.) If this field has the appearance of a Call Number, the tag 'CAL' for Call Number is stored in the Record Directory entry. Otherwise, the tag 'ME-' for Main Entry is stored in the entry. In addition, for the Call Number case, the first character of the input field is tested for being an open bracket. If so, the bracket is removed from the data and the starting position and length are adjusted accordingly in the Record Directory entry. A flag is set in the entry as well, to indicate that the field was in brackets. Similarly, the last character preceding the end-of-field character is tested for being a close bracket. If so, it is removed from the data and the length of the field is again adjusted in the entry.

VI.A.4.   Procedure 4 - Collation Statement Occurs as 4th Input Field, Continued

b]   A second Record Directory entry is created and the starting position, length, and site number of the second input field are stored in the entry. If the first input field was established as being a Call Number, then the tag 'ME-' for Main Entry is stored in this newly-created entry. Otherwise, the tag 'UTI' for Uniform Title is stored in the entry. In addition, for the Uniform Title case, the first character of the input field is tested for being an open bracket. If so, it is removed from the data and the starting position and length are adjusted accordingly in the Record Directory entry. A flag is set in the entry as well, to indicate that the field was in brackets. Similarly, the last character preceding the end-of-field character is tested for being a close bracket. If so, it is removed from the data and the length of the field is again adjusted in the entry.

c]   A Record Directory entry is created with the tag 'TIL' for the Title Statement and its starting position (the beginning of the third input field) and its site number are stored in the entry.

d]   The Title Paragraph (third input field) is inspected for the first occurrence of the standard delimiter, '‡', (which sets off the Title Statement from the rest of the Title Paragraph) or the occurrence of the end-of-field indication. One of the following is now completed:

1]   Delimiter found - The length of the Title Statement is computed through the delimiter character and stored in the Record Directory entry. The delimiter is replaced with an end-of-field character.

2]   Delimiter not found - The length of the Title Statement is computed through the end-of-field character and stored in the Record Directory entry. The processing is continued at f].

VI.A.4.   Procedure 4 - Collation Statement Occurs as 4th Input Field, Continued

e]   The Title Paragraph is now inspected forward from the current
position, at the end of the Title Statement, for the occurrence of
another standard delimiter or the end-of-field indication. One of
the following is now completed:

1]   Delimiter found - A Record Directory entry is created with the
tag 'EDN' for the Edition Statement and its starting position
(the first non-blank character following the Title Statement)
and its site number are stored in the entry. The length of
this field is computed through the second delimiter and also
stored in the entry. The delimiter is replaced by the end-of-
field character. Processing continues at e]2], immediately
following.

2]   Delimiter not found - A Record Directory entry is created with
the tag 'IMP' for Imprint and its starting position (the first
non-blank character after the last field encountered) and its
site number are stored in the entry. The length of this field
is computed through the end-of-field character and also stored
in the entry.

f]   A Record Directory entry is created with the tag 'COL' for the
Collation Statement and its starting position (the beginning of the
fourth input field) and its site number are stored in the entry.

g]   The Collation Paragraph (fourth input field) is now inspected for
the ending of the Size Subfield of the Collation Statement
(Subfield c - which should always be present) or the end-of-field
indication. One of the following is now completed:

1]   End-of-Subfield found - The length of this field is computed throug
the blank following the 'cm.' or 'mm.' not followed by 'end' in the
Size Subfield and is stored in the Record Directory entry; the las
blank character is replaced by the end-of-field character.

VI.A.4. <u>Procedure 4 - Collation Statement Occurs as 4the Input Field, Continued</u>

2] <u>End-of-Field found</u> - The length of this field is computed through the end-of-field character and stored in the Record Directory entry. The processing of this First Substep of Step 2 is now complete.

h] The Collation Paragraph is now inspected forward from the current position, at the end of the Collation Statement proper, for the occurrence of one or both of the following:

1] <u>A text statement enclosed in parentheses or brackets</u> - A Record Directory entry is created with the tag 'SE-' for Series Statement and its starting position (at the open parenthesis or bracket), its length (through the space or end-of-field character following the close parenthesis or bracket), and its site number are stored in the entry. If the last character of this field is a blank, it is replaced by an end-of-field character.

2] <u>Any other statement</u> - A Record Directory entry is created with the tag 'PRI' for Bibliographic Price and its starting position (first non-blank character following the Collation or Series Statement), its length, and its site number are stored in the entry. The processing of the First Substep of Step 2 is now complete.

VI.A.5. Procedure 5 - Collation Statement Occurs as the Fifth Input Field

When the Collation Statement is the fifth input field, the only possible field occurrence is: Call Number, Main Entry, Uniform Title, Title Paragraph, and Collation Paragraph. This procedure includes the following tests. When completed, the processing should continue at Substep 2 of this Step.

a]   A Record Directory entry is created with the tag 'CAL' for Call Number and the starting position, length, and site number of the first input field are stored in the entry. In addition, the first character of the field is tested for being an open bracket. If so, it is removed from the data and the starting position and length are adjusted accordingly in the Record Directory entry. A flag is set in this entry as well, to indicate that the field was in brackets. Similarly, the last character preceding the end-of-field character is tested for being a close bracket. If so, it is removed from the data and the length of the field is again adjusted in the entry.

b]   A second Record Directory entry is created with the tag 'ME-' for Main Entry and the starting position, length, and site number of the second input field are stored in the entry.

c]   A third Record Directory entry is created with the tag 'UTI' for Uniform Title and the starting position, length, and site number of the third input field are stored in this entry. In addition, the first character of the input field is tested for being an open bracket. If so, it is removed from the data and the starting position and length are adjusted accordingly in the Record Directory entry. A flag is set in this entry as well, to indicate that the field was in brackets. Similarly, the last character preceding the end-of-field character is tested for being a close bracket. If so, it is removed from the data and the length of field is again adjusted in the entry.

VI.A.5.   Procedure 5 - Collation Statement Occurs as 5th Input Field, Continued

d]   A Record Directory entry is created with the tag 'TIL' for the Title Statement and its starting position (the beginning of the fourth input field) and the site number are stored in the entry.

e]   The Title Paragraph (fourth input field) is inspected for the first occurrence of the standard delimiter, '‡', (which sets off the Title Statement from the rest of the Title Paragraph) or the occurrence of the end-of-field indication. One of the following is now completed:

   1]   Delimiter found - The length of the Title Statement is computed through the delimiter character and stored in the Record Directory entry. The delimiter is replaced with an end-of-field character.

   2]   Delimiter not found - The length of the Title Statement is computed through the end-of-field character and stored in the Record Directory entry. The processing is continued at g].

f]   The Title Paragraph is now inspected forward from the current position, at the end of the Title Statement, for the occurrence of another standard delimiter or the end-of-field indication. One of the following is now completed:

   1]   Delimiter found - A Record Directory entry is created with the tag 'EDN' for the Edition Statement and its starting position (the first non-blank character following the Title Statement) and its site number are stored in the entry. The length of this field is computed through the second delimiter and stored in this entry. The delimiter is replaced by the end-of-field character. Processing continues at f]2], immediately following.

   2]   Delimiter not found - A Record Directory entry is created with the tag 'IMP' for Imprint and its starting position (the first non-blank character after the last field encountered) and its site number are stored in the entry. The length of this field is computed through the end-of-field character and also stored in the entry.

VI.A.5. Procedure 5 - Collation Statement Occurs as 5th Input Field, Continued

g] A Record Directory entry is created with the tag 'COL' for the Collation Statement and its starting position (the beginning of the fifth input field) and its site number are stored in the entry.

h] The Collation Paragraph (fifth input field) is now inspected for the ending of the Size Subfield of the Collation Statement (Subfield c - which should always be present) or the end-of-field indication. One of the following is now completed:

1] End-of-Subfield found - The length of this field is computed through the blank following the 'cm.' or 'mm.' not followed by 'and' in the Size Subfield and is stored in the Record Directory entry; the last blank character is replaced by the end-of-field character.

2] End-of-Field found - The length of this field is computed through the end-of-field character and stored in the Record Directory entry. The processing of this First Substep of Step 2 is now complete.

i] The Collation Paragraph is now inspected forward from the current position, at the end of the Collation Statement proper, for the occurrence of one or both of the following:

1] A text statement enclosed in parentheses or brackets - A Record Directory entry is created with the tag 'SE-' for Series Statement and its starting position (at open parenthesis or bracket), its length (through the space or end-of-field character following the close parenthesis or bracket), and its site number are stored in the entry. If the last character of the field is a blank, it is replaced by the end-of-field character.

2] Any other statement - A Record Directory entry is created with the tag 'PRI' for Bibliographic Price and its starting position (first non-blank character following the Collation or Series Statement), its length, and its site number are stored in the entry. The processing of the First Substep of Step 2 is now complete.

VI.A.6.   Procedure 6 - Collation Cannot Be Recognized Among First Five Input Fields

This is not a valid case; however, an attempt will be made to identify the input fields. This is feasible, even though no foothold has been established, since most of the fields in the record are self-identifying.

At this point, the most probable situation is that the LC Call Number and Main Entry fields are both present in the record. Therefore, the following arbitrary choice is made, based on the bracket test for a Uniform Title in the 3rd input field:

1.   If the 3rd input field begins with an open bracket, assume Collation is the 5th input field and go to Procedure 5.

2.   If the 3rd input field does not begin with an open bracket, assume Collation is the 4th input field and go to Procedure 4.

It should be noted that none of the first five input fields contain 'cm.' or 'mm.', since this is one of the identifying features of a Collation Statement. Therefore, in Procedures 4 and 5, where the attempt is made to locate text in parentheses or brackets (i.e. - Series Statement), following the Size Subfield of the Collation Statement, end-of-field will be encountered before this subfield, terminating the testing on that field with no further action.

VI.B.   Substep 2 - Identifying Remaining Input Fields Past Collation

This process identifies the remaining input fields following the Collation
Paragraph. These fields are read, one at a time, and identified. (Initially,
any fields following the Collation which have been input as one of the first
5 fields are processed first.) If an input field cannot be identified, the
tag 'UNK' for Unknown Field is stored in the Record Directory entry created
for the field and its starting position, length, and site number are stored
in the entry.

The only remaining input field which represents a cluster of fields is the
Series Added Entry Paragraph; this is broken into its separate Entries when
encountered.

The set of non-LC Subject Added Entries and the set of Children's Subject
Added Entries are grouped within a single enclosing pair of brackets, even
though each entry is input as a separate input field, with the open bracket
included with the first such field and the close bracket included with the
last. Therefore, when these bracketed Subject Entries are encountered in
Step 2, the Record Directory entry for each such field is flagged that the
data was in brackets.

Only two of the remaining input fields are always present in a record: the LC
Card Number and the Cataloging Source. Following the Collation Paragraph, there
is expected a regular ordering of the input fields, when they occur, down to
near the bottom of those appearing on a manuscript card. These are: Numbers
(National Bibliography Number, Standard Book Number, Overseas Acquisition Number),
Series Notes and other Notes, Subject Added Entries, (Other) Added Entries, and
Series Added Entries. However, following these fields, other fields may occur
which may be input in no regular order. These are: Romanized Title, Uniform
Title - Type 3, Copy Statement, Bracketed LC Call Number, Non-LC Call Number,
Second Class Number, and Non-LC Cataloging Source. The remaining fields are
again well-ordered when they occur, since in general they fall within boxes on
a manuscript card specifically allocated for them. These are: Dewey Decimal
Number, LC Card Number, Cataloging Source (LC), and (on back of Manuscript Card)
Uniform Title - Type 2, Non-LC Subject Entries, and possibly Non-LC Call Number.

VI.B.   Substep 2 - Identifying Remaining Fields Past Collation, Continued

Also, several input fields can occur in two places, based on their appearance
on a Manuscript Card. The Cataloging Source may occur before the Dewey Decimal
Number or following the LC Card Number. The bracketed Subject Added Entries
may occur as a set either replacing or following the normal Subject Entries
or may follow the Uniform Title - Type 2, appearing on the back of the Manuscript
Card. The Non-LC Call Number may occur following the Non-LC Subject Added
Entries set within their enclosing brackets or before the LC Card Number without
brackets. The Bracketed LC Call Number sometimes occurs when there is no
Call Number, in its place as the first input field.

Since some input fields have no fixed order of input and some may occur in
several places, it would therefore appear that it is not feasible to rely on
input field order past the Collation Paragraph for the identification of the
remaining input fields. However, since most of these fields are self-identifying,
the remaining input fields can be identified with a high degree of success. The
procedure for their identification begins with an initial test on the beginning
portion of the input field's data to classify it into one of eight categories:

Initial Character	Procedure Identification	Possible Candidates
Open Bracket	1	Series Notes, Subject Added Entries (including Non-LC), LC Call Number, Second Class Number, Dewey Decimal Number, Non-LC Call Number
Open Parenthesis	2	National Bibliography Number, Overseas Acquisition Number, Series Added Entries, Uniform Title - Type 3
Quotation Mark	3	Notes
Multiple Hyphens	4	Copy Statement
Arabic Numeral	5	Subject Added Entries
Roman Numeral	6	(Other) Added Entries
Numeric Digit	7	LC Card Number, Dewey Decimal Number
Alpha Character	8	National Bibliography Number, Standard Book Number, Overseas Acquisition Number, Notes, Cataloging Source, Romanized Title, Uniform Title - Type 2, LC Card Number, Non-LC Call Number

VI.B.1.   Procedure 1 - Initial Character is an Open Bracket

The following tests are performed on these input fields following the Collation
Paragraph which begin with an open bracket in order to distinguish between them
and identify them to complete the processing of Step 2.

a]   If the data immediately following the bracket is one of the following:

1]   DNAL: Arabic Numeral*

2]   DNLM: Arabic Numeral*

3]   Arabic Numeral*

then the field is a Subject Added Entry. A Record Directory entry is
created with the tag 'SU-' and the starting position, length, and site
number of the input field is stored in the entry. The initial open
bracket and the phrase through the blank following the colon, when
present, are removed from the data and the length adjusted accordingly
in the entry. The entry is also flagged that the data was in brackets.

If the data in this field ends with a close bracket, it is removed
from the data and the length in the Record Directory entry is again
adjusted accordingly; the identification process for this field is now
complete. If the input field does not end with a close bracket, the
next input field is tested as to whether it begins with an Arabic
Numeral. If it does, then another Record Directory entry is created
for that field with the tag 'SU-' and the starting position, length,
and incremented site number of the input field are stored in the
entry. The entry is flagged that the data was in brackets. The close
bracket test is again made, as per the start of this paragraph, and
the process continues until either a close bracket is found ending a
field or an input field occurs which does not start with an Arabic
Numeral.

---

*An Arabic Numeral is defined as: Numeric digit(s), followed by period, followed
by space.

VI.B.1.   Procedure 1 - Initial Character is an Open Bracket, Continued

If the next input field is not a Subject Entry, it is tested as to whether it is a call number, that is - it consists of 1-3 capital letters, followed by 1-4 numbers (optionally followed by a period and more numbers), followed by a period or space, and finally followed by a capital letter and more numbers and letters. If this field is a Call Number, then a new Record Directory entry is created with the pseudo-tag 'NLC' for Non-LC Call Number and the starting position, length, and site number of the field are stored in the entry.

This completes the lookahead process whether or not the field ends with a close bracket. However, it must be tested for, and, if present, removed from the data, with the length in the Record Directory entry being adjusted accordingly. The entry is flagged as having been input in brackets.

If the next input field is not a Call Number, then it must be assumed that the close bracket of the preceding bracketed Subject Added Entries was omitted by error. This new field should now be handled independently, based on the nature of its first character.

b]   If the data following the bracket is one of the following:

1]   Fic

2]   E

3]   B

4]   all numeric digits (may also contain 'j', 's', slashes, parentheses, or a decimal point)

then the field is a Dewey Decimal Number. A Record Directory entry is created for this input field with the tag 'DDC' and the starting position, length, and site number of the field are stored in the entry. This completes the identification processing for this input field.

VI.B.1. **Procedure 1 - Initial Character is an Open Bracket, Continued**

c] If the data following the bracket contains a mix of numeric digits and alpha characters, the input field may be either an LC Call Number or a Second Class Number. The Call Number is identical to a Class Number in the beginning of its expression; this form is: 1-3 capital letters, followed by 1-4 numbers, optionally followed by a period and more numbers. Both a Call Number and a Class Number may continue past this point, so the following test is used to distinguish between them:

    1] Test if the Directory contains a Call Number entry (tag CAL). If yes, then consider this field the Second Class Number. A Record Directory entry is created with the pseudo-tag 'CAL+' and the starting position, length, and site number of the field are stored in the entry. The enclosing brackets are removed from the data, and the starting position and length in the Directory entry are adjusted accordingly. This completes the identification processing for this field.

    2] If the Directory does not already contain a Call Number entry (tag CAL), consider this field the LC Call Number and create a Record Directory entry with the tag 'CAL'. The starting position, length, and site number of the field are stored in the entry. The enclosing brackets are removed from the data, and the starting position and length in the entry are adjusted accordingly. This completes the identification processing for this field.

d] If the data following the open bracket is not one of the above cases, then the beginning character test is again made on the character following the bracket on the off chance that the bracket represents an insertion by a Cataloger. The appropriate procedure is then executed as a result of this test.

VI.B.2. Procedure 2 - Initial Character is an Open Parenthesis

The following tests are performed on those input fields following the Collation Paragraph which begin with an open parenthesis, in order to distinguish among them and identify them to complete the processing of Step 2.

a] If the first word following the open parenthesis is 'Title: ', then this field is a Uniform Title - Type 3. A Record Directory entry is created with the tag 'UTI' and the starting position, length, and site number of the field are stored in the entry. This completes the identification processing for this field.

b] If the first word following the open parenthesis is 'Series.' or 'Series: ', then this field is the Series Added Entries Paragraph. A Record Directory entry is created with the tag 'SA-' and the starting position and site number of the field are stored in the entry

From the current position in the Series Added Entries Paragraph, a scan is made through the input field until one of the following is encountered:

1] Close parenthesis - This terminates the Series Added Entries Paragraph and should be followed by an end-of-field character. It is processed as in b]2] below.

2] End-of-field - This terminates the Series Added Entries Paragraph. The length of this input field is computed from the starting position in its Record Directory entry through the end-of-field character and stored in the entry. This completes the identification processing for this field.

3] The word 'Series: ' is encountered - This marks the start of another Series Added Entry field. First, however, the length of the current Series Added Entry field is computed from the starting position in its Record Directory entry through the first non-blank character preceding the word 'Series: ' and stored in the entry. The terminal blank charcter is then replaced by the end-of-field

VI.B.2.   **Procedure 2 - Initial Character is an Open Parenthesis, Continued**

character. Now a new Record Directory entry is created with the tag 'SA-' and the starting position of the word 'Series: ' and the incremented site number are stored in the entry. The process from the beginning of this paragraph is continued until all of the individual entries of the Series Added Entries Paragraph are broken out and identified.

c] If the data following the open parenthesis has the form: 1-5 letters, followed by a space or no space or a hyphen, followed by 2 letters or 2 numbers, followed by a hyphen, etc., then the input field is either a National Bibliography Number or an Overseas Acquisition Number. The following test is made:

1] Test for the presence of the term 'LACAP'. If found, the input field is an Overseas Acquisition Number. A Record Directory entry is created with the tag 'OAN', and the starting position length, and site number of the input field are stored in the Directory entry. This completes the identification processing for this field.

2] All others will be tagged as a National Bibliography Number. A Record Directory entry is created with the tag 'NBN', and the starting position, length, and site number of the input field are stored in the entry. This completes the identification processing for this field. Note: Data such as 'C***' would be considered a National Bibliography Number.

d] If the data following the parenthesis is not one of the above cases, then the flat assumption is made that this is a Series Statement which was entered by the typist separately since it did not appear to be a part of the Collation Paragraph on the Manuscript Card. A Record Directory entry is created with the tag 'SE-' and the starting position, length, and site number of the field are stored in the entry. This completes the identification processing for this field.

VI.B.3. Procedure 3 - Initial Character is a Quotation Mark

The only field which may begin with a quotation mark is a Note field. A Record Directory entry is created with the tag 'NO-' and the starting position, length, and site number of this input field are stored in the entry. This completes the identification processing for this field.

VI.B.4.   Procedure 4 - Initial Characters are Multiple Hyphens

The only field which is preceded directly by multiple hyphens is one of the two forms of the Copy Statement. A Record Directory entry is created with the tag 'COP' and the starting position, length, and site number of this input field are stored in the entry. This completes the identification processing for this field.

VI.B.5.   Procedure 5 - Initial Portion of Field is an Arabic Numeral

The only input field which is preceded directly by an Arabic Numeral is a Subject Added Entry. The form of this numeral is Arabic digit(s), period, and space. A Record Directory entry is created with the tag 'SU-' and the starting position, length, and site number of this input field are stored in the entry. This completes the identification processing for this field.

VI.B.6. Procedure 6 - Initial Portion of Field is a Roman Numeral

The only input field which is preceded directly by a Roman Numeral is an (Other) Added Entry. The form of this numeral is: the appropriate alphabetic character(s), period, and space. A Record Directory entry is created with the tag 'AE-' and the starting position, length, and site number of this input field are stored in the entry. This completes the identification processing for this field.

VI.B.7. Procedure 7 - Initial Character is a Numeric Digit (Not an Arabic Numeral)

There are three input fields which may start with a numeric digit: the LC Card Number, the Dewey Decimal Number, and a Standard Book Number from which the prefix 'SBN' has been omitted. To distinguish among the three, the input data is scanned for the presence of hyphens. If none is found, then the input field is a Dewey Decimal Number and a Record Directory entry is created with the tag 'DDC'. If one hyphen is found, the input field is the LC Card Number and a Record Directory entry is created with the tag 'CRD'. Otherwise, the input field is a prefixless Standard Book Number and a Record Directory entry is created with the tag 'SBN'. In each case, the starting position, length, and site number of the input field are stored in the Record Directory entry. This completes the identification processing for this input field.

VI.B.8.   Procedure 8 - Initial Character is an Alpha Character (Not a Roman Numera

Since all remaining unidentified input fields fall into this category, it is
necessary to make additional discrete tests to further categorize these fields.
In all cases, a Record Directory entry is created and the starting position,
length, and appropriate site number of the input field are stored in the entry.
The tag assignment is made as per the following, which completes the identification processing of Step 2.

a]   Identifiable Prefixes

1]   SBN - The input field is a Standard Book Number and the tag
assigned to the Record Directory entry is 'SBN".

2]   LACAP - The input field is an Overseas Acquisition Number and
the tag assigned to the Record Directory entry is 'OAN'.

3]   PL480 - The input field is an Overseas Acquisition Number and
the tag assigned to the Record Directory entry is 'OAN'.

4]   'j' followed by numbers - The input field is a Dewey Decimal
Number and the tag assigned to the Record Directory entry is
'DDC'.

b]   Distinctive Initial Phrases

1]   Title romanized: - The input field is a Romanized Title and
the tag assigned to the Record Directory entry is 'ROM'.

2]   Title transliterated: - The input field is a Romanized Title and
the tag assigned to the Record Directory entry is 'ROM'.

3]   Filing title: - The input field is a Uniform Title - Type 2
and the tag assigned to the Record Directory entry is 'UTI'.

4]   Shared Cataloging with DLNM. - The input field is the (non-LC)
Cataloging Source and the tag assigned to the Record Directory
entry is 'CAS'.

VI.B.8. **Procedure 8 - Initial Character is an Alpha Character, Continued**

    5] <u>Shared Cataloging for DNAL.</u> - The input field is the (Non-LC) Cataloging Source and the tag assigned to the Record Directory entry is 'CAS'.

    6] <u>Library of Congress.</u> - The input field is the (LC) Cataloging Source and the tag assigned to the Record Directory entry is 'CAS'.

c] <u>Distinctive Ending Phrases</u>

    1] <u>... for Library of Congress.</u> - The input field is the (Cooperating Library) Cataloging Source and the tag assigned to the Record Directory entry is 'CAS'.

d] <u>Short Text (1-2 words) Containing Alpha and Numeric Data</u>

The five possible input fields in this category are: Copy, Non-LC Call Number, Overseas Acquisition Number, National Bibliography Number, and LC Card Number. To distinguish among them, the text is scanned for the occurrences of single hyphens, multiple hyphens, and asterisks, with the following interpretation:

    1] <u>No single hyphens</u> - If the field contains asterisks, it is taken to be a National Bibliography Number and the tag 'NBN' is assigned to the Record Directory entry. If the field contains multiple hyphens, it is taken to be a Copy Statement and the tag 'COP' is assigned to the Record Directory entry. Otherwise, the field is assumed to be a Non-LC Call Number and the tag 'NLC' is assigned to the Record Directory entry.

    2] <u>More than one single hyphen</u> - The input field is a National Bibliography Number and the tag assigned to the Record Directory entry is 'NBN'.

VI.B.8. __Procedure 8 - Initial Character is an Alpha Character, Continued__

3] __One single hyphen__ - The input field is either a National Bibliography Number or an LC Card Number. The following list must be matched against the initial letter(s) of the input field to identify it as a National Bibliography Number. If a match is found, the tag assigned to the Record Directory entry is 'NBN'. Otherwise, the field is considered to be an LC Card Number, and the tag 'CRD' is assigned.

The National Bibliography Number Country Code prefixes are as follows:

Au	C	Fi	N	Sw
Aus	Cz	GDB	Ne	SANB
B	CzS	GDNB	NeB	SANL
Be	D	It	NZ	USSR
BB	F	Ja	S	Yu

It should be noted that two ambiguities exist between the possible initial letters for these two types of numbers; these are: 'C' and 'Fi'. For National Bibliography Numbers, these prefixes identify Canada and Finland, respectively; whereas, for LC Card Numbers, these prefixes identify "cards printed in the Chinese language" and "cards for motion pictures and filmstrips", respectively. Since the Format Recognition process is currently only concerned with monographs in the English language, the assignment of these two prefixes to the National Bibliography Number has been made.

e] __Undistinguishable Text__

All fields in this category which have not otherwise been identified are considered to be Notes. (The Series Notes are included with the other Notes at this time; they are differentiated in Step 3.) A Record Directory entry is created with the tag 'NO-' and the starting position, length, and site number of the field are stored in the entry. This completes the identification processing for this field.

VII.   STEP 3 - PROCESS VARIABLE FIELDS

At this point in processing, the input fields have been identified to a greater or lesser degree, those which contain a cluster of more than one variable field have been broken up into their components, and a preliminary Record Directory has been built, containing an entry for each variable field, with its tag (or partial tag), starting position, length, site number, and a flag set if the field was in brackets. The processing of each type of variable field is given in the following procedures in this section:

Input Field Order	Procedure Identification	Tag	Field	
1	A	CAL	Call Number	
2	B	ME-	Main Entry	
3	C	UTI	Uniform Title - Type 1	
4	D	TIL	Title Statement	Title Paragraph
	E	EDN	Edition Statement	
	F	IMP	Imprint	
5	G	COL	Collation Statement	Collation Paragraph
	H	SE-	Series Statement	
	I	PRI	Bibliographic Price	
6	J	NBN	National Bibliography No.	Numbers
	K	SBN	Standard Book No.	
	L	OAN	Overseas Acquisition No.	
7	M	NO-	Series Notes and other Notes	
8	N	SU-	Subject Added Entries	
9	O	AE-	(Other) Added Entries	
10	P	SA-	Series Added Entries	
11	C	UTI	Uniform Title - Type 3	
12	Q	COP	Copy Statement	
13	R	ROM	Romanized Title	
14	A	CAL	Bracketed LC Call Number	
15	S	'NLC'	Non-LC Call Number	
16	T	'CAL+'	Second Class Number	
17	U	DDC	Dewey Decimal Number	
18	V	CRD	LC Card Number	
19	W	CAS	Cataloging Source	
20	C	UTI	Uniform Title - Type 2	
21	N	SU-	Non-LC Subject Added Entries	
22	S	'NLC'	Non-LC Call Number	

VII.A.   Call Number Procedure

This field has 1 indicator. Therefore, 2 character positions are created preceding the start of text; the 1st character position is set to 'blank' and the standard delimiter, '‡', is stored in the 2nd character position. The following steps are then performed.

1.   Delimit the Call Number and accumulate subfield codes, using the Delimit Call Number and Copy Statement Algorithm given in Appendix I.

2.   Insert the accumulated subfield code(s), followed by the standard delimiter, into the field immediately preceding the start of text.

3.   Perform the following Special Tests:

    a]   If the Record Directory entry for this field is flagged that the Call Number was in brackets, set the 1st indicator for this field to 'X'; otherwise, leave it set to 'blank'.

    b]   If the class portion of this number is in the range PZ5 through PZ10.7, set the fixed field Intellectual Level (Juvenile) Indicator to 'J'.

    c]   If the class portion of this number is in the range PZ1 through PZ4, or is PZ7, set the fixed field Fiction Indicator to 'X'.

    d]   If no Subject Added Entries exist* and if the Call Number does not start with 'A' or 'P', set the fixed field Main Entry is Subject Indicator to 'X'.

    e]   If the Call Number begins with 'Microfilm', set the fixed field Form of Reproduction Code to 'A'.

---

*This is determined by searching forward in the preliminary Record Directory and not detecting an 'SU-' tagged Directory entry.

VII.B.   Main Entry Procedure

This field has 2 indicators. Therefore, 3 character positions are created preceding the start of text; the first 2 character positions are set to 'blank' and the standard delimiter, '⧧', is stored in the 3rd character position. The following steps are then performed.

1.   Perform the initial analysis of the field, using the Preliminary Scan Algorithm given in Appendix A.

2.   Determine the 3rd letter of the tag in the Record Directory entry for this field and assign the 1st indicator to the field, using the Identify Entry Algorithm given in Appendix B.

3.   Delimit the field and accumulate subfield codes, **using** the Delimit Entry Algorithm given in Appendix C.

4.   Insert the accumulated subfield code(s), followed by the standard delimiter, into the field immediately preceding the start of text.

5.   Perform the following Special Tests:

    a]   If this is a Meeting Main Entry (tag is MEM), set the fixed field Conference Indicator to 'X'.

    b]   Set the 2nd indicator for the Main Entry field equal to the fixed field Main Entry is Subject Indicator.

VII.C.   Uniform Title Procedure

This field has 1 indicator. Therefore, 2 character positions are created preceding the start of text; the 1st character position is set to 'blank' and the standard delimiter, '‡', is stored in the 2nd character position. Also, since this field is not broken into subfields, the subfield code 'a', followed by the standard delimiter, is automatically inserted between the delimiter following the indicator position and the start of text. The following Special Tests are then performed.

a]   If the Record Directory entry for this field is flagged that the field was in brackets, set the 1st indicator for this field to 'A'. Otherwise, proceed to the next Special Test.

b]   If the field is enclosed in parentheses and the text is preceded by 'Title: ', set the 1st indicator for this field to 'N' and remove the parentheses and 'Title: ' from the data. Otherwise, proceed to the next Special Test.

c]   If the text of this field is preceded by 'Filing Title: ', set the 1st indicator for the field to 'N' and remove 'Filing Title: ' from the data.

VII.D.   Title Statement Procedure

This field has 1 indicator. Therefore, 2 character positions are created preceding the start of text; the 1st character position is set to 'blank' and the standard delimiter, '‡', is stored in the 2nd character position. The following steps are then performed.

1.   Delimit the field and accumulate subfield codes, using the Delimit Title Statement Algorithm given in Appendix E.

2.   Insert the accumulated subfield code(s), followed by the standard delimiter, into the field immediately preceding the start of text.

3.   Perform the following Special Tests:

   a]   If the Main Entry field is a Personal Name (its Record Directory entry tag is MEP) and its Surname (or Forename, if no Surname) occurs in the Title Statement's Short Title (Subfield a) or Remainder of Title (Subfield b), set the fixed field Biography Indicator to 'A'. Also, set the fixed field Main Entry in Body Indicator to 'X', set the fixed field Main Entry is Subject Indicator to 'X', and set the 2nd indicator of the Main Entry field to 'X'.

   b]   If the fixed field Fiction Indicator has been set to 'X', skip this test. Otherwise, if one of the key phrases in Keyword List 5F in Appendix L occurs, set the fixed field Festschrift Indicator to 'X'.

   c]   If the fixed field Fiction Indicator has been set to 'X', skip this test. Otherwise, if the keyword 'autobiography', 'autobiographical', 'diary', 'diaries', or 'memoirs' occurs, set the fixed field Biography Indicator to 'A'. Also, set the fixed field Main Entry is Subject Indicator to 'X' and set the 2nd indicator of the Main Entry field to 'X'.

   d]   If the keyword 'biography' occurs, set the fixed field Biography Indicator to 'B'.

   e]   If the keyword 'biographies' occurs, set the fixed field Biography Indicator to 'C'.

- 101 -

VII.D.   Title Statement Procedure, Continued

f]   If the fixed field Fiction Indicator has been set to 'X', skip this test. Otherwise, if the keyword 'bibliography' or 'bibliographies' occurs, insert the code 'B' in the fixed field Form of Contents Codes, in order of precedence.*

g]   If the fixed field Fiction Indicator has been set to 'X', skip this test. Otherwise, if the keyword '(indexes)' occurs, insert the code 'I' in the fixed field Form of Contents Codes, in order of precedence.*

h]   If the fixed field Fiction Indicator has been set to 'X', skip this test. Otherwise, if the keyword 'Directory' occurs, insert the code 'R' in the fixed field Form of Contents Codes, in order of precedence.*

i]   If the key phrase '(romanized form)' occurs, set the fixed field Modified Record Indicator to 'X' and set the 1st indicator of the Title Statement field to 'N'.

Alternatively, the transliterated form of any part of the Short Title (Subfield a) may appear in double brackets without the phrase '(romanized form)'; for example - the spelling out of a Greek letter. In this case, one set of brackets is deleted from the data and the fixed field Modified Record Indicator (only) is set to 'X'.

j]   If the last sentence of the Title Statement field has the appearance of an Imprint in its entirety (place, publisher, and date), set the fixed field Publication Key to 'R', and store the date from this imprint in the DATE 2 fixed field.

---

*The Form of Contents Codes have the following precedence order: B, C, I, A, D, E, R, Y, S, P. Up to four codes of those which could be assigned are kept, and, when over four are possible, the four with the highest precedence are kept. Therefore, a code is inserted in the Form of Contents Codes fixed field to the right of any higher precedence codes, if any, moving the remaining codes to the right one position and discrading the rightmost fifth code, if present. If four codes of higher precedence are already in the field, the new code is discarded.

VII.D.   Title Statement Procedure, Continued

k]   If the keyword 'Translated' or 'translation' occurs in Subfield c, set the Translation Indicator Byte to 'X'. If the keyword is followed (not necessarily immediately) by the name of a foreign language, store the three-letter code equivalent to the language in the Language Code Subfield A Working Buffer. If a foreign language name does not follow, store 'UND' (for Undetermined) in the Working Buffer. (If the Working Buffer was empty, the code should be stored in the second position to allow room for the language into which the work was translated.)

l]   Perform the appropriate following search and set the fixed field Main Entry in Body Indicator to 'X' if the result is a match:

1]   If the Main Entry is a Personal Name, use the Surname (tag/indicator MEPS, MEPM), Forename (MEPF), or Family Name (MEPN) to search against the Title Statement.

2]   If the Main Entry is an Inverted Order Corporate or Meeting Name (tag/indicator MECS, MEMS), search that portion of the Entry preceding the left parenthesis against the Title Statement.

3]   If the Main Entry is a Direct Order Corporate or Meeting Name (tag/indicator MECN, MEMN), omit words such as 'Corporation' or 'Company' from the first subgroup of the first group* in the Entry and search it against the Title Statement. If there is no match, build an acronym from the first letters of all capitalized words and repeat the search.

4]   If the Main Entry is a Place-type Corporate or Meeting Name (tag/indicator MECP, MEMP) search the last 'b' group* (for MECP) or the second group* (for MEMP) against the Title Statement, using Test l]2] above if the group contains parentheses, and Test l]3] if it does not.

---

*Roughly speaking, a 'group' is a portion of an Entry field which ends with a 'significant' period and a 'subgroup' is a part of a group which ends with a comma. For a full discussion of dividing an Entry field into groups and subgroups, see the Preliminary Scan Algorithm given in Appendix A.

VII.E.   Edition Statement Procedure

This field has no indicators. Therefore, 1 character position is created preceding the start of text and the standard delimiter, '‡', is stored in this position. The following steps are then performed.

1.   Delimit the field and accumulate subfield codes, using the Delimit Edition Statement Algorithm given in Appendix F.

2.   Insert the accumulated subfield code(s), followed by the standard delimiter, into the field immediately preceding the start of text.

3.   Perform the following Special Tests:

   a]   If the last sentence in this field has the appearance of an Imprint in its entirety (place, publisher, and date), set the fixed field Publication Key to 'R' and store the date from this imprint in the DATE 2 fixed field.

   b]   If there is no embedded imprint in this field, but the keyword 'reprint' occurs, set the fixed field Publication Key to 'R' and set the DATE 2 fixed field equal to any date accompanying the keyword; otherwise, set DATE 2 to 'blanks'.

   c]   If the key phrase 'large type' occurs, set the fixed field Form of Reproduction Code to 'D'.

   d]   If the fixed field Main Entry in Body Indicator is not already set to 'X', perform the appropriate following search and set this Indicator if the search results in a match:

      1]   If the Main Entry is a Personal Name, use the Surname (tag/indicator MEPS, MEPM), Forename (MEPF), or Family Name (MEPN) to search against the Edition Statement.

VII.E.   <u>Edition Statement Procedure, Continued</u>

2]   If the Main Entry is an Inverted Order Corporate or Meeting Name (tag/indicator MECS, MEMS), search that portion of the Entry preceding the left parenthesis against the Edition Statement.

3]   If the Main Entry is a Direct Order Corporate or Meeting Name (tag/indicator MECN, MEMN), omit words such as 'Corporation' or 'Company' from the first subgroup of the first group* in the Entry and search it against the Edition Statement. If there is no match, build an acronym from the first letters of all capitalized words and repeat the search.

4]   If the Main Entry is a Place-type Corporate or Meeting Name (tag/indicator MECP, MEMP), search the last 'b' group* (for MECP) or the second group* (for MEMP) against the Edition Statement, using Test d]2] above if the group contains parentheses, and Test d]3] if it does not.

----

*Roughly speaking, a 'group' is a portion of an Entry field which ends with a 'significant' period and a 'subgroup' is a part of a group which ends with a comma. For a full discussion of dividing Entry fields into groups and subgroups, see the Preliminary Scan Algorithm given in Appendix A.

VIII.F.   Imprint Procedure

This field has 1 indicator. Therefore, 2 character positions are created preceding the start of text; the 1st character position is set to 'blank' and the standard delimiter, '‡', is stored in the 2nd character position. The following steps are then performed.

1.   Delimit the field and accumulate subfield codes, using the Delimit Imprint Algorithm given in Appendix G.

2.   Insert the accumulated subfield code(s), followed by the standard delimiter, into the field immediately preceding the start of text.

3.   Perform the following Special Tests:

a]   The first Place of Publication (Subfield a) is searched against the appropriate place lists in Appendix L: 4A - Common U.S. Cities, 4B - Common Foreign Cities, 4C - U.S. State Name and Abbreviations, 4D - British County Names and Abbreviations, and 4E - Foreign Countries; using 1] and 2] below. An exact match is required. The process continues until a match is attained ar the subfield is exhausted.

1]   Where the subfield is not divided by punctuation, it is matched against U.S. and Foreign Cities, in that order.

2]   Where the subfield is divided by punctuation, the portion after the punctuation is matched against U.S. States, British Counties, and Foreign Countries, in that order.

3]   If a match is attained, the corresponding place of publication code is stored in the Place of Publication Code fixed field and the corresponding language of publication code is stored in the first position of the Language Code Subfield A Working Buffer.

4]   If the matching portion of the subfield is followed by a question mark, the rightmost letter of the Place of Publication Code is changed as follows: 'blank' goes to 'Q', 'C' goes to 'D', 'K' goes to 'L', 'R' goes to 'S', and 'U' goes to 'V'.

5]   If no match is attained, 'XX ' is stored in the Place of Publication Code fixed field (only).

VII.F.   <u>Imprint Procedure, Continued</u>

b]   If the fixed field Publication Key has <u>not</u> been set to 'R', test
       if the Publisher (Subfield b) of this field contains the **keyword**
       'Reprint' or 'Reprints'. If it does, set the fixed field Publication
       Key to 'R' and store 'blanks' in the DATE 2 fixed field; otherwise
       take no action.

c]   If the Imprint Date (Subfield c) is '[n.d.]', store 'blanks'
       in the DATE 1 fixed field. Also, if the fixed field Publication
       Key is <u>not</u> 'R', set this fixed field to 'N' and store 'blanks'
       in the DATE 2 fixed field.

d]   If the Imprint Date (Subfield c) is a single date*, test if any of
       the digits have been replaced by hyphens, as follows:

   1]   If hyphen(s) occur, set the Publication Key fixed field to 'Q',
          replace the hyphen(s) with '0's, and store the modified date in
          the DATE 1 fixed field. The DATE 2 fixed field is built by
          replacing the hyphen(s) with '9's, unless the result is larger
          than the current processing date. In this latter case, the DATE 2
          fixed field is built by substituting for the hyphen(s) the
          appropriate digit(s) of the LC Card Number Year, unless it is a
          '7-Series', in which case, the appropriate digit(s) from the current
          processing year are used.

   2]   If no hyphens occur, store the Imprint Date in the DATE 1 fixed
          field. If the fixed field Publication Key is <u>not</u> 'R', set this
          fixed field to 'S' and store 'blanks' in the DATE 2 fixed field.

---

*An Imprint Date of the type: 'date$_1$ [i.e. date$_2$] or 'date$_1$ [date$_2$] is taken
as a single date, with the latter date in brackets being the one used.
Also, dates of the type: 1967 or 8, 1967/68 are considered to be single dates,
with the first date being the one used.

VII.F.   <u>Imprint Procedure, Continued</u>

e]   If the Imprint Date (Subfield c) of this field is an open or
closed date range*, test if the <u>first</u> date is incomplete (as
evidenced by missing digits), as follows:

1]   If the first date is incomplete, follow Step d]1] on the
previous page, assuming the appropriate number of trailing
hyphens in the first date, and ignoring the presented
second date, if any.

2]   If the first date is not incomplete, store it in the DATE 1
fixed field. If the fixed field Publication Date Key is
<u>not</u> 'R', set this fixed field to 'M' and either (for closed
date range) store the second date in the DATE 2 fixed field,
or (for open date range) store '9999' in the DATE 2 fixed
field.

f]   If the Imprint Date (Subfield c) of this field contains a copyright date** only, treat it as a single date, using Step d] on
the previous page. Otherwise, test if any digits in the other
date (the publication date) have been replaced by hyphens, as
follows:

1]   If the publication date contains hyphens, follow Step d]1]
on the previous page, ignoring the copyright date.

2]   If the publication date does not contain hyphens, store it in
the DATE 1 fixed field. If the fixed field Publication Date
Key is <u>not</u> 'R', set this fixed field to 'C' and store the
copyright date in the DATE 2 fixed field.

---

*An open date range consists of a single date followed by a hyphen. A closed
date range consists of two dates separated by a hyphen. A closed date range
of the type: '1946-47' is not considered to be incomplete, and the first two
digits of the first date are 'borrowed' to complete the second date.

**A copyright date is preceded by 'c'.

VII.F.   <u>Imprint Procedure, Continued</u>

g]   If Subfield b (Publisher) does <u>not</u> exist in this field <u>and</u> the Main Entry is a Corporate Name (tag MEC) or a Meeting (MEM), set the first indicator of the Imprint field to 'X' and set the fixed field Publisher is Main Entry Indicator to 'X'. Otherwise, set both of these indicators to 'blank'.

h]   If the fixed field Main Entry in Body Indicator is not already set to 'X', perform the appropriate following search and set this indicator to 'X' if the search results in a match:

  1]   If the Main Entry is an Inverted Order Corporate or Meeting Name (tag/indicator MECS, MEMS), search that portion of the Entry preceding the left parenthesis against the Imprint Publisher (Subfield b).

  2]   If the Main Entry is a Direct Order Corporate or Meeting Name (tag/indicator MECN, MEMN), omit words such as 'Corporation' or 'Company' from the first subgroup of the first group* in the Entry and search it against the Imprint Publisher (Subfield b). If there is no match, build an acronym from the first letters of all capitalized words and repeat the search.

  3]   If the Main Entry is a Place-type Corporate or Meeting Name (tag/indicator MECP, MEMP), search the last 'b' group* (for MECP) or the second group* (for MEMP) against the Imprint Publisher (Subfield b), using Test h]1] above if the group contains parentheses, and Test h]2] if it does not.

---

*Roughly speaking, a 'group' is a portion of an Entry field which ends with a 'significant' period and a 'subgroup' is a part of a group which ends with a comma. For a full discussion of dividing an Entry field into groups and subgroups, see the Preliminary Scan Algorithm given in Appendix A.

VII.G. Collation Statement Procedure

This field has no indicators. Therefore, 1 character position is created preceding the start of text and the standard delimiter, '‡', is stored in this position. The following steps are then performed.

1. Delimit the field and accumulate subfield codes, using the Delimit Collation Statement Algorithm given in Appendix H.

2. Insert the accumulated subfield code(s), followed by the standard delimiter, into the field immediately preceding the **start** of text.

3. Perform the following Special Test:

    From keywords in the Illustration Subfield (Subfield b) of this field, assign up to four codes to the fixed field Illustration Forms Codes, followed by as many 'blanks' as necessary to pad the fixed field to four characters. Only one of each code may be assigned and the codes are assigned in descending order of precedence from 'a' to 'm', as shown (this is a restatement of List 5C in Appendix L):

Code	Identification	Keywords
a	Illustrations Diagrams Tables Photographs	'illus.' 'diagr.', 'diagrs.' 'table', 'tables' 'photo.', 'photos.'
b	Maps	'map', 'maps'
c	Portraits	'port.', 'ports.', 'group port.', 'group ports.'
d	Charts	'chart', 'charts'
e	Plans	'plan', 'plans'
f	Plates	'plate', 'plates'
g	Music	'music'
h	Facsimiles	'facsim.', 'facsims.'
i	Coats of Arms	'coat of arms', 'coats of arms'
j	Genealogical Tables	'geneal. table', 'geneal. tables'
k	Forms	'form', 'forms'
l	Samples	'samples'
m	Phono	'phonocylinder', 'phonodisc', 'phonofilm', 'phonoroll', 'phonotape', 'phonowire'

VII.H.   Series Statement Procedure

The parentheses surrounding this field, if any, are removed from the data.

This field has 2 indicators. Therefore, 3 character positions are created preceding the start of text; the first 2 character positions are set to 'blank' and the standard delimiter, '‡', is stored in the 3rd character positions. If this is the first 'SE-' field in the record, go to Step 1; otherwise, Step 2.

1.   Search forward in the Record Directory and determine whether a Series Added Entry field (tag 'SA-') exists:

   a]   If no, set the tag of this field to 'SER', its 1st indicator to 'U', insert 'a‡' before the start of text, and go to Step 6.b].

   b]   If yes, test if the text of the first Series Added Entry field begins with '(Series: '. If yes, set the tag of this field to 'SER', its 1st indicator to 'D', insert 'a‡' before the start of text, and go to Step 6.b]. If no, go to Step 2.

2.   Perform the initial analysis of this field, using the Preliminary Scan Algorithm given in Appendix A.

3.   Determine the 3rd letter of the tag in the Record Directory entry for this field and assign the 1st indicator to the field, using the Identify Entry Algorithm given in Appendix B.

4.   Delimit the field and assign subfield codes, using the Delimit Entry Algorithm given in Appendix C.

5.   Insert the accumulated subfield code(s), followed by the standard delimiter, into the field immediately preceding the start of text.

6.   Perform the following Special Tests:

   a]   If the field begins with the keyword 'His', 'Her', **'Their'**, or 'Its', set the 2nd indicator of this field to 'X'; otherwise, leave it blank.

   b]   If the keyword 'reprint' or 'reissue' occurs in this field, test if the fixed field Publication Key is set to 'Q'. If so, leave it as it is and take no further action. If not, set the Publication Key to 'R'.

VII.I.   Bibliographic Price Procedure

This field has no indicators. Therefore, 1 character position is created preceding the start of text and the standard delimiter, '‡', is stored in this position. The following steps are then performed.

1.   Search the text of the field for semicolons; replace each semicolon found with the standard delimiter and remove any immediately following blanks from the text.

2.   Construct a subfield code string consisting solely of 'a's, and containing one more 'a' than the number of semicolons encountered in Step 1. Insert this subfield code string, followed by the standard delimiter, immediately preceding the start of text.

VII.J.   <u>National Bibliography Number Procedure</u>

This field has no indicators. Therefore, 1 character position is created preceding the start of text and the standard delimiter, '‡', is stored in this position. The following steps are then performed.

1.   If this field is enclosed in parentheses, they are removed from the text.

2.   Search the text of the field for semicolons; replace each semicolon found with the standard delimiter and remove any immediately following blanks from the text.

3.   Construct a subfield code string consisting solely of 'a's, and containing one more 'a' than the number of semicolons encountered in Step 2. Insert this subfield code string, followed by the standard delimiter, immediately preceding the start of text.

4.   Search the field for 'v. ', followed by an Arabic Numeral, a colon, and a space, occurring before any National Bibliography Number. If found, remove it from the text and insert the 'v.' and Numeral, enclosed in parentheses and preceded by a blank, into the text immediately before the next standard delimiter (or end-of-field character). Also, search the field for the notation 'pbk.' and, if found, enclose it in parentheses.

5.   Perform the following Special Test:

      If the fixed field Publication Country Code is set to 'XX ' (Unknown), replace it with the Publication Country Code equivalent to the country identification in the first NBN in the field, using Keyword List 4L in Appendix L. Since the Publication Country Codes for Canada, Great Britain, and the U.S.S.R. contain subdivisions as well, the following codes are equated to their NBN country identification:

Canada	'ONC'	(Ontario assumed)
Great Britain	'ENK'	(England assumed)
U.S.S.R	'RUR'	(Russian SFSR assumed)

VII.K.   Standard Book Number Procedure

This field has no indicators. Therefore, 1 character position is created preceding the start of text and the standard delimiter, '‡', is stored in this position. The following steps are then performed.

1.   If this field is enclosed in parentheses, they are removed from the text.

2.   Search the text of the field for semicolons; replace each semicolon found with the standard delimiter and remove any immediately following blanks from the text.

3.   Construct a subfield code string consisting solely of 'a's, and containing one more 'a' than the number of semicolons encountered in Step 2. Insert this subfield code string, followed by the standard delimiter, immediately preceding the start of text.

4.   Search the field and remove from the text all spaces, hyphens, and occurrences of the code 'SBN'. Enclose the notation 'pbk.', if found, in parentheses.

VII.L.   Overseas Acquisition Number Procedure

This field has no indicators. Therefore, 1 character position is created preceding the start of text and the standard delimiter, '‡', is stored in this position. Also, since this field is not broken into subfields, the subfield code 'a', followed by the standard delimiter, is automatically inserted between this delimiter and the start of text. The following Special Tests are then performed:

a]   If the field is enclosed in parentheses, they are removed from the data.

b]   If the field is a 'PL480' number or an East African Accession Number, and the fixed field Publication Country Code is set to 'XX ' (Unknown), the code is replaced with the Publication Country Code equivalent to the country identification in this field.

c]   If the field is an East African Accession Number, and the first position of the Language Code Subfield A Working Buffer has not been filled, the three-letter Language Code equivalent to the language identification in the field is stored in this position.

VII.M.   Series Notes and (other) Notes Procedure

Both Series Notes and the six other types of Notes are assigned the
preliminary tag identification 'NO-' in their respective Record Directory
entries in Step 2. However, the Series Statement will already have been
identified and processed by Procedure VII.H., if that field is present.
Therefore, the following steps are taken.

1.   Search backwards in the Record Directory from the entry for this field:
      If no Directory entry tag beginning with 'SE' is encountered, or if a
      Directory entry tag beginning with 'NO' is encountered before one
      beginning with 'SE', go to the 3rd step of this procedure. Otherwise
      go to the 2nd step of this procedure to test for a Series Note.

2.   The following tests are used to identify a Series Note:

      a]   If the field begins with a quotation mark it cannot be a Series
            Note. Go to Step 3 of this procedure.

      b]   If the field begins with 'His', 'Her', 'Their', or 'Its', change
            the preliminary tag in the Record Directory entry for this field to
            'SE-', and go to the Series Statement Procedure (VII.H.).

      c]   If the keyword 'Series', 'series', 'Studies', or 'studies' occurs
            in the field, change the preliminary tag in the Record Directory entry
            for this field to 'SE-', and go to the Series Statement Procedure
            (VII.H.).

      d]   Following any intial 'A', 'An', or 'The' in the field, if the next
            word is capitalized, change the preliminary tag in the Record
            Directory entry for this field to 'SE-', and go to the Series
            Statement Procedure (VII.H.).

VII.M.   Series Notes and (other) Notes Procedure, Continued

3.   From this step on, the field is assumed to be a Note. A Note field has
at most 1 indicator. Therefore 2 character positions are created preceding
the start of text; the 1st character is set to 'blank' and the standard
delimiter, '‡', is stored in the 2nd character position. Also, since
this field is not broken into subfields, the subfield code 'a', followed
by the standard delimiter, is automatically inserted between the delimiter
following the indicator position and the start of text.

4.   Determine the 3rd letter of the tag in the Record Directory entry for
this field and assign the 1st indicator to the field, using the Identify
Note Algorithm given in Appendix D. If the Note is not determined to
be a Contents Note (tag NOC), remove the 1st indicator position which was
built in Step 3 from the text.

5.   Perform the following Special Tests:

a]   If the field is a Bibliography Note (tag NOB), insert the code 'B'
in the Form of Contents Codes fixed field, in order of precedence.*

b]   If the keyword 'Catalog', 'catalog', 'Catalogue', or 'catalogue'
occurs in a General Note (tag NOG), insert the code 'C' in the Form
of Contents Codes fixed field, in order of precedence.*

c]   If the keyword 'Directory' or 'directory' occurs in a General Note
(tag NOG), insert the code 'R' in the Form of Contents Codes fixed
field, in order of precedence.*

---

*The Form of Contents Codes have the following precedence order: B, C, I, A,
D, E, R, Y, S, P. Up to four codes of those which could be assigned are kept,
and, when over four are possible, the four with the highest precedence are kept.
Therefore, a code is inserted in the Form of Contents Codes fixed field to the right
of any higher precedence codes, if any, moving the remaining codes to the right
one position and discarding the rightmost fifth code, if present. If four codes
of higher precedence are already in the field, the new code is discarded.

VII.M.   <u>Series Note and (other) Notes Procedure, Continued</u>

d]   If the keyword 'Microfilm' occurs in a General Note (tag NOG),
set the Form or Reproduction fixed field to 'A'.

e]   If the keyword 'Microfilm' occurs together with a height in 'cm.'
occurs in a General Note (tag NOG), set the Form of Reproduction
fixed field to 'B'.

f]   If the keyword 'Microopaque' occurs in a General Note (tag NOG),
set the Form of Reproduction Code fixed field to 'C'.

g]   If the keyword 'Reprint', 'reprint', 'Reprinted', 'reprinted',
'Republished', 'republished', or 'Original t.p. has imprint'
occurs in a General Note (tag NOG) and the fixed field Publication
Key is <u>not</u> 'Q', set this fixed field to 'R' and set the DATE 2
fixed field equal to the first of any dates found in the Note;
if no date, set the DATE 2 fixed field to 'blanks'.

h]   If the keyword 'translated' or 'translation' occurs in a General
Note (tag NOG), set the Translation Indicator Byte to 'X'.
If the name of a foreign language also occurs in the note, store
the three-letter code equivalent to the foreign language (given
in List 5G of Appendix L) in the Language Code Subfield A Working
Buffer. If there is no foreign language name, store the code
'UND' (for Undetermined) in the Working Buffer. In either case,
if the Working Buffer was empty, this code should be stored in the
2nd position in the Working Buffer.

i]   If the name of one or more foreign languages occurs in a General
Note (tag NOG), together with the word 'English', store the code
'ENG' in the first position of the Language Code Subfield A Working
Buffer and store the three-letter code equivalent(s) to the foreign
language(s) (given in List 5G of Appendix L) in subsequent positions
of the Working Buffer.

VII.M.   <u>Series Notes and (other) Notes, Continued</u>

j]   If the name of <u>any</u> language occurs in a General Note (tag NOG),
      after a key phrase such as 'abstracts in', 'reviews in',
      'chronicle in', or 'summaries in', store the three-letter code
      equivalent to the language (given in List 5G of Appendix L) in
      the Language Code Subfield A Working Buffer.

k]   If the fixed field Fiction Indicator has been set, skip this test.
      Otherwise, if the keyword 'autobiography' or 'autobiographical',
      'diary', 'diaries', or 'memoirs' occurs in any Notes field, set the
      fixed field Biography Indicator to 'A'. Also, set the fixed field
      Main Entry is Subject Indicator to 'X', and set the 2nd indicator
      of the Main Entry field to 'X'.

l]   If the keyword '(romanized form)' or '(romanized)' occurs in any
      Notes field, set the Modified Record Indicator fixed field to 'X'.

VII.N.   Subject Added Entry Procedure

This field has 2 indicators. Therefore, 3 character positions are created preceding the start of text; the first 2 character positions are set to 'blanks' and the standard delimiter, '‡', is stored in the 3rd character position. The following steps are then performed.

1.   Remove the Arabic Numeral and the following period and space from the beginning of the field.

2.   Perform the initial analysis on the field, using the Preliminary Scan Algorithm given in Appendix A.

3.   Determine the 3rd letter in the tag in the Record Directory entry for this field and assign the 1st indicator to the field, using the Identify Entry Algorithm given in Appendix B.

4.   Delimit the field and accumulate subfield codes, using the Delimit Entry Algorithm given in Appendix C.

5.   Insert the accumulated subfield code(s), followed by the standard delimiter, into the field immediately preceding the start of text.

6.   Perform the following Special Tests:

a]   Test if the Record Directory entry for this field is flagged that the field was entered in brackets. If not, set the 2nd indicator for this field to 'L'. Otherwise, set the 2nd indicator according to the following state of the fixed field Cataloging Source Code:

Cataloging Source Code	Field 2nd Indicator
binary zero	(do not set indicator)
'blank'	'C'
'M'	'M'
'A'	'A'
'C'	'V'

VII.N. Subject Added Entry Procedure, Continued

b] If this Subject Entry is a Personal Name (tag SUP) and its Surname
(or Forename, if no Surname) occurs in the Short Title (Subfield a)
or Remainder of Title (Subfield b) of the Title Statement, set the
fixed field Biography Indicator to 'B', unless either of these
subfields also contains the keyword 'Hearing', 'hearing', 'Hearings',
or 'hearings'.

Note - if more than one of the Personal Name Subject Entries in the
record match the Title Statement in this way, the fixed field
Biography Indicator should be set to 'C'.

c] If the Subject Subdivision 'Biography' occurs, set the fixed field
Biography Indicator to 'C'.

d] If the Subject Subdivision 'Juvenile literature' occurs, set the
fixed field Intellectual Level (Juvenile) Indicator to 'J'.

e] If the keyword 'Bibliography' or 'Bibliographies' occurs as a
Subject Subdivision, insert the code 'B' in the fixed field
Form of Contents Codes, in order of precedence.*

f] If the Subject Subdivision 'Catalog' occurs, insert the code 'C'
in the fixed field Form of Contents Codes, in order of precedence.*

g] If the Subject Subdivision 'Abstracts' occurs, insert the code 'A'
in the fixed field Form of Contents Codes, in order of precedence.*

h] If the Subject Subdivision 'Indexes' occurs, insert the code 'I'
in the fixed field Form of Contents Codes, in order of precedence.*

---

*The Form of Contents Codes have the following precedence order: B, C, I, A,
D, E, R, Y, S, P. Up to four codes of those which could be assigned are kept,
and, when over four are possible, the four with the highest precedence are kept.
Therefore, a code is inserted in the Form of Contents Codes fixed field to the
right of any higher precedence codes, if any, moving the remaining codes to the
right one position and discarding the rightmost fifth code, if present. If four
codes of higher precedence are already in the field, the new code is discarded.

VII.N.   Subject Added Entry Procedure, Continued

i]   If the Subject Subdivision 'Dictionaries, indexes, etc.' occurs,
       insert both the codes 'I' and 'D' in the fixed field Form of
       Contents Codes in order of precedence.*

j]   If the Subject Subdivision 'Dictionaries' occurs, insert the code 'D'
       in the fixed field Form of Contents Codes, in order of precedence.*
       Also, in this case, if the name(s) of language(s) occur as further
       subdivision(s), store the equivalent three-letter codes (given in
       List 5G in Appendix L) in the Language Code Subfield A Working Buffer.

k]   If the Sunject Subdivision 'Dictionaries and encyclopedias' occurs,
       without further subdivision, a test is made for the occurrence of
       the keyword 'Dictionary' in the Title Statement. If a match is
       found, the code 'D' is inserted in the fixed field Form of Contents
       Codes, in order of precedence.* Otherwise, the code 'E' is inserted
       in this fixed field, similarly.*

l]   If the Subject Heading 'Encyclopedias and dictionaries' occurs,
       with no subdivision, insert the code 'E' in the fixed field Form
       of Contents Codes, in order of precedence.*

m]   If the Subject Subdivision 'Directories' occurs, insert the code 'R'
       in the fixed field Form of Contents Codes, in order of precedence.*

n]   If the Subject Subdivision 'Yearbooks' occurs, insert the code 'Y'
       in the fixed field Form of Contents Codes, in order of precedence.*

o]   If the Subject Subdivision 'Statistics' occurs, insert the code 'S'
       in the fixed field Form of Contents Codes, in order of precedence.*

p]   If the Subject Subdivision 'Programmed instruction' occurs, insert
       the code 'P' in the fixed field Form of Contents Codes, in order of
       precedence.*

---

*See footnote on preceding page.

VII.N.   Subject Added Entry Procedure, Continued

In the three Special Tests q], r], and s], the following keyword lists from Appendix L are used:

> 4A - U.S. Cities
>
> 4B - Foreign Cities
>
> 4C - U.S. State Names and Abbreviations
>
> 4D - British County Names and Abbreviations
>
> 4E - Foreign Countries
>
> 4F - Geographic Area Names
>
> 4I - Possessing Countries

q] If this Subject Entry is a Geographic Name (tag SUG), make the following tests:

1] Search the Subject Heading for an exact match against Lists 4A through 4F, in that order.

2] If no match in q]1], and the Subject Heading contains a comma:

i] Search the text following the comma against Lists 4C, 4E, and 4I.

ii] If no match in q]2]i], search the text up to the comma for a match against Lists 4C and 4E.

At the first match, searching is terminated and the Geographic Area Code associated with the matched place name in the list is stored in the Geographic Area Code Working Buffer.

r] Only for Topical Subjects (tag SUT) which contain a comma, search the text following the comma for exact match against List 4I (Possessing Countries). Store the equivalent Geographic Area Code associated with the country name in the Geographic Area Code Working Buffer.

s] Repeat Test q] for the 'z' Subdivisions of all Subject Entries.

VII.0.   (Other) Added Entry Procedure

If the text of this field (following the Roman Numeral) consists in its entirety of the word 'Title.', no further processing is conducted on this field. If the text of the field consists of 'Title.(through "word')', only the special test on the following page is conducted. (Note - 'thru' may also be rendered as 'Thru', 'Through', or 'through'.)

This field has 2 indicators. Therefore, 3 character positions are created preceding the start of text; the first 2 character positions are set to 'blank' and the standard delimiter, '‡', is stored in the 3rd character position. The following steps are then performed.

1.   Remove the Roman Numeral and the following period and space from the beginning of the field.

2.   Perform the initial analysis of the field, using the Preliminary Scan Algorithm given in Appendix A.

3.   Determine the 3rd letter of the tag in the Record Directory entry for the field and assign the 1st indicator to the field, using the Identify Entry Algorithm given in Appendix B.

4.   Delimit the field and accumulate subfield codes, using the Delimit Entry Algorithm given in Appendix C.

5.   Insert the accumulated subfield code(s), followed by the standard delimiter, into the field immediately preceding the start of text.

6.   Assign the 2nd indicator to the field using the (Other) Added Entry 2nd Indicator Algorithm given in Appendix J.

7.   Perform the following Special Test:

    If this field is a Meeting Name (tag AEM), set the fixed field Conference Indicator to 'X'

VII.0   (Other) Added Entry Procedure, Continued

Special Test for 'Title.(thru "word")' Added Entry

All of the text following 'Title.' is removed from the field. The "word" from the parentheses is now used to check the delimitation of the Title Statement.

As a result of the Delimit Title Statement Algorithm, the Title Statement has been broken up into subfields using the standard delimiter, '‡', with the subfields being identified by codes. The subfield code cases are:

```
      'a'        - no embedded delimiter
'ab' or 'ac' - one embedded delimiter, which begins Subfield b or c
     'abc'      - two embedded delimiters, 1st begins Subfield b, 2nd - Subfield c
```

The "word" from the parentheses is searched against the field and the position of the next blank following it is noted as the "new delimiter" position. Depending on the subfield code case and the relation of the "new delimiter" position to the existing delimiter(s) (or end-of-field character), appropriate action is taken, as indicated below with the following conventions:

By "move b" or "move c" is meant to replace the character at the "new delimiter" position with the standard delimiter and to replace the delimiter formerly beginning Subfield b or c with 'blank'.

By "delete b" or "delete c" is meant to replace the character formerly beginning Subfield b or c with 'blank' and remove the 'b' or 'c' from the field's subfield codes.

By "create b" or "create c" is meant to replace the character at the "new delimiter" position with the standard delimiter and insert 'b' or 'c' in sequence in the field's subfield codes.

"New Delimiter" Position	Action for Subfield Code Cases			
	a	ab	ac	abc
left of 1st delimiter*	create b	move b	create b	move b
at 1st delimiter	-	none	none	none
between 1st & 2nd delimiter**	-	move b	move c	move b
at 2nd delimiter	-	-	-	delete b
right of 2nd delimiter	-	-	-	delete b, move c
at end-of-field character	none	delete b	delete c	delete b & c

*left of end-of-field for 'a'
**between delimiter and end-of-field for 'ab' and 'ac'

VII.P.   Series Added Entry Procedure

An open parenthesis beginning this field and/or a close parenthesis ending
this field are removed from the data. At this point the field will consist
in its entirety of the word 'Series' or 'Series.', or will begin with
'Series: ' followed by text. In the former two cases, no further processing
is conducted on the field; in the latter case, the initial 'Series: ' is
removed from the data and processing continues.

This field has 1 indicator position. Therefore, 2 character positions are
created preceding the start of text; the 1st position is set to 'blank'
and the standard delimiter, '‡', is stored in the 2nd. The following steps
are then performed.

1.   Perform the initial analysis of the field, using the Preliminary Scan
      Algorithm given in Appendix A.

2.   Determine the 3rd letter of the tag in the Record Directory entry for this
      field and assign the 1st indicator to the field, using the Identify Entry
      Algorithm given in Appendix B.

3.   Delimit the field and accumulate subfield codes, using the Delimit Entry
      Algorithm given in Appendix C.

4.   Insert the accumulated subfield code(s), followed by the standard
      delimiter, into the field immediately preceding the start of text.

VII.Q.   Copy Statement Procedure

This field has no indicators. Therefore, 1 character position is created preceding the start of text and the standard delimiter, '$\neq$', is stored in this position. The following steps are then performed.

1.   Delimit the Copy Statement and accumulate subfield codes, using the Delimit Call Number and Copy Statement Algorithm given in Appendix I.

2.   Insert the accumulated subfield code(s), followed by the standard delimiter, into the field immediately preceding the start of text.

VII.R.   Romanized Title Procedure

This field has 1 indicator. Therefore, 2 character positions are created preceding the start of text; the 1st character position is set to 'blank' and the standard delimiter, '‡', is stored in the 2nd character position. Also, since this field is not broken into subfields, the subfield code 'a', followed by the standard delimiter, is automatically inserted between the delimiter following the indicator position and the start of text. The following steps are then performed.

1.   Remove the initial phrase 'Title romanized: ' or 'Title transliterated: ' from the beginning of the field.

2.   Set the fixed field Modified Record Indicator to 'X'.

VII.S.   Non-LC Call Number Procedure

This field has no indicators. Therefore, 1 charactor position is created preceding the start of text and the standard delimiter, '$\ddagger$', is stored in this position. The following steps are then performed.

1.   The originating library's delimitation of its call number is accepted. Therefore, search the call number for an embedded standard delimiter. If one is found, accumulate the subfield codes 'ab'; otherwise, accumulate the subfield code 'a'.

2.   Insert the accumulated subfield code(s), followed by the standard delimiter, into the field immediately preceding the start of text.

3.   Perform the following Special Test:

      if the fixed field Cataloging Source has not been set (is still binary zero), take no further action. Otherwise, change the pseudo-tag 'NLC' in the Record Directory entry for this field according to the following:

Cataloging Source Code	New Tag for Call Number
'M'	'NLM'
'A'	'NAL'

VII.T.   Second Class Number Procedure

This field does not remain a separate variable field, but is appended to the
end of the LC Call Number field, separated by the standard delimiter, '‡'.
In addition, the subfield code 'a' is inserted at the end of the Call Number
field's subfield codes. The Record Directory entry for the Second Class
Number is flagged as deleted. The following Special Test is then made:

If the Second Class Number begins with a 'P' classification which
indicates literature in a foreign language, as given in List 5B in
Appendix L, set the Translation Indicator Byte to 'X' and store the
code 'ENG' and the three-letter code equivalent to that of the language
implied in the Second Class Number into the first and second positions
of the Language Code Subfield A Working Buffer, respectively.

VII.U.   Dewey Decimal Number Procedure

This field has no indicators. Therefore, 1 character position is created preceding the start of text and the standard delimiter, '‡', is stored in this position. The following steps are then performed.

1.   Search the field for the notations '[B]', '[92]', or '[920]'. For each such notation found, insert the standard delimiter before the notation and remove the enclosing brackets and any blanks preceding the notation.

2.   Construct a subfield code string consisting solely of 'a's, and containing one more 'a' than the number of standard delimiters inserted in the text in Step 1. Insert the subfield code string, followed by the standard delimiter, into the field immediately preceding the start of text.

3.   Perform the following Special Tests:

   a]   If the letter 'j' occurs in this field, set the fixed field Intellectual Level (Juvenile) Indicator to 'J'.

   b]   If this field consists of the notation '[E]', set the fixed field Intellectual Level (Juvenile) Indicator to 'J'.

   c]   If this field consists of the notation '[Fic]', set the fixed field Intellectual Level (Juvenile) Indicator to 'J', set the Fiction Ind. to 'X'.

   d]   If this field contains the notation 'B', '(B)', '920'; or contains '092' within a number, set the fixed field Biography Indicator to 'B'.

VII.V.   LC Card Number Procedure

The majority of this field is moved to fixed fields in the Record Control Area of the Bookkeeping Areas of the record. This is accomplished by the following steps:

1. Since only 3 positions are available for the Card Number Prefix, those prefixes which are longer must be modified. The fixed field Form of Reproduction Indicator may also be set at the same time, as follows:

If Prefix is:	Change Prefix to:	Set Form of Reproduction Indicator to:
'Mic'	(leave as is)	'A'
'MicA'	'MID'	'A'
'MicP'	'MIE'	'C'
'MicpA'	'MIF'	'C'
'PhoM'	'PHP'	(not pertinent)

2. Store the Prefix, Year (or Series Number), Serial, and Supplement Number in the appropriate fixed field areas of the Record Control Area. If there is no Prefix, store 'blanks' instead. If there is no Supplement Number, store 'subscript 0' (65_{16}); for Supplements 1-9, store 'subscript 1-9' ($71\text{-}79_{16}$); for Supplements 10-35, store 'a-z'.

3. Remove all portions of the Card Number moved to the Record Control Area from the data, plus the 'blank' between the Prefix and Year, the hyphen between the Year and Serial, and the parentheses surrounding the Supplement Number. If nothing remains of the field, flag its Record Directory entry as deleted. Otherwise, as the remaining Suffix has no indicators and is not divided into subfields, 3 character positions are created preceding the start of the remaining text; the standard delimiter, '≠', is stored in the 1st and 3rd positions and the subfield code 'a' is stored in the 2nd position.

VII.V. LC Card Number Procedure, Continued

4. Perform the following Special Tests:

a] If the LC Card Number has the prefix 'AC' or has a suffix containing 'AC', set the Intellectual Level (Juvenile) Indicator to 'J'.

b] If the LC Card Number has the prefix 'AC' or has a suffix containing 'AC', inspect the tags of the Record Directory entries for Notes fields as follows: if the first note is a General Note (tag NOG) and no Contents Note (tag NOC) exists in the record, then change the tag of the first Note from NOG to NOA (Annotation or Abstract Note).

VII.W.   Cataloging Source Procedure

This field is used primarily to set the fixed field Cataloging Source Code, as follows:

1. If this field consists only of the phrase 'Library of Congress', store 'blank' in the fixed field Cataloging Source Code, and flag the Record Directory entry for this field as deleted.

2. If this field consists of the phrase 'Shared Cataloging for 'DNAL', store code 'A' in the fixed field Cataloging Source Code, and flag the Record Directory entry for this field as deleted.

3. If this field consists of the phrase 'Shared Cataloging with DNLM', store code 'M' in the fixed field Cataloging Source Code, and flag the Record Directory entry for this field as deleted.

4. If this field ends with the phrase 'for Library of Congress', remove this phrase (only) from the data and store the code 'C' in the fixed field Cataloging Source Code. Since the remaining CAS variable field has no indicators and is not divided into subfields, 3 character positions are created preceding the start of text; the standard delimiter, '≠', is stored in the 1st and 3rd positions and the subfield code 'a' is stored in the 2nd position.

(Steps continue on the following page.)

VII.W.   Cataloging Source Procedure, Continued

5.   Perform the following Special Tests:

a]   Search backward in the Record Directory from the entry for this
field and test if any previously-encountered Subject Added Entries
are flagged as having been input in brackets. If not, take no
further action in this Special Test. Otherwise, set the 2nd
indicator of each such field according to the fixed field
Cataloging Source Code, as follows:

Cataloging Source Code	Field 2nd Indicator
'blank'	'C'
'M'	'M'
'A'	'A'
'C'	'V'

b]   Search backward in the Record Directory from the entry for this
field and test if there is a previously-encountered Non-LC Call
Number field (pseudo-tag 'NLC'). If not, take no further action
in this special test. Otherwise, change the tag in the Directory
entry for the Non-LC Call Number according to the fixed field
Cataloging Source Code, as follows:

Cataloging Source Code	New Tag
'M'	'NLM'
'A'	'NAL'

VIII.   STEP 4 - COMPLETE PROCESSING OF VARIABLE FIELDS

After the individual variable fields have been processed, it is necessary
to execute three additional procedures which correlate variable fields or
process data accumulated in Step 3. These procedures are:

A.   Correlate Series Added Entries and Series Statement/Notes Procedure

B.   Set 1st Indicator of Title Statement and Romanized Title Procedure

C.   Assemble the Language and Geographic Area Codes Fields Procedure

VIII.A.   Correlate Series Added Entries with Series Statement/Notes Procedure

The Series Statement and first Series Added Entry, if they exist, have already been correlated when the Series Statement was processed in Procedure VII.H. At this point, any remaining Series Notes and Series Added Entries are correlated.

1.   If there are no Series Added Entries, change the tag and indicators of any remaining Series Notes to 'SERU-', remove all standard delimiters marking off subfields, and remove all subfield codes except 'a'. This completes the processing of Procedure VIII.A.

2.   If the text of the first Series Added Entry field consists in its entirety of the word 'Series' or 'Series.', flag the Record Directory entry for this field as deleted.

3.   Any Series Notes are now correlated with the remaining Series Added Entries, as follows:

    a]   If there are no further Series Note fields, this completes the processing of Procedure VIII.A. Otherwise, continue.

    b]   If no Series Added Entry field remains in the record, change the tag and indicators of any remaining Series Note fields to 'SERU-', remove all standard delimiters marking off subfields, and remove all subfield codes except 'a'. This completes the processing of Procedure VIII.A.

    c]   Compare the text of the current Series Note field against the text of any remaining Series Added Entry fields.* If a match is found, flag the Record Directory entry for the Series Added Entry field as deleted. If there is no match, change the tag and indicators of the Series Note field to 'SERD-', remove all standard delimiters marking off subfields, and remove all subfield codes except 'a'. Go to Step 3.a] above for next Series Note field.

---

*Normally, this comparison is made from left to right. However, if the Series Note begins with 'His', 'Her', 'Their', or 'Its', this initial word is ignored and the comparison is made from right to left, using the remaining length of the Series Note field.

VIII.B.   <u>Set 1st Indicator of Title Statement and Romanized Title Procedure</u>

The setting of these indicators depends on the existence of an (Other) Added Entry field whose text (following the Roman Numeral) consists in its entirety of the word 'Title.'. Since this field is bypassed in Step 3, it can be easily detected by the fact that the tag in its Record Directory Entry is still of the form 'AE-'.

The setting of the 1st indicator of the Title Statement (tag TIL) and the Romanized Title (tag ROM) is accomplished by the appropriate one of the following steps.

1.   If the 'Title.' Added Entry exists and there is a Romanized Title, set the 1st indicator of the Title Statement field to 'N', set the 1st indicator of the Romanized Title field to 'A', and flag the Record Directory entry for the 'Title.' Added Entry field as deleted.

2.   If the 'Title.' Added Entry exists and there is no Romanized Title, set the 1st indicator of the Title Statement field to 'A', <u>unless</u> it is already set to 'N'. Also, flag the Record Directory entry for the 'Title.' Added Entry field as deleted.

3.   If the 'Title.' Added Entry does not exist, set the 1st indicator of the Title Statement field to 'N'. If there is also a Romanized Title field, set its 1st indicator to 'N'.

VIII.C.   Assemble the Language and Geographic Area Codes Fields Procedures

The data for building the Language Codes variable field (tag LAN) and the
Geographic Area Codes variable field (tag GAC) is accumulated in working
buffers in Step 3. The Language Codes are somewhat unusual in that a
variable field may or may not result, depending on the results of this
accumulation.

Before processing the accumulated data, the two buffers for Language Codes
and the single buffer for Geographic Area Codes are inspected and duplicate
codes within each buffer are removed. In addition, for the Language Code
Subfield A Working Buffer:

1.   If the first position of the Buffer is empty, store the code 'ENG'
      in it on the a priori assumption that the work is in English.*
      Also, in this case, if the code 'ENG' occurs in any other position
      in this Buffer, remove it.

2.   If two or more legitimate language codes now occur in the Buffer,
      remove all 'UND' (Undefined) codes.

The two subprocedures on the following pages will then determine these two
fields.

---

*As long as only English-language works are being processed, there is an override
on this step, i.e. - 'ENG' is stored in the first position of the Buffer whether
it is empty or not.

VIII.C.1.   Assemble the Language Codes Variable Field Subprocedure

In the special (if most common) case where the Language Code Subfield A Working Buffer contains 1 code, the Language Code Subfield B Working Buffer contains no codes, and the Translation Indicator Byte has not been set to 'X', the code in the A Working Buffer is simply stored in the Publication Language Code fixed field in the record's Fixed Field Area and no further processing in this Subprocedure is necessary.

In all other cases, the following steps are preformed:

1.   A working buffer is set up. If the Translation Indicator Byte has been set to 'X', it is moved to the working buffer; if not, 'blank' is moved to the working buffer. This is the 1st indicator for the variable field and is followed by the standard delimiter, '≠'.

2.   The subfield code 'a' is stored in the working buffer. If the Subfield B Buffer count is non-zero, the subfield code 'b' is also stored in the working buffer. The subfield code(s) are followed by the standard delimiter, '≠'.

3.   The code(s) in the Subfield A Buffer are moved to the working buffer.

4.   If the Subfield B Buffer count is zero, processing continues at Step 5. Otherwise, the standard delimiter, '≠', is stored in the working buffer and then the code(s) in the Subfield B Buffer are moved to the working buffer.

5.   The contents of the working buffer (followed by an end-of-field character) are added to the record's variable field data and a Record Directory entry is created for the variable field, containing the tag 'LAN' and the appropriate starting position, length, and site number.

VIII.C.2.   Assemble the Geographic Area Codes Variable Field Subprocedure

The Geographic Area Codes are 7-byte codes which are accumulated in the Geographic Area Codes Working Buffer in Step 3. Since no more than 3 Codes may be carried in a record, the following three cases may arise:

1.   No Codes in buffer - No further action is taken.

2.   1 to 3 Codes in buffer - A number of character positions are created before the Working Buffer equal to the number of Codes plus 2, the standard delimiter, '≠', is stored in the first and last positions, and the subfield code 'a' is stored in the remaining positions. The standard delimiter is also inserted between the Area Codes and the end-of-field character is added at the end. The entire constructed field is then added to the record's variable field data and a Record Directory entry is created for the variable field, containing the tag 'GAC' and the appropriate starting position, length, and site number.

3.   Over 3 Codes in buffer - Taking advantage of the Codes' hierarchical left-to-right structure, the Codes are 'collapsed' together until 3 or fewer remain. They are then treated as in Case 2.

      (The 'collapsing' substeps are given on the following page.)

VIII.C.2.   <u>Assemble the Geographic Area Codes Field Subprocedure, Continued</u>

The 'collapsing' of Geographic Area Codes utilizes the structure of the codes, whose bytes, numbered from left to right, have the following significance:

1	Continent
2	Area of continent
3-4	Country
5	Area of country
6-7	State or Province

The substeps for collapsing Geographic Area Codes are as follows:

a]   All codes identical through country (bytes 1-4) are collapsed by replacing them with a single code whose first 4 bytes are identical with theirs, but with hyphens in bytes 5-7.

b]   If over 3 codes remain, all codes identical through area of continent (bytes 1-2) are collapsed by replacing them with a single code whose first 2 bytes are identical with theirs, but with hyphens in bytes 3-7. In addition, the country bytes (bytes 3-4) in any other remaining codes are also replaced by hyphens.

c]   If over 3 codes remain, all codes identical through continent (byte 1) are collapsed together by replacing them with a single code whose first byte is identical with theirs, but with hyphens in bytes 2-7.

d]   If over 3 codes remain, all codes past the first 3 are discarded.

(See the following page for an example of the collapsing process.)

VIII.C.2.   <u>Assemble the Geographic Area Codes Field Subprocedure, Continued</u>

As an example of collapsing Geographic Area Codes, consider the following seven codes:

1.	N-US-NY	New York (State)
2.	N-US-NJ	New Jersey
3.	N-USN--	New England
4.	N-CN-ON	Ontario
5.	N-CN-QU	Quebec
6.	N-MX---	Mexico
7.	NWTR---	Trinidad & Tobago

Substep 3.a] would collapse codes 1-3 together and 4-5 together, leaving:

1'.	N-US---	U.S.
2'.	N-CN---	Canada
3'.	N-MX---	Mexico
4'.	NWTR---	Trinidad & Tobago

Substep 3.b] would collapse codes 1'-3' together and would remove the country bytes from code 4', leaving:

1".	N------	North America
2".	NW-----	West Indies

The two remaining codes may now be processed by Substep 2.

IX.   STEP 5 - FINAL RECORD ASSEMBLY

Two additional procedures are necessary to complete the record processing.
They are:

A.   Sort the Record Directory Procedure

B.   Assemble and Output the Record Procedure

Procedure IX.B. assumes a single-block output record. For considerations
of segmenting large record, see the final subsection in this section:

C.   Segmentation of Records

IX.A.   Sort the Record Directory Procedure

The following steps are pertinent to sorting the Record Directory:

1.   Sort the Record Directory entries on tag and site number.*

2.   Go through the Directory, removing special processing flags used
      by the Format Recognition process from the entries and counting the
      entries, until either the end-of-field character ending the Directory
      is encountered, or until the first entry flagged as deleted is
      encountered. (The deleted entries are flagged in such a way that they
      will sort to the bottom.) Store an end-of-field character following
      the last valid Record Directory entry.

3.   Store the count of undeleted entries in the Directory Entry count fixed
      field in the Communications Area of the record.

---

*A site number is assigned in its Record Directory entry to each variable field
of a given type, in order of input. For example, if there are five Subject
Added Entries, they will be assigned the site numbers 1-5. These are included
in the Directory entry because sorting on tags generally changes the input
order; the site numbers can subsequently be used to restore this order when
desired.

IX.B.   Assemble and Output the Record Procedure

The final steps in completing the record are as follows:

1.   Assemble the record from the Bookkeeping Areas, the Fixed Field Area,
       the Record Directory, and the variable fields.

2.   Replace the end-of-field character following the last field in the record
       with the end-of-record character and store the total record length in
       the Record Length fixed field in the Record Leader.

3.   Test if the LC Catalog Card Number Year and Serial fixed fields
       (bytes 27-34) in the Record Control Area have been filled (are no longer
       binary zeros). If not, a pseudo-card number must be constructed and
       stored in these fields, since a record without these fields cannot be
       accessed. This pseudo-card number must have the twin attributes of
       not possibly duplicating any legitimate LC Card Number and still being
       unique from any other pseudo-card number. This can be accomplished by
       using the current date/time of processing which is available from the
       computer's operating system, and encoding the pseudo-card number as
       follows:

                                    MDDHH###

       where: M = Month code, A-L = Jan-Dec
                  DD = Day, 01-31
                  HH = Hour, 00-23
                  ### = Serial number of pseudo-card numbers generated during
                         this processing run, 000-999

The alphabetic month code serves to prevent the pseudo-card number from
duplicating a legitimate LC Card Number, which always has a numeric
digit in this position. The remainder should serve to unique the
pseudo-number, since the necessity of generating over 1000 of them in
any one processing hour seems extremely unlikely.

IX.B.   <u>Assemble and Output the Record Procedure, Continued</u>

In addition to the building of the pseudo-card number, the Prefix field (bytes 24-26) is set to 'blanks' and the Supplement Number (byte 35) is set to 'subscript zero' (65_{16}), since these are the expected values when these portions of the LC Card Number do not appear.

4.   Store FF_{16} for 'first and only segment' in the Segment Number byte in the Record Control Area. (However, see also the segmentation of records discussion in Section IX.C.)

5.   Output the completed MARC II Internal Processing Format record.

Processing is now completed on the record.

IX.C.   Segmentation of Records

Procedure IX.B. of Step 5, which assembles the final MARC II Internal Processing
Format record, assumes the general case where the record occupies one block, or
physical, record on the output magnetic tape. While it is not the purpose of
this report to consider segmentation of records extensively, it must be
recognized that a maximum block (physical record) size must be defined, in order
to assign buffer space in computer programs used for processing. The probability
that a record will exist which will be larger than any reasonable block size
is virtually a certainty. For example, the block size in current MARC processing
is 2040 bytes, yet on rare occasions records have occurred which have exceeded
this size, generally due to voluminous Contents Notes. A record of this type
over 18,000 bytes in length has been noted.

In the case where the logical record exceeds the maximum block size, the logical
record must be broken up into physical blocks called segments. Each segment
will contain a Segment Number byte, which will be a binary number, running
sequentially from 01_{16}, with the last segment's Segment Number byte being FF_{16}.
It can be seen that the case in Procedure IX.B. of Step 5, which assigns FF_{16}
to this byte, represents the special (if most common) case where the record
consists of one segment.

Since the instance of an oversize record stems from length variable fields
rather than a large number of variable fields, it seems feasible to pick a
segment size of reasonable size such that it would be able to contain the
Bookkeeping Areas and Fixed Field Area (98 bytes total), plus the entire
Record Directory, 100% of the time. Based on this premise, from a computer
programming point of view, segmentation would be handled in the following
manner:

There would be essentially three buffers: one for holding the Bookkeeping
Areas, the Fixed Field Area, and the Record Directory as it is built; one to
contain records being input; and one for building output records.

IX.C.   Segmentation of Records, Continued

During Step 2, in the case where the input fields exceed the input buffer, the buffer contents are dumped off as a record on auxiliary storage. This could be magnetic tape, since these fields are to be read back in the same order in Step 3.

In Step 3, the blocks of input fields are read back into the input buffer and the fields are processed. The formatted variable fields resulting are packed in the output buffer. When they exceed the output buffer, the buffer contents are dumped off on auxiliary storage. (It would be best in this case if this were addressable storage, such as magnetic disk, since the correlations among fields in Step 3 and Step 4 processing may require the accessing of a variable field in a block which has already been written out.)

The assembling process in Step 5 would now consist of reading the blocks of processed fields back from auxiliary storage and constructing record segments. The initial segment would consist of the Bookkeeping Areas, the Fixed Field Area, the Record Directory, and as much of the variable field text as would extend the segment to the maximum block size. The Bookkeeping Areas would also be carried in the subsequent (continuation) segments with more of the variable field text until it is exhausted.

The following general considerations apply:

a]   The variable field area in any segment is simply chopped to the maximum block size, with no attempt being made to break between variable fields. Therefore, in a multi-segment record, all segments will be maximum length except the last one, which will be variable-length (the length required to contain the final extent of variable fields).

IX.C.   Segmentation of Records, Continued

b]   The Bookkeeping Areas (bytes 'minus 6' through 37) carried in
each continuation segment (those after the first segment) will be
identical to that in the first segment except for the following:

1]   The Record Length field (bytes 0-1) in the Record Leader will
give the length of that segment. (The Record Length field in
the first segment will give its length, not the total length
of the complete logical record.)

2]   The Record Directory Location field (bytes 12-13) and the
Directory Entry Count field (bytes 14-15) in the
Communications Area will both be binary zero in continuation
segments.

3]   The Segment Number field (byte 37) in the Record Control
Area will increase sequentially from 01_{16} through FF_{16} from
the first segment on, except that the last segment will
always be numbered FF_{16}.

c]   The Bookkeeping Areas in all segments after the first will be
'transparent' to the Record Directory, that is - the relative
starting locations of variable fields in the Directory will be
assigned as if the segments were actually one complete logical
record of the appropriate size, and that the Bookkeeping Areas
in all continuation segments were actually not present.

APPENDIX A.   PRELIMINARY SCAN ALGORITHM

Step 2 of the Format Recognition process has the purpose of identifying the functional nature of each input field. Those fields which are Entries, however, are only partially identified by Step 2; all that is known for them is the first two letters of their alphabetic tags, as follows:

> ME- = Main Entry
>
> SE- = Series Statement
>
> SU- = Subject Added Entry
>
> AE- = (Other) Added Entry
>
> SA- = Series Added Entry

What is now necessary is to determine the third letter of the field's tag, its indicator(s), etc. This is a two-step process. First, the Algorithm in this Appendix performs a preliminary scan of the field and accumulates specific data from it. Then the further identification of the Entry is performed by the Identify Entry Algorithm given in Appendix B, which draws on the data from the Preliminary Scan, as well as conducting further tests on the field's data itself.

The Preliminary Scan Algorithm functions by conducting a complete search of the Entry field and accumulating the existence, location, and number of the following:

   1.   Groups in the field

and, within the leftmost group:

   2.   Subgroups
   3.   Single dates
   4.   Type 1 date ranges
   5.   Type 2 date ranges
   6.   Type 3 date ranges
   7.   Significant ordinal numbers
   8.   Initials
   9.   Roman Numerals
   10. Terms in parentheses

A.1.   Determining Groups

In order to avoid confusion in discussion of subdivisions of an Entry field, two terms have been coined: 'group' and 'subgroup'. These are defined as follows:

a)   A group is a portion of an Entry field, usually terminated by a 'significant' period (or by end-of-field).

b)   A subgroup is a portion of a group, usually terminated by a comma (or by end-of-group).

c)   In referring to groups within an Entry, they are considered to be numbered, starting from 1, from left to right. Subgroups are considered to be numbered within groups in the same manner.

It is apparent that, in defining a group, two things need further definition - 'significant' periods and the qualification 'usually'.

For the purpose of terminating a group, all periods are significant, with the following exceptions:

a)   Any period followed by close parentheses or other punctuation (such as comma) is not significant.

b)   A period in an initial is not significant. An initial is defined as a single capital letter, followed by period, followed by a space or other punctuation (but not close parenthesis).

c)   A period occurring in a small set of certain specific abbreviations is not significant. At present, this set of abbreviations is the following: 'St.', 'Ft.', 'Mt.', 'Gt.', 'Pres.', 'Mrs.', 'Abp.', 'Bp.', 'Rev.', 'Hon.', 'no.', 'v.', 'etc.', 'Dept.' and the month abbreviations 'Jan.'-'Dec.'.* (Note that other abbreviations, such as 'inc.' and 'ltd.', do terminate a group.)

---

*In addition, 'Mrs.', 'Rev.', and 'Hon.', when detected, must be moved as a separate subgroup following the subgroup they begin. This must be done for the non-abbreviations 'Sir', 'Lord', 'Lady', and 'Dame' as well.

A.1.   <u>Determining Groups, Continued</u>

d)   An 'embedded' period is not significant. An embedded period is one
falling between two alphabetic characters. This happens in the
abbreviation for United States and several of the states (U.S., N.H.,
N.J., N.Y., N.C., S.C., N.D., S.D., W.Va.). In these cases, the
first period is not significant. Note, however, that the <u>second</u>
period <u>is</u> significant, as are those in other place abbreviations,
such as: 'Brit.', 'Tex.', 'Tenn.', etc., unless they also fall
under Rule a) on the preceding page.

In addition to a 'significant' period terminating a group, a group may be
terminated by the following three occurrences:

a)   Certain specific terms in parentheses determine the end of a group.
These are defining terms which follow Corporate Place Names and other
defining terms which follow Direct Order Corporate Names. The former
category includes '(State)', '(City)', '(Diocese)', etc.; a full list
is given in Keyword List 4K in Appendix L. The latter category
includes '(Ship)', '(Society)', etc.; a full list is given in Keyword
List 1C in Appendix L. If the term in parentheses is followed by
a period, the period is considered to be part of, and the last
character in, the group defined by the term in parentheses.

b)   An 'open' date range (4 digits, followed by a hyphen, not followed by
more digits) determines the end of a group if it is followed by a
blank, except in two cases: if the blank is followed by a lower-case
letter (the date range determines the end of a subgroup within the
group), or the blank is followed by open parenthesis (nothing is
determined). If an open date range itself is enclosed in parentheses,
it definitely determines an end-of-group, with the end of the group
being the close parenthesis or any punctuation following it.

A.1.   <u>Determining Groups, Continued</u>

c)   The double hyphens which set of a Subject Subdivision determine the
end of a group. This is a 'special' end-of-group condition which is
recorded so as to distinguish it from the other 'normal' end-of-group
conditions. This is done because the Delimit Entry Algorithm given in
Appendix C treats the 'normal' and 'special' cases differently, while
the Identify Entry Algorithm given in Appendix B handles the 'special'
case as <u>end-of-field</u>.

The preceding rules determine how the Preliminary Scan locates and numbers the
groups in the Entry field. All other punctuation, except comma, period, double
hyphens, and parentheses, are treated as if they were not there; i.e. - 'O'Brien'
is treated like 'OBrien'. Except for its occurrence in date ranges, single
hyphen is treated like a space.

A.2.   Determining Subgroups

A subroup is a portion of a group, usually terminated by a comma (or end-of-group). Only the subgroups in the first group are significant. All commas are significant in determining the end of a subgroup. However, there are two other occurrences which determine the end of a subgroup; these are:

a)   An 'open' date range (4 digits, followed by a hyphen, not followed by more digits) may determine the end of a subgroup. It is always followed by a blank. If the blank is followed by open parenthesis, a subgroup is not determined. If the blank is followed by a lower-case letter, a subgroup is determined. If the blank is followed by any other character, the date range not only determines the end of a subgroup but the end of a group as well. If the date range is enclosed in parentheses, both end-of-subgroup and end-of-group are also determined, with the end being the close parenthesis or any punctuation following it.

b)   A term in parentheses determines the end of a subgroup, if it is not one of the special Corporate Name terms, such as '(State)' or '(Ship)', and if it is followed by either a date range or a relator ('ed.', 'jt. author', etc.). This special case arises when a married woman's maiden name is included after her forename(s). In such a case, the comma normally following the forename(s) is omitted.

For a listing of all expected combinations of subgroups occurring in the first group of an Entry field, see page A-9 of this Appendix.

A.3.   Determining Single Dates

A single date is defined as a 4-digit number preceded by a punctuation mark and a space and followed by a punctuation mark (or end-of-field). The only exception to this is when, in a known Series Statement, the 4-digit number is preceded by a comma and followed by either end-of-field or period and end-of-field. In this case, the number is considered to be a number in the series, not a single date.

A single date subgroup is significant because it almost always excludes the Entry from being a Personal Name. Note that when such terms as 'b.', 'd.', 'fl.', etc. are included with the 4-digit number between the punctuation, it is not a 'single' date, as defined here. These cases are included in the Type 1 date range category.

A.4.   Determining Type 1 Date Ranges

A Type 1 date range is an 'open' date range, that is - a 4-digit number followed by a hyphen and a blank. The number may be preceded by 'ca. ', or be followed before the hyphen by '?', or may be in the form '1836 or 7- '. In addition (quite rarely), it may also be followed before the hyphen by a month abbreviation with or without a day, all in parentheses. The qualification of being an open date range is that digits (or digits preceded by 'ca. ') do not immediately follow the hyphen.

The significance of an open date range is that it almost always determines the Entry to be a Personal Name. For that reason, included in the Type 1 date range are cases in which a date range is implied, such as a single date preceded by 'b.', 'd.', 'fl.', etc. Also included are notations which do not actually contain a 4-digit number at all, such as '12th cent.' or '14th century'.

A.5. & 6.   Determining Type 2 and Type 3 Date Ranges

Type 2 and Type 3 date ranges are identical in form; they are both 'closed' date ranges. A closed date range consists of two 4-digit numbers separated by a hyphen. The same variation in each date may arise as those occurring in the single date in an open date range. Either date may be preceded by 'ca. ', be followed by '?', be followed by a month abbreviation with or without day in parentheses, or be of the form '1836 or 7'. The important qualification is that two dates separated by a hyphen are present.

A date range is significant in that it generally implies that the Entry is a Personal Name. However, Meetings may also occur over a span of years, and, therefore, the distinction between Type 2 and Type 3 date ranges lies in the numeric difference between the second and first date. If the difference is greater than or equal to 20 years, it is a Type 2 date range, and a Personal Name Entry is assumed. If the difference is less than 20 years, it is a Type 3 date range, and a Meeting Entry is assumed.

It is rather difficult to determine the precise cutoff to be used between these two types of date ranges. The figure of 20 years is a tentative one and was chosen on the assumption that most persons of bibliographic or historical significance will have reached that age. Note, however, that this would falsely exclude as a person Jeanne d'Arc (1412-1431). However, lowering the dividing line much more would begin to falsely include as a person meetings such as the Councel of Trent (1545-1563).

A.7.   Determining Significant Ordinal Numbers

An ordinal number (1st, 2nd, 3rd, etc.) is only 'significant' if it is preceded by punctuation and a blank and followed by punctuation (or end-of-field). Such an ordinal number 'all by itself' is a subgroup, and is a good indication that the Entry is a Meeting. On the other hand, no particular significance can be attached to an ordinal number which occurs with other text in a subgroup.

A.8.   Determining Initials

An initial is defined as a single capital letter, followed by period, followed by either a blank or other punctuation (except close parenthesis). Initials are significant because, when one occurs in the second subgroup of the first group of a field, it gives a strong indication that the Entry is a Personal Name. What would otherwise be an initial, but which occurs in parentheses, is not regarded as an initial, however, since this is a common occurrence in Inverted Order Corporate Names.

A.9.   Determining Roman Numerals

A Roman Numeral can be detected using the special algorithm given in Appendix K. Such a numeral is significant if it occurs in the first subgroup of the first group of a field, since it identifies the field as a Personal Forename Entry.

A.10.   Determining Terms in Parentheses

The existence of terms, other than those denoting Corporate Place Names, etc. (See page A-3), in parentheses is noted, since this is a strong indication that the field is an Inverted Order Corporate Name or Meeting Entry.

A.11.   Types of Entries by Subgroups in First Group

The following lists the expected occurrences of subgroups within the first group in entry fields:

Number of Subgroups	Type of Field	Cases	Codes	
1	Personal Name	Forename only	--PF	
		Family name	--PN	
	Corporate Name	Place [common city, state, or country]	--CP	
		Name*	--CN,	--CS
	Meeting	Place [common city, state, or country]	--MP	
		Name*	--MN,	--MS
	Uniform Heading	Title	--U-	
	Geographic Subject	Area name	SUG-	
	Topical Subject	Subject	SUT-	
2	Personal Name	Forename, title		
		Forename, date	--PF	
		Forename, relator		
		Surname, forename**	--PS,	--PM
	Corporate Name	Place [city, state or city, country]	--CP	
		Name, foreign city		
		Name, date	--CN,	--CS
		Name, relator		
		Name, name		
	Meeting	Place [city, state or city, country]	--MP	
		Name, place	--MN,	--MS
		Name, date		
	Geographic Subject	Area name, area name	SUG-	
	Topical Subject	Subject, subject	SUT-	

---

*Either Direct Order Name (--CN, --MN) or Inverted Order Name (--CS, --MS).

**Either Single Surname (--PS) or Multiple Surname (--PM).

A.11.   Types of Entries by Subgroups in First Group, Continued

Number of Subgroups	Type of Field	Cases	Codes
3	Personal Name	Forename, title, dates Forename, title, relator Forename, dates, relator	--PF
		Surname, forename, dates Surname, forename, title Surname, forename, relator	--PS, --P
	Corporate Name	Name, name, date Name, name, relator Name, name, name	--CN, --C
	Meeting	Name, number, place Name, number, date Name, place, date Name, place, place Name, name, number Name, name, place Name, name, date	--MN, --M
	Topical Subject	Subject, subject, subject	SUT-
4	Personal Name	Forename, title, dates, relator Forename, title, title, dates	--PF
		Surname, forename, title, dates Surname, forename, title, relator Surname, forename, dates, relator	--PS, --P
	Corporate Name	Name, name, name, date Name, name, name, relator Name, name, name, name	--CN, --C
	Meeting	Name, number, place, date Name, place, place, date Name, name, number, date Name, name, number, date Name, name, place, date Name, name, place, place Name, name, name, number Name, name, name, place Name, name, name, date	--MN, --M
	Topical Subject	Subject, subject, subject, subject	SUT-

A.11.   Types of Entries by Subgroups in First Group, Continued

Number of Subgroups	Type of Field	Cases	Codes
5	Personal Name	Forename, title, title, dates, relator Forename, title, title, title, dates	--PF
		Surname, forename, title, dates, relator Surname, forename, title, title, relator* Surname, forename, title, title, dates*	--PS, --PM
	Corporate Name	Name, name, name, name, date Name, name, name, name, relator Name, name, name, name, name	--CN, --CS
	Meeting	Name, number, place, place, date Name, name, number, place, date Name, name, place, place, date Name, name, name, number, place Name, name, name, number, date Name, name, name, place, date Name, name, name, place, place Name, name, name, name, number Name, name, name, name, place Name, name, name, name, date	--MN, --MS
6	Corporate Name	Name, name, name, name, name, date Name, name, name, name, name, relator Name, name, name, name, name, name	--CN, --CS

---

*The 'title, title' referred to here is in reality a title with an embedded place name, which, to the algorithm, looks like two subgroups of 'title'.

APPENDIX B.   IDENTIFY ENTRY ALGORITHM

The Identify Entry Algorithm adds the 3rd tag letter to the Record Directory entry for an Entry field and inserts its 1st indicator in the appropriate position in the field. In the notation used in the following flowcharts, this is indicated by an arrow pointing to a 4-letter tag and 1st indicator for the Entry. For clarity, all four letters are given whenever this can be done unambiguously. In most cases, however, the first 2 tag letters are replaced by hyphens, indicating that the 3rd letter and indicator are to be assigned for whatever the 2 initial tag letters in the Entry's Record Directory entry happen to be. For those cases where the Entry has no 1st indicator, a 'b' with a line through its stem is used as the conventional symbol for 'blank'.

At the time the Identify Entry Algorithm is executed, the first 2 letters of the Entry's tag have been identified, as follows:

> ME = Main Entry
>
> SE = Series Statement/Note
>
> SU = Subject Added Entry
>
> AE = (Other) Added Entry
>
> SA = Series Added Entry

In addition, it is expected that the Preliminary Scan Algorithm given in Appendix A has been executed. This accumulates the following information on the Entry field, which is utilized by the Identify Entry Algorithm:

The existence, location, and number of:

1. Groups in the field

and, within the leftmost group:

2. Subgroups	5. Type 2 date ranges	8. Initials
3. Single dates	6. Type 3 date ranges	9. Roman Numerals
4. Type 1 date ranges	7. Significant ordinal numbers	10. Terms in parentheses

It should be noted that the 'special' end-of-group condition arising from Subject Subdivisions is treated as end-of-field in this algorithm.

APPENDIX B.   IDENTIFY ENTRY ALGORITHM Continued

In addition to the data accumulated by the Preliminary Scan Algorithm, the Identify Entry Algorithm makes extensive use of the keyword lists given in Appendix L.

Flowchart Notes

(1) A Type 1 date range is an open date range, as : 1900-. A Type 2 date range is a closed date range spanning 20 years or more, as: 1900-1960. See the Preliminary Scan Algorithm in Appendix A for a discussion of dates and date ranges.

(2) A 'significant' ordinal number is one preceded by punctuation and a space and followed by either punctuation or end-of-field.

(3) These prefixes are those, such as 'De', 'De La', 'Van', etc., which are not to be regarded as separate names. Since the Preliminary Scan Algorithm generally treats a hyphen as a blank, multiple names, such as 'Leon-Dufour' would be correctly handled, since they would be treated as two words.

(4) A single date is a 4-digit number. A type 3 date range is a closed date range spanning less than 20 years, as 1964-1967. See the Preliminary Scan Algorithm in Appendix A for a discussion of dates and date reanges.

(5) In addition to detecting those fields which end in place-type terms, such as '(City)','(State)', etc., this would detect cases, such as:

> Germany (Third Reich)
> Germany (Federal Republic)
> Germany (Democratic Republic)

APPENDIX B.   IDENTIFY ENTRY ALGORITHM, Continued

Flowchart Notes, Continued

(6) 'Personal Name' Relators can only pertain to persons, such as 'jt. author', etc.   'Legal' Relators can pertain to both persons and corporations, such as 'plaintiff', etc.

(7) These are the only two places where testing is done outside of the first group, to handle the obsolescent Meeting Name form:

>   Place.   Meeting Name, Number, Date.

Note that if the Meeting Name does not include a Meeting keyword, this will be handled incorrectly. A small number of such cases is assumed. If this is not so, then tests for Meeting Number and Date in the second group must be conducted at this point as well.

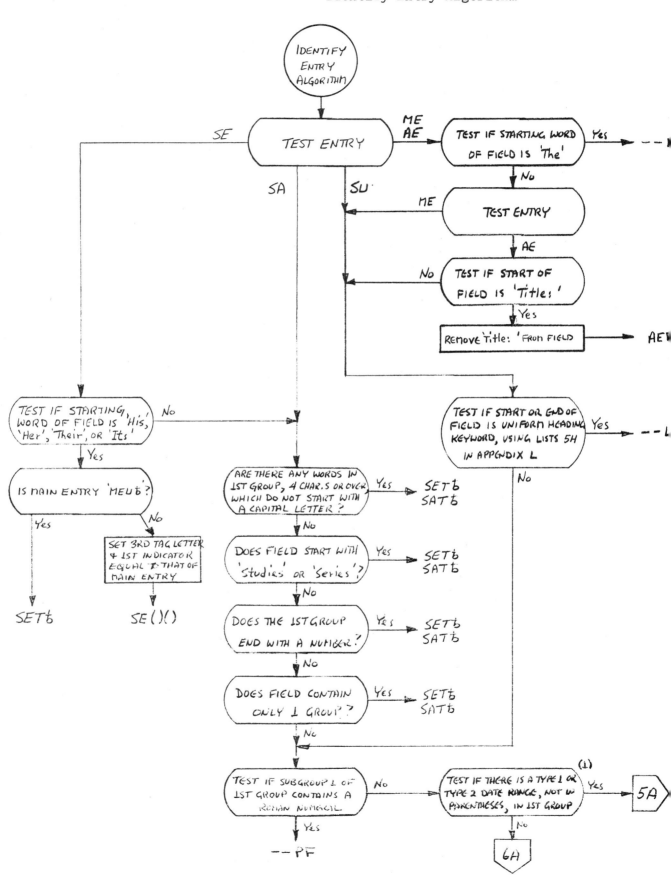

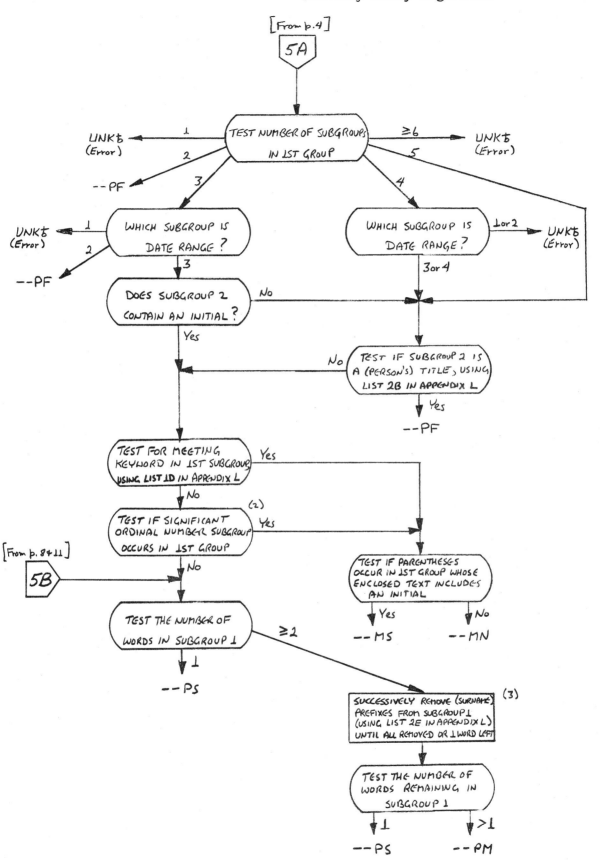

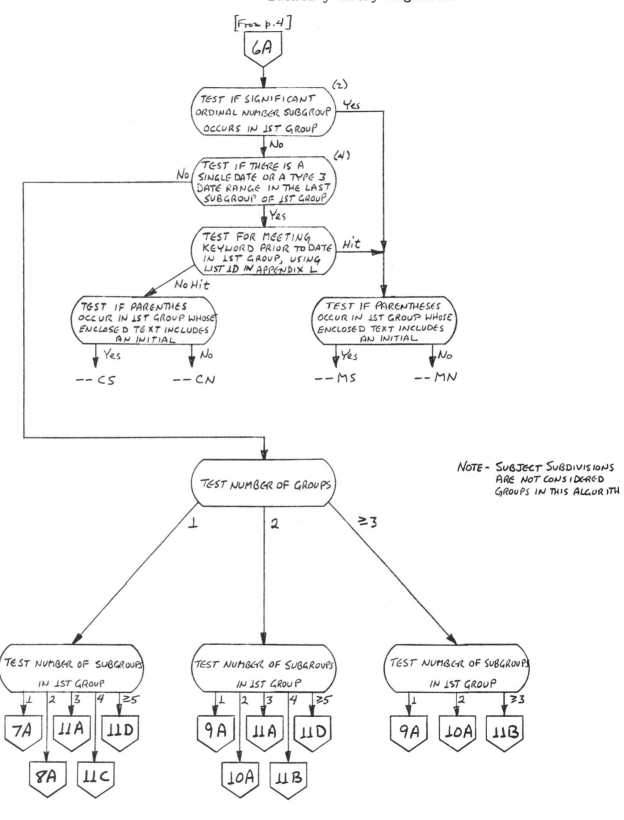

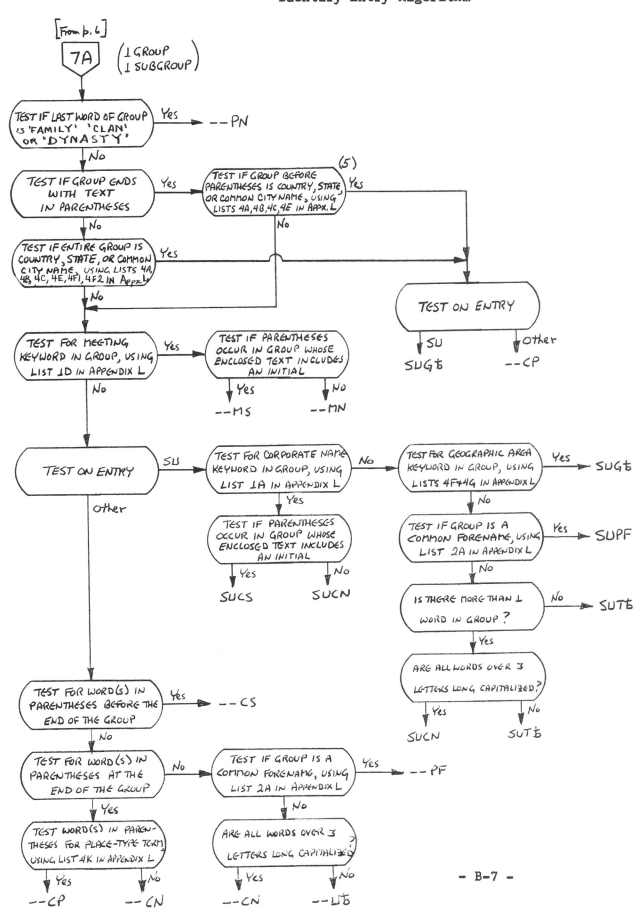

- B-7 -

[From p. 6]

8A (1 GROUP
2 SUBGROUPS)

State Abbreviation or Country

TEST FOR COMMON CITY, STATE ABBREVIATION, OR COUNTRY IN SUBGROUP 2, USING LISTS 4A, 4BI, 4C, 4E, 4CE → Other

Common U.S. or Foreign City

TEST FOR MEETING KEYWORD IN SUBGROUP 1, USING LIST 1D IN APPENDIX L

Yes / No

TEST IF PARENTHESES OCCUR IN GROUP WHOSE ENCLOSED TEXT INCLUDES AN INITIAL

Yes → --CS   No → --CN

TEST IF PARENTHESES OCCUR IN GROUP WHOSE ENCLOSED TEXT INCLUDES AN INITIAL

--MS   --MN

TEST ON ENTRY → Other → --CP

SU

SUGЪ

8B

[From p. 10]

TEST ON ENTRY → SU

Other

No

TEST IF SUBGROUP 2 IS COMPASS-TYPE SUBDIVISION OR COMMON POSSESSING COUNTRY, USING LISTS 4H+4I IN APPENDIX L

Yes

TEST FOR PLACE-KEYWORD OR AREA-TYPE KEYWORD IN SUBGROUP 1, USING LISTS 4F3, 4F4, 4F7, 4F8, 4G

Yes → SUGЪ   No → SUTЪ

DOES SUBGROUP 2 CONTAIN AN INITIAL? → Yes → 5B (--P-)

No

TEST IF SUBGROUP 2 IS A (PERSON'S) TITLE, USING LIST 2B IN APPENDIX L → Yes → --PF

No

TEST FOR MEETING KEYWORD IN GROUP, USING LIST 1D IN APPENDIX L → Yes → TEST IF PARENTHESES OCCUR IN GROUP WHOSE ENCLOSED TEXT INCLUDES AN INITIAL

Yes → --MS   No → --MN

No

(6)

TEST IF SUBGROUP 2 IS A PERSONAL NAME RELATOR, USING LIST 2C IN APPENDIX L → Yes → --PF

No

TEST FOR CORPORATE NAME KEYWORD IN GROUP, USING LIST 1A IN APPENDIX L → Yes → TEST IF PARENTHESES OCCUR IN GROUP WHOSE ENCLOSED TEXT INCLUDES AN INITIAL

Yes → --CS   No → --CN

No

(6)

TEST IF SUBGROUP 2 IS A LEGAL RELATOR, USING LIST 5A IN APPENDIX L → YES → --PF

No

DOES SUBGROUP 2 CONTAIN 1-3 WORDS → No → --CN

Yes

TEST ON ENTRY → SU → SUTЪ

Other

5B (--P-)

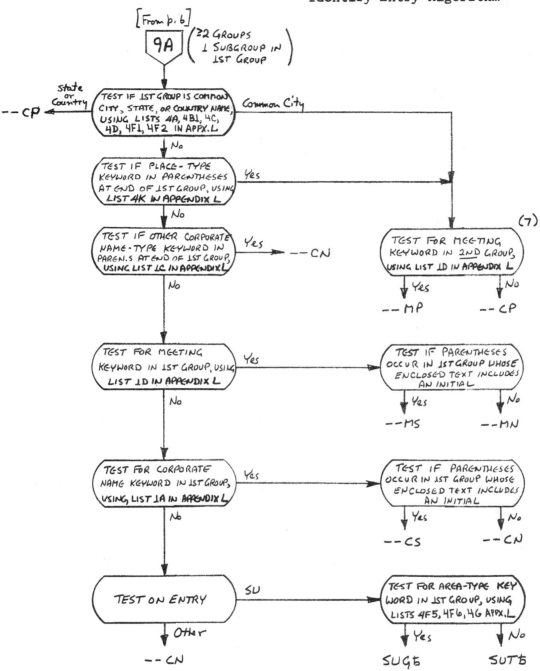

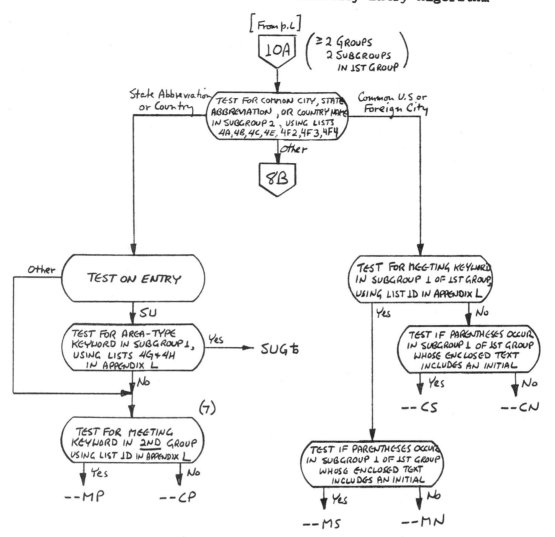

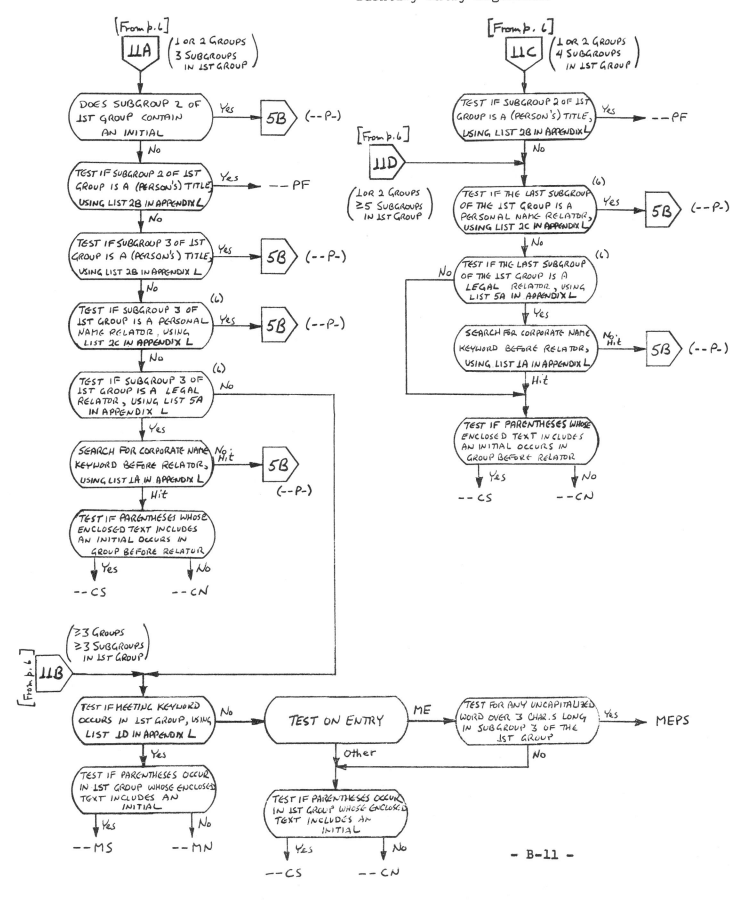

- B-11 -

APPENDIX C.   DELIMIT ENTRY ALGORITHM

The Delimit Entry Algorithm divides the presented Entry field into subfields by inserting the standard delimiter, '≠', and accumulates the associated subfield codes in a working buffer. The flowcharts are written in the form of a subroutine, with the notation 'Return' being used to signify that the algorithm is completed, with the accumulated subfield codes being available in the buffer for use by the calling procedure.

At the time the Delimit Entry Algorithm is entered, it is expected that the full 3-letter tag plus the 1st indicator have been determined for the Entry field by executing the Identify Entry Algorithm given in Appendix A.

In addition, it is expected that the Preliminary Scan Algorithm given in Appendix A has been executed. This accumulates the following information on the Entry field, which is utilized by the Delimit Entry Algorithm:

The existence, location, and number of:

1.   Groups in the field

and, within the leftmost group:

2.   Subgroups
3.   Single dates
4.   Type 1 date ranges

5.   Type 2 date ranges
6.   Type 3 date ranges
7.   Significant ordinal numbers

8.   Initials
9.   Roman Numerals
10.   Terms in parentheses

It should be noted that the normal end-of-group condition and the 'special' end-of-group condition arising from Subject Subdivisions are handled uniquely in the Delimit Entry Algorithm.

In addition to the data accumulated by the Preliminary Scan Algorithm, the Delimit Entry Algorithm makes extensive use of the keyword lists given in Appendix L.

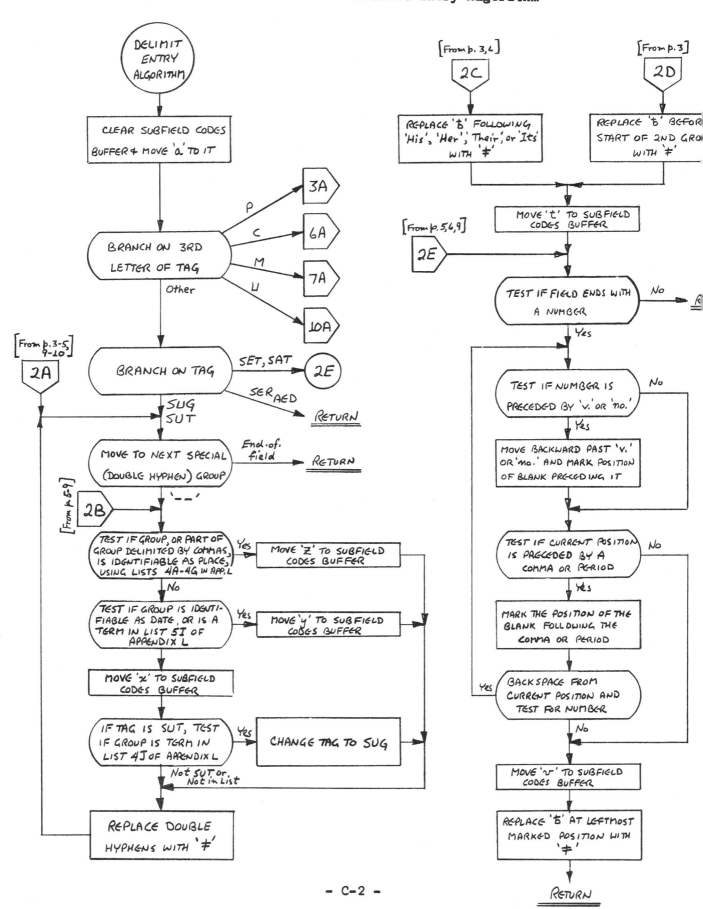

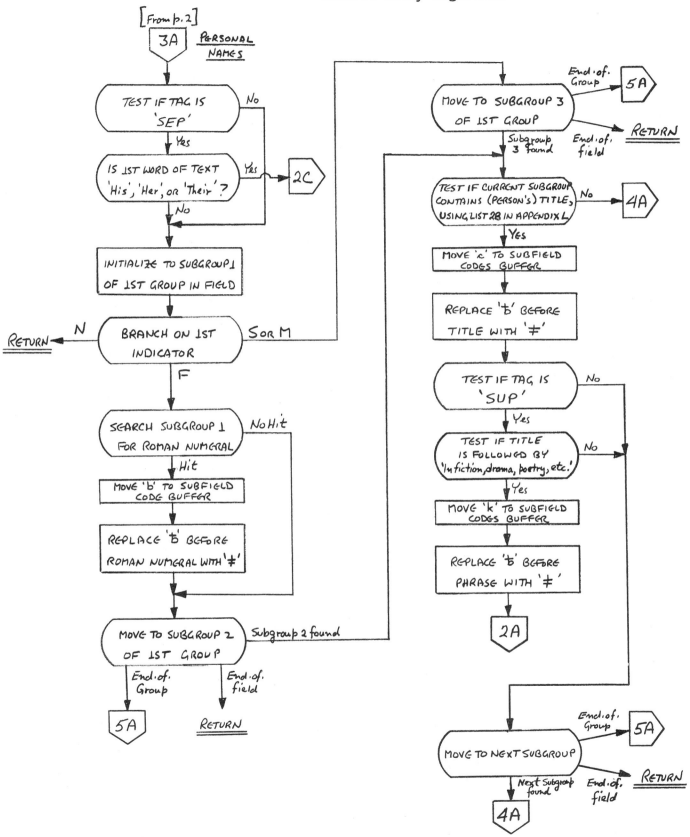

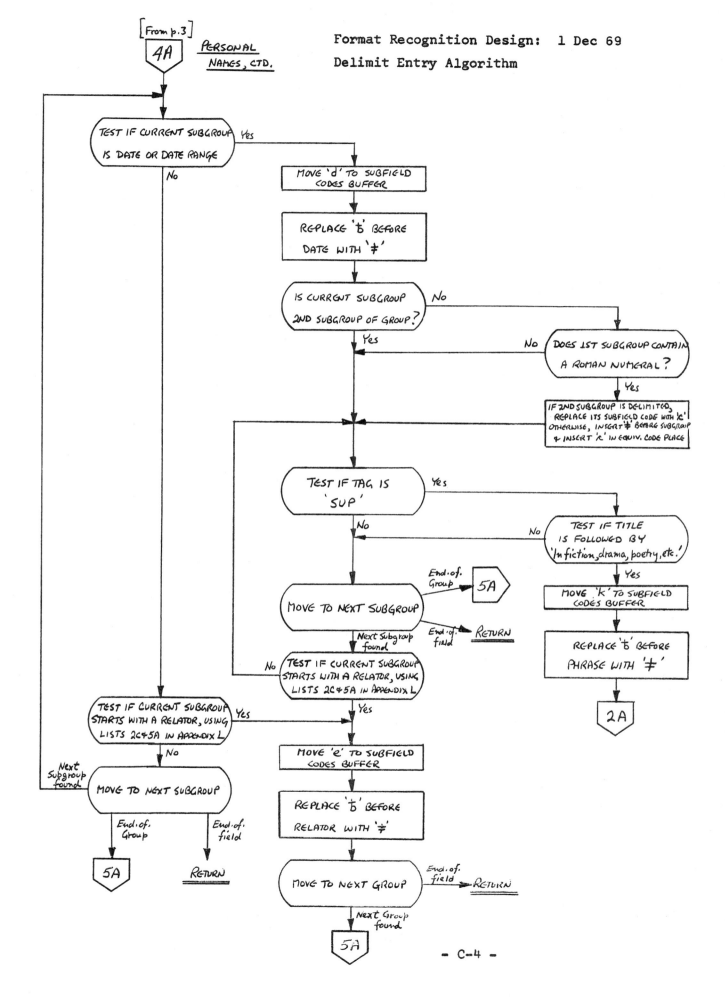

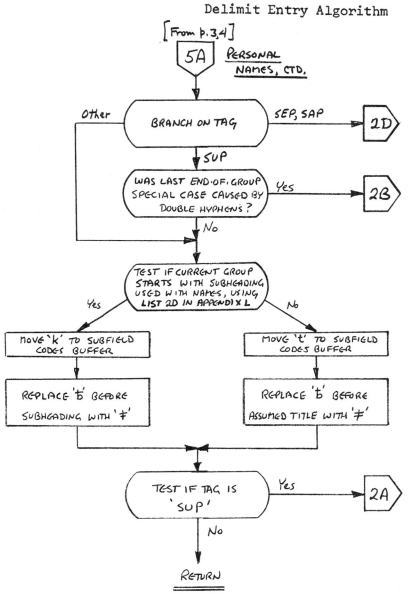

[From p.3,4]

5A   PERSONAL
      NAMES, CTD.

Other   BRANCH ON TAG   SEP, SAP → 2D

SUP

WAS LAST END·OF·GROUP
SPECIAL CASE CAUSED BY   Yes → 2B
DOUBLE HYPHENS ?

No

TEST IF CURRENT GROUP
STARTS WITH SUBHEADING
USED WITH NAMES, USING
LIST 2D IN APPENDIX L

Yes   No

MOVE 'k' TO SUBFIELD   MOVE 't' TO SUBFIELD
CODES BUFFER   CODES BUFFER

REPLACE 'ƀ' BEFORE   REPLACE 'ƀ' BEFORE
SUBHEADING WITH '≠'   ASSUMED TITLE WITH '≠'

TEST IF TAG IS
'SUP'   Yes → 2A

No

RETURN

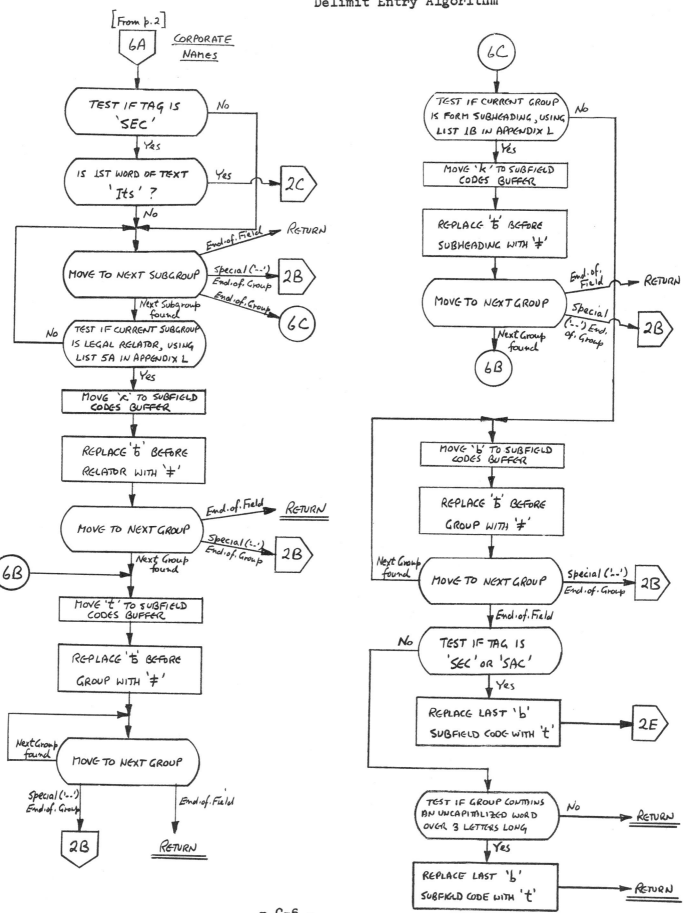

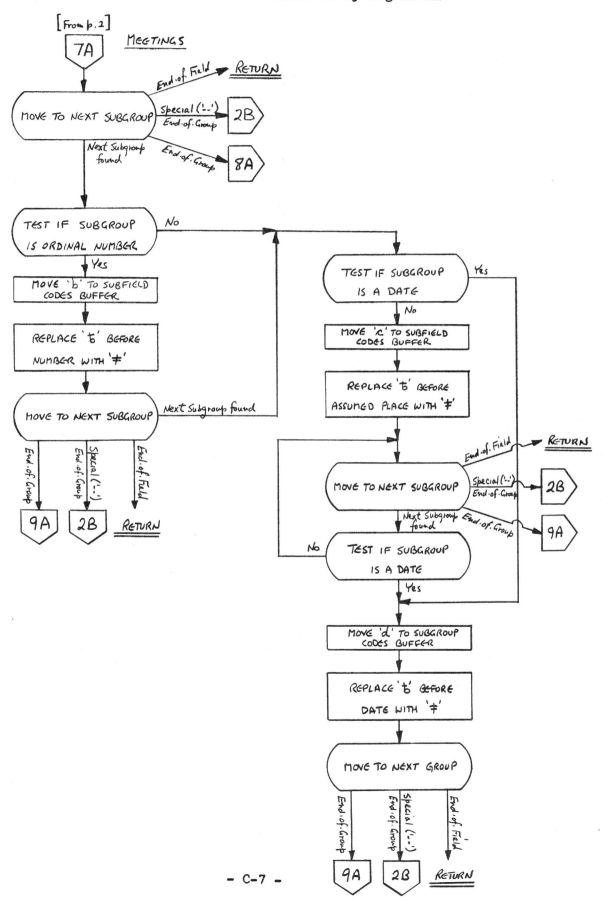

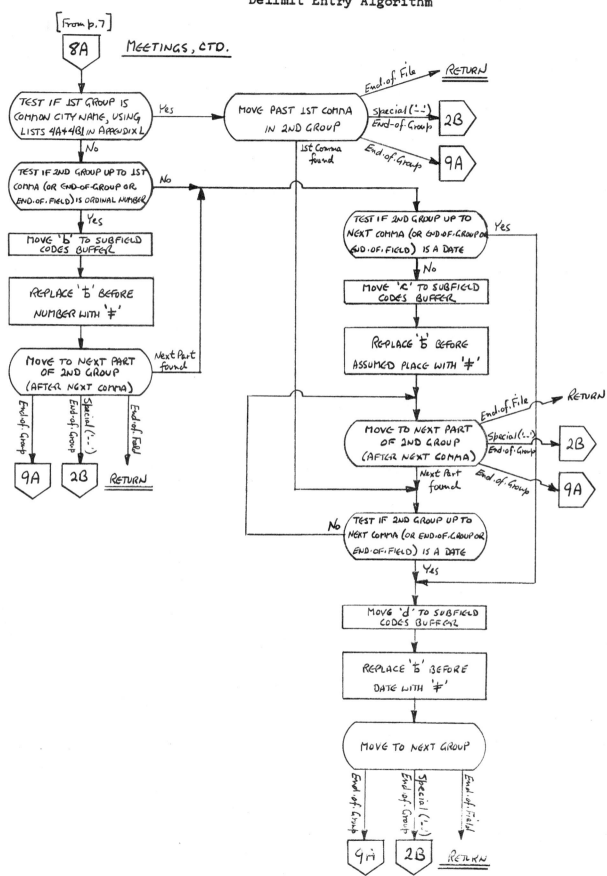

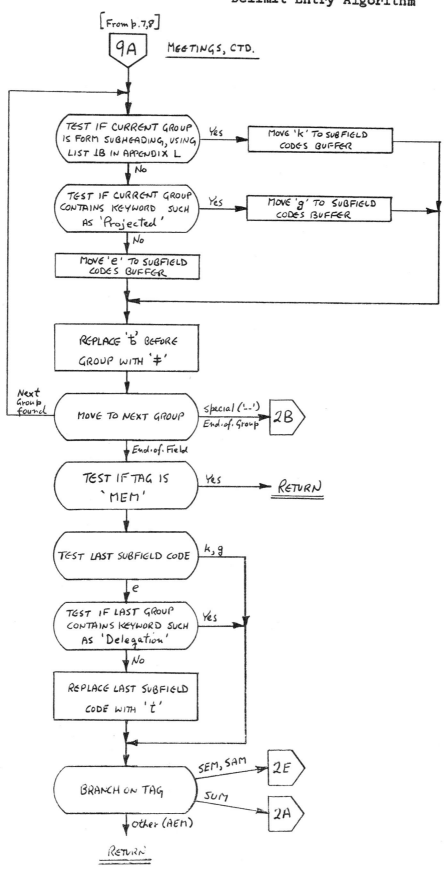

[From p.7,8]

9A   MEETINGS, CTD.

TEST IF CURRENT GROUP IS FORM SUBHEADING, USING LIST 1B IN APPENDIX L — Yes → MOVE 'k' TO SUBFIELD CODES BUFFER

No

TEST IF CURRENT GROUP CONTAINS KEYWORD SUCH AS 'Projected' — Yes → MOVE 'g' TO SUBFIELD CODES BUFFER

No

MOVE 'e' TO SUBFIELD CODES BUFFER

REPLACE 'b' BEFORE GROUP WITH '≠'

Next Group found

MOVE TO NEXT GROUP — Special ('--') End of Group → 2B

End of Field

TEST IF TAG IS 'MEM' — Yes → RETURN

TEST LAST SUBFIELD CODE — k, g

e

TEST IF LAST GROUP CONTAINS KEYWORD SUCH AS 'Delegation' — Yes

No

REPLACE LAST SUBFIELD CODE WITH 't'

BRANCH ON TAG — SEM, SAM → 2E
— SUM → 2A

Other (AEM)

RETURN

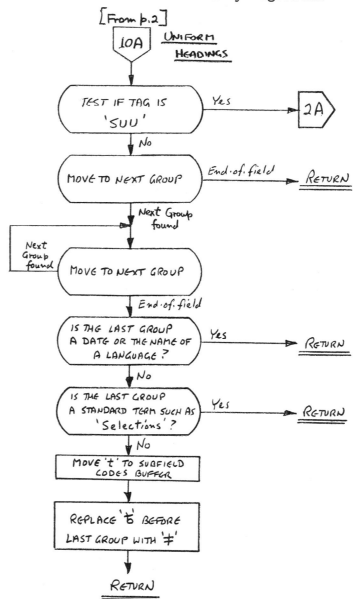

[From p.2]

10A   UNIFORM
           HEADINGS

TEST IF TAG IS
'SUU'   —Yes→   2A

No

MOVE TO NEXT GROUP   —End·of·field→   RETURN

Next Group
found

Next
Group
found

MOVE TO NEXT GROUP

End·of·field

IS THE LAST GROUP
A DATE OR THE NAME OF   —Yes→   RETURN
A LANGUAGE?

No

IS THE LAST GROUP
A STANDARD TERM SUCH AS   —Yes→   RETURN
'Selections'?

No

MOVE 't' TO SUBFIELD
CODES BUFFER

REPLACE 'ƀ' BEFORE
LAST GROUP WITH '≠'

RETURN

APPENDIX D   IDENTIFY NOTE ALGORITHM

The purpose of this algorithm is to determine into which of five of the six
possible Note field categories a given Note field falls:

> NOB - Bibliography Note
> NOC - Contents Note
> NOD - Dissertation (Thesis) Note
> NOG - General Note
> NOW - "Bound With" Note

(The Annotation or Abstract Note (tag NOA) is determined by a Special Test in
the Step 3 processing of the LC Card Number, as is described in Section VII.V.)

In general, all Note fields are identified by the occurrence of keywords
within them, with NOG being assigned to any field not so identified. None
of the Note fields are delimited, so the accumulation of subfield codes is
not involved. The only Note field having and indicator is NOC, to which is
assigned as its 1st indicator either 'C' (Complete Contents), 'P' (Partially
Complete Contents), or 'I' (Incomplete Contents).

Flowchart Notes

(1) These keywords are removed from the data of the variable field.

(2) NOW terms are: Bound with

> With, as issued
>
> In case, as issued, with

(3) NOB keywords are given in List 5D of Appendix L; NOD keywords are given in
List 5E of Appendix L.

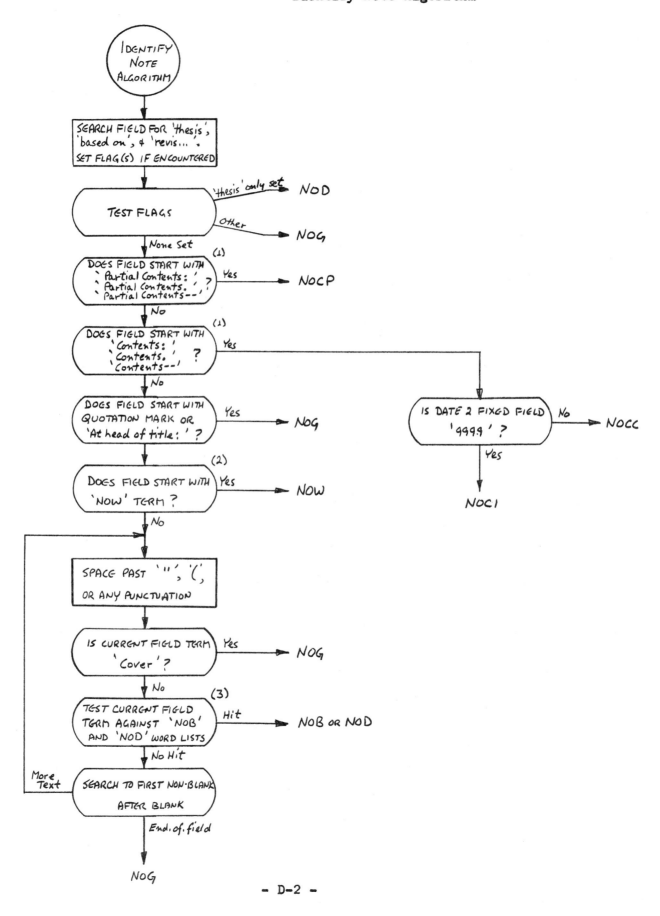

APPENDIX E.   DELIMIT TITLE STATEMENT ALGORITHM

The Delimit Title Statement Algorithm performs the delimiting function for
the Title Statement. The one indicator of this field is determined by
Special Tests in both Steps 3 and 4. The complete three-letter tag has
been assigned to this field in Step 2. There are three possible subfields
to the Title Statement:

> Subfield 'a' - Short Title
>
> Subfield 'b' - Remainder of Title
>
> Subfield 'c' - Remainder of Title Page Transcription

Subfield 'c' is more readily identifiable due to keywords used only in this
subfield, such as 'by'. The Subfield 'b', on the other hand, is not so easily
identified due to its free form nature as the continuation of the Title. It
can be derived from observed keywords which follow certain punctuation, but
these are not necessarily unique terms.

Flowchart Notes

(1) The subfield codes accumulation area is three characters in length.

(2) Decisions as to the start of a new subfield are suspended between paren-
     theses and quotation marks. These counters are used to determine whether
     either punctuation is currently operative. See explanation (6) also.

(3) When there is more than one sentence to a Title Statement, the second
     sentence automatically starts a new subfield. Also, if a 'semicolon'
     occurs after the fourth word in the Short Title, or a 'question mark' or
     'explanation point' occurs, anyone should be considered to end the first
     subfield. In these cases, the subfield code to be assigned to the text
     following the end of the first subfield, either 'b' or 'c', should be analyzed
     for, ignoring starting punctuation, when there.

APPENDIX E.   DELIMIT TITLE STATEMENT ALGORITHM Continued

(4)   The 'parens counter' is maintained merely for knowing at any point during the processing of the Title Statement whether 'parentheses' are operative. As 'open parens' are encountered, the 'parens counter' is advanced by one count; when 'close parens' are encountered, the 'parens counter' is reduced by one count. It **has no** meaning to reduce this counter below zero and such cases are ignored.

(5)   The 'quotes counter' is maintained merely for knowing at any point during the processing of the Title Statement whether 'quotation marks' are operative. Since there is no way of knowing if a 'quotation mark' is 'open' or 'close', a sequential count is maintained in this counter. When the counter is an odd number, then it can be interpreted to mean that the 'quotation mark' is an 'open' one; similarly, when the counter is an even number, the 'quotation mark' is a 'close' one.

(6)   The 'parens or quotes "in process" counter' is maintained for quick testing as to whether either 'parentheses' or 'quotation marks' or both are operative. As described in (2) above, certain decisions are suspended when this counter contains a number greater than zero. It **has no** meaning to reduce this counter below zero and such cases are ignored. When either an 'open parens' or 'open quotation mark' is encountered, this counter is advanced by one count; when **either** a 'close parens' or 'close quotation mark' is encountered, this counter is reduced by one count.

(7)   This punctuation is not expected to break the 'b' and 'c' subfields.

(8)   Since the Title Paragraph is broken up at the discretion of the input typist, the end of the Title Statement may occur at a point not necessarily ending with a 'period', so the test for 'end-of-field' character must be made following all of the punctuation.

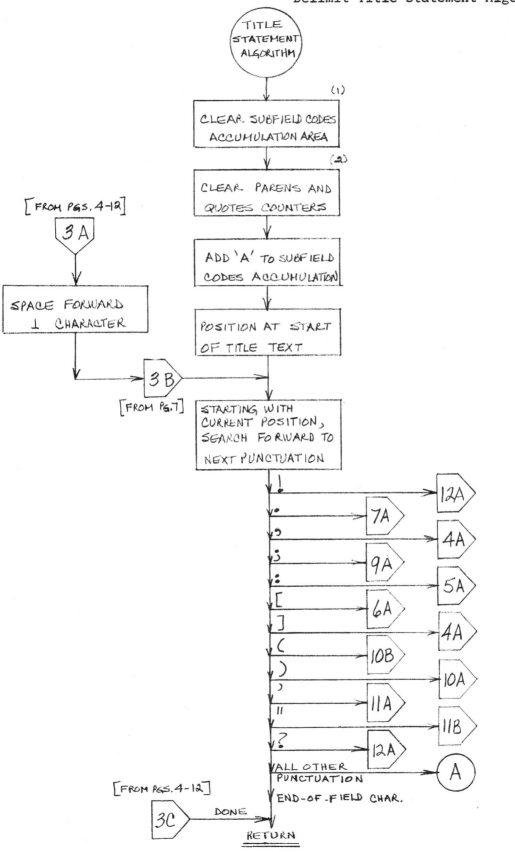

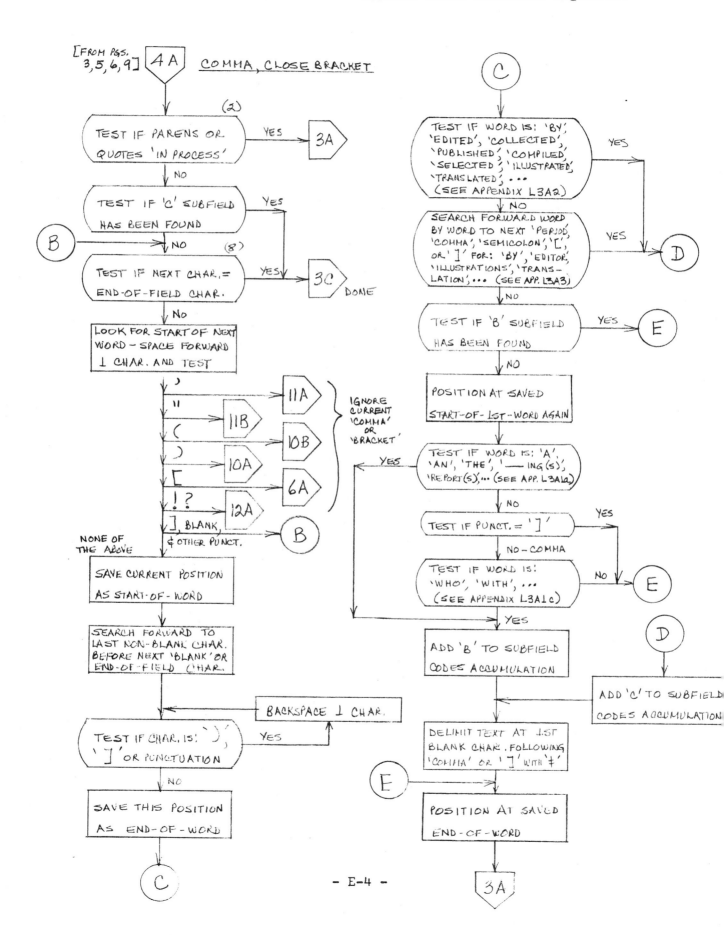

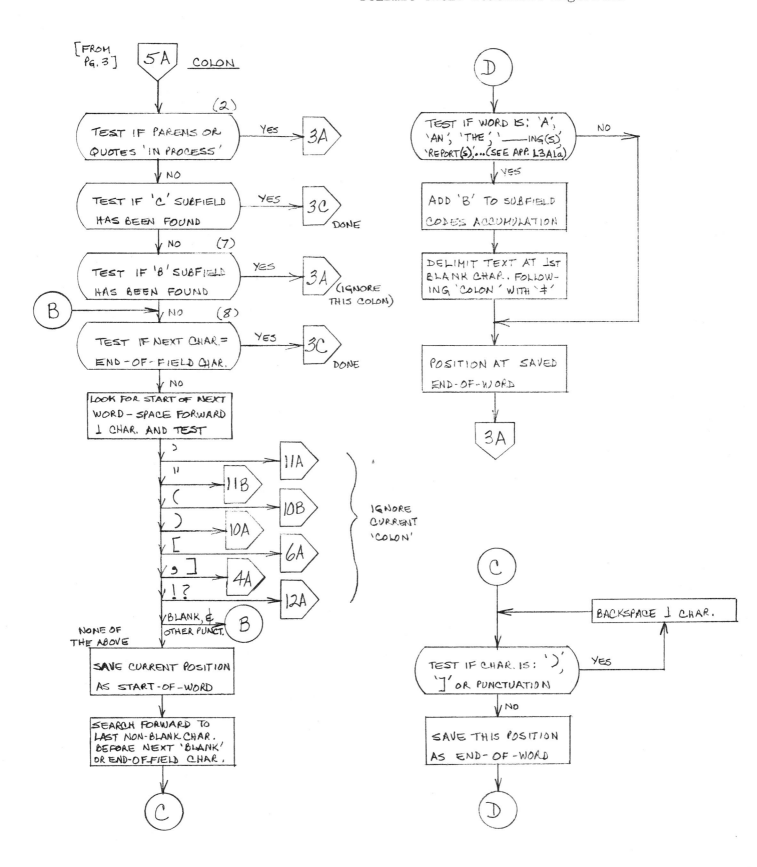

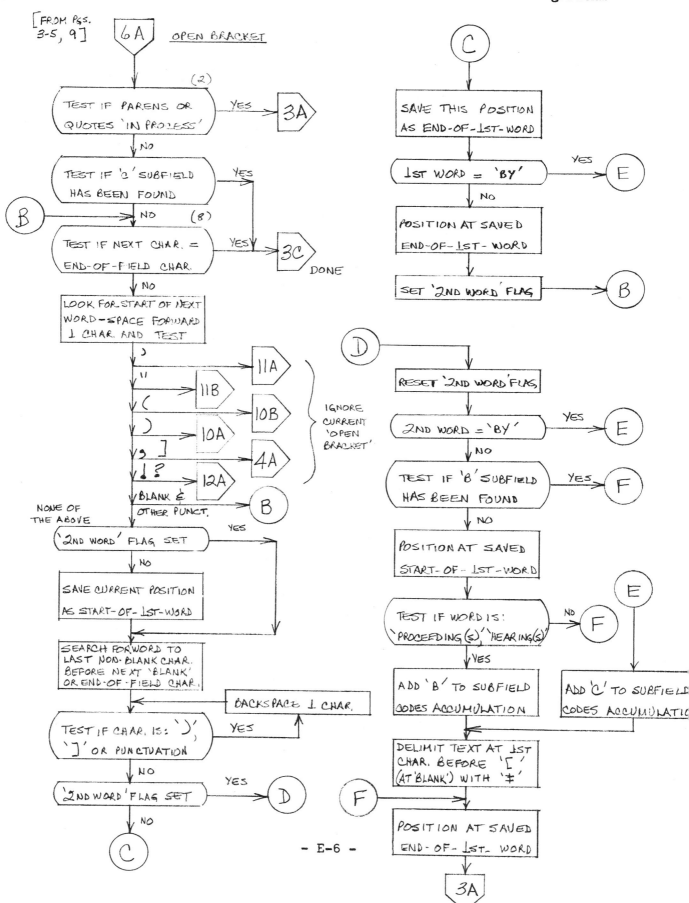

[FROM PGS. 3-5, 9] 6A OPEN BRACKET

(2)
TEST IF PARENS OR QUOTES 'IN PROCESS' — YES → 3A
NO

TEST IF 'C' SUBFIELD HAS BEEN FOUND — YES
NO   (8)

B →

TEST IF NEXT CHAR. = END-OF-FIELD CHAR. — YES → 3C DONE
NO

LOOK FOR START OF NEXT WORD — SPACE FORWARD 1 CHAR. AND TEST

' → 11A
" → 11B
(→ 10B
) → 10A
;] → 4A
! ? → 12A

IGNORE CURRENT 'OPEN BRACKET'

BLANK & OTHER PUNCT. → B

NONE OF THE ABOVE

'2ND WORD' FLAG SET — YES
NO

SAVE CURRENT POSITION AS START-OF-1ST-WORD

SEARCH FORWARD TO LAST NON-BLANK CHAR. BEFORE NEXT 'BLANK' OR END-OF-FIELD CHAR.

BACKSPACE 1 CHAR.

TEST IF CHAR. IS: ')' ']' OR PUNCTUATION — YES ↗
NO

'2ND WORD' FLAG SET — YES → D
NO

C

C

SAVE THIS POSITION AS END-OF-1ST-WORD

1ST WORD = 'BY' — YES → E
NO

POSITION AT SAVED END-OF-1ST-WORD

SET '2ND WORD' FLAG → B

D →

RESET '2ND WORD' FLAG

2ND WORD = 'BY' — YES → E
NO

TEST IF 'B' SUBFIELD HAS BEEN FOUND — YES → F
NO

POSITION AT SAVED START-OF-1ST-WORD

TEST IF WORD IS: 'PROCEEDING(S)' 'HEARING(S)' — NO → F
YES

ADD 'B' TO SUBFIELD CODES ACCUMULATION

E

ADD 'C' TO SUBFIELD CODES ACCUMULATIO

DELIMIT TEXT AT 1ST CHAR. BEFORE '[' (AT 'BLANK') WITH '≠'

F →

POSITION AT SAVED END-OF-1ST-WORD

3A

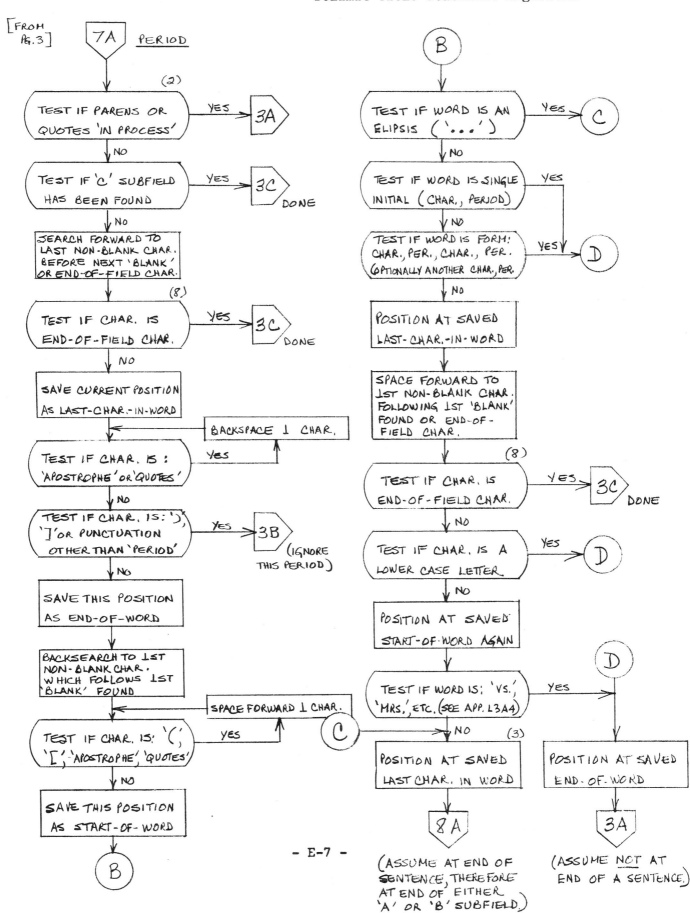

- E-7 -

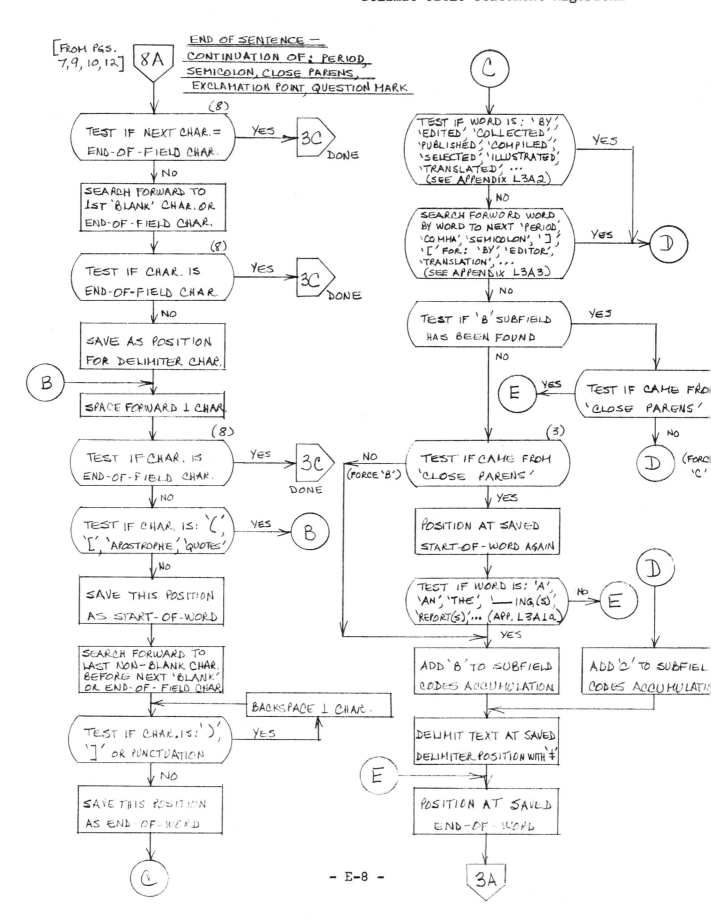

- E-8 -

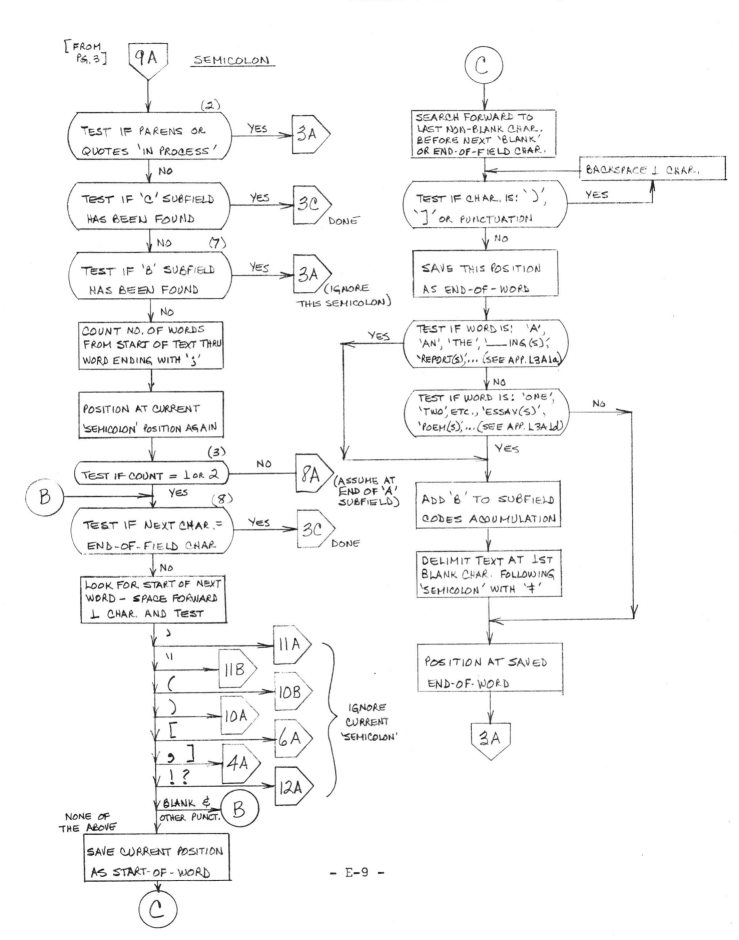

- E-9 -

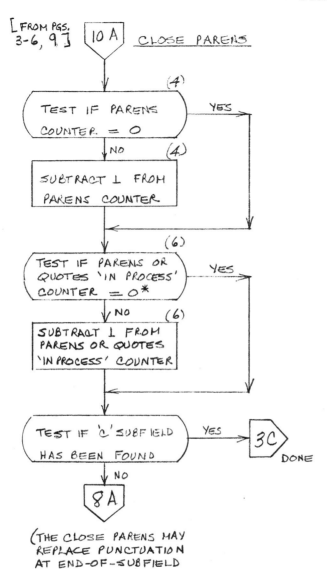

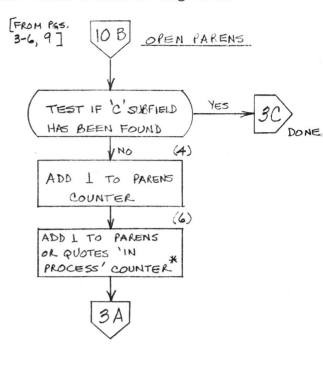

(THE CLOSE PARENS MAY
REPLACE PUNCTUATION
AT END-OF-SUBFIELD
OR END-OF-FIELD, SO
MAKE TESTS ACCORDINGLY.)

* WHEN THE PARENS OR QUOTES
'IN PROCESS' COUNTER >0, EITHER
PARENS OR QUOTES OR BOTH ARE
CURRENTLY OPERATIVE. WHEN THIS
COUNTER = 0, NEITHER ARE OPERATIVE.

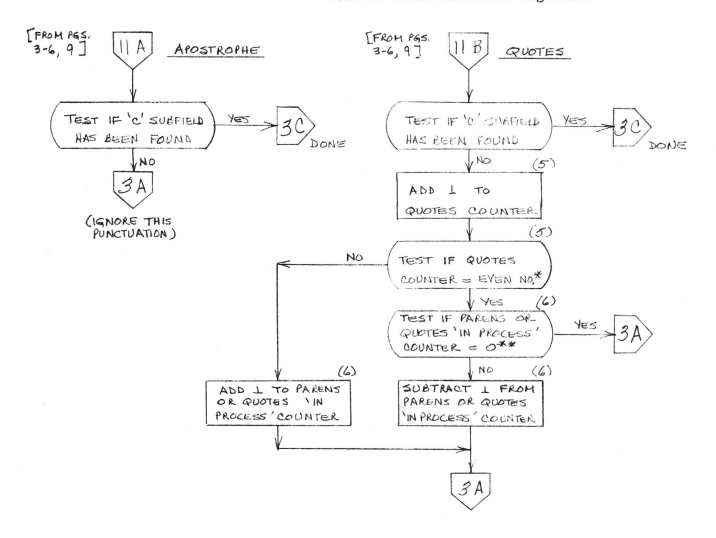

* WHEN THE QUOTES COUNTER IS AN ODD NO.,
THE QUOTATION MARK IS AN 'OPEN' ONE; WHEN
THIS COUNTER IS AN EVEN NO., THE QUOTATION
MARK IS A CLOSING ONE.

** WHEN THE PARENS OR QUOTES 'IN PROCESS'
COUNTER > 0, EITHER PARENS OR QUOTES
OR BOTH ARE CURRENTLY OPERATIVE. WHEN
THIS COUNTER = 0, NEITHER ARE OPERATIVE.

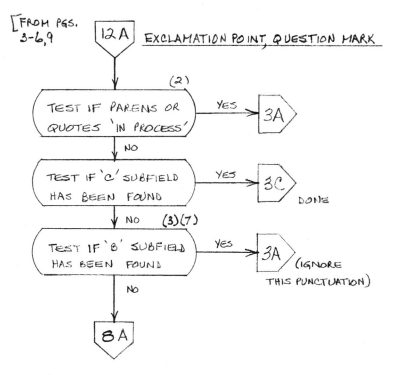

FROM PGS. 3-6, 9

12 A   EXCLAMATION POINT, QUESTION MARK

(2)

TEST IF PARENS OR QUOTES 'IN PROCESS' — YES → 3A

NO

TEST IF 'C' SUBFIELD HAS BEEN FOUND — YES → 3C   DONE

NO   (3)(7)

TEST IF 'B' SUBFIELD HAS BEEN FOUND — YES → 3A (IGNORE THIS PUNCTUATION)

NO

8 A

(ASSUME AT END OF SENTENCE, THEREFORE AT END OF 'A' SUBFIELD)

APPENDIX F.   DELIMIT EDITION STATEMENT ALGORITHM

The Delimit Edition Statement Algorithm performs the delimiting function
for the Edition Statement. There are no indicators for this field. The
complete three-letter tag has been assigned to this field in Step 2. There
are two possible subfields to the Edition Statement:

<blockquote>
Subfield 'a' - Edition Statement proper
Subfield 'b' - Remainder of Edition Statement
</blockquote>

Flowchart Notes

(1) The subfield codes accumulation area is two characters in length.

(2) Decisions as to the start of a new subfield are suspended between
     parentheses. A counter is used to determine whether parentheses
     are currently operative. See explanation (4) as well.

(3) Since multiple initials are of the form: character, period, character,
     period, etc., the first period encountered may not be the end of word.
     Periods interior to multiple initials are ignored until the one at
     the end of the word is encountered.

(4) The 'parens counter' is maintained merely for knowing at any point during
     the processing of the Edition Statement whether 'parentheses' are operative.
     As an 'open parens' is encountered, the 'parens counter' is advanced by
     one count; when a 'close parens' is encountered, the 'parens counter'
     is reduced by one count. It has no meaning to reduce this counter below
     zero and such cases are ignored.

(5) This test is successful quite often to identify the 'b' subfield.

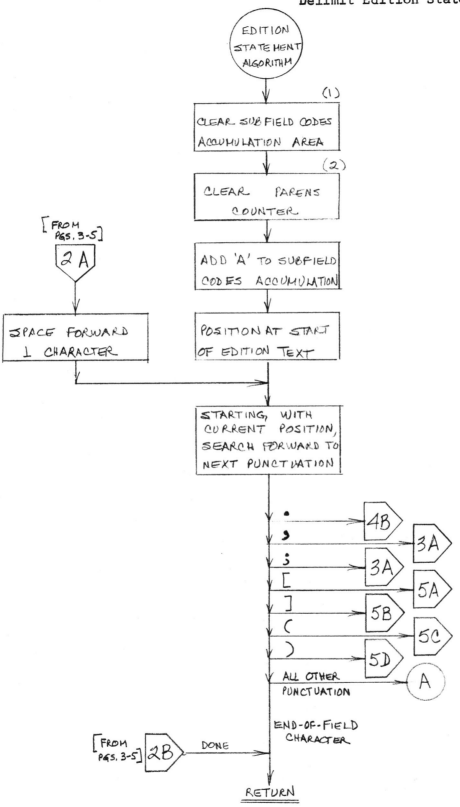

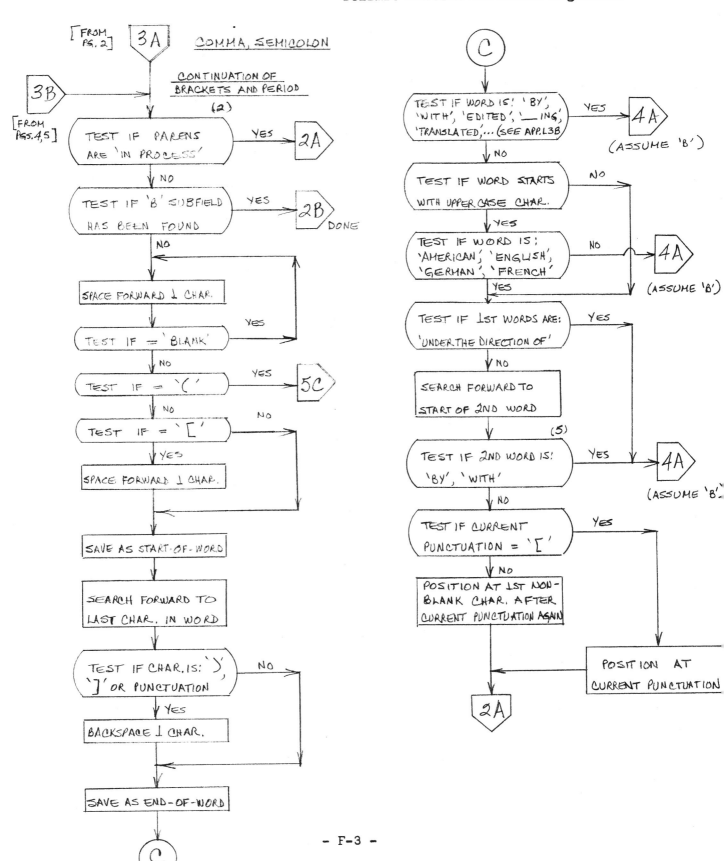

COMMA, SEMICOLON

CONTINUATION OF
BRACKETS AND PERIOD
(2)

[FROM PG. 2] 3A

3B [FROM PGS. 4,5]

TEST IF PARENS ARE 'IN PROCESS' — YES → 2A
NO ↓

TEST IF 'B' SUBFIELD HAS BEEN FOUND — YES → 2B DONE
NO ↓

SPACE FORWARD 1 CHAR.
↓
TEST IF = 'BLANK' — YES →
NO ↓
TEST IF = '(' — YES → 5C
NO ↓
TEST IF = '[' — NO →
YES ↓
SPACE FORWARD 1 CHAR.
↓
SAVE AS START-OF-WORD
↓
SEARCH FORWARD TO LAST CHAR. IN WORD
↓
TEST IF CHAR. IS: ')', ']' OR PUNCTUATION — NO →
YES ↓
BACKSPACE 1 CHAR.
↓
SAVE AS END-OF-WORD
↓
C

C
↓
TEST IF WORD IS: 'BY', 'WITH', 'EDITED', '___ING', 'TRANSLATED',... (SEE APP. L3B) — YES → 4A (ASSUME 'B')
NO ↓
TEST IF WORD STARTS WITH UPPER CASE CHAR. — NO →
YES ↓
TEST IF WORD IS: 'AMERICAN', 'ENGLISH', 'GERMAN', 'FRENCH' — NO → 4A (ASSUME 'B')
YES ↓
TEST IF 1ST WORDS ARE: 'UNDER THE DIRECTION OF' — YES →
NO ↓
SEARCH FORWARD TO START OF 2ND WORD
↓ (5)
TEST IF 2ND WORD IS: 'BY', 'WITH' — YES → 4A (ASSUME 'B')
NO ↓
TEST IF CURRENT PUNCTUATION = '[' — YES →
NO ↓
POSITION AT 1ST NON-BLANK CHAR. AFTER CURRENT PUNCTUATION AGAIN
↓
POSITION AT CURRENT PUNCTUATION
↓
2A

- F-3 -

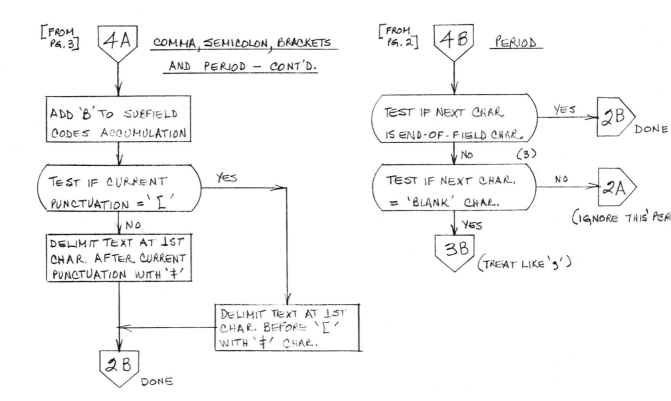

[FROM PG. 3] **4A** COMMA, SEMICOLON, BRACKETS AND PERIOD — CONT'D.

ADD 'B' TO SUBFIELD CODES ACCUMULATION

TEST IF CURRENT PUNCTUATION = '[' — YES

NO

DELIMIT TEXT AT 1ST CHAR. AFTER CURRENT PUNCTUATION WITH '‡'

DELIMIT TEXT AT 1ST CHAR. BEFORE '[' WITH '‡' CHAR.

2 B DONE

[FROM PG. 2] **4B** PERIOD

TEST IF NEXT CHAR. IS END-OF-FIELD CHAR. — YES — **2B** DONE

NO (3)

TEST IF NEXT CHAR. = 'BLANK' CHAR. — NO — **2A** (IGNORE THIS PER

YES

3B (TREAT LIKE 'S')

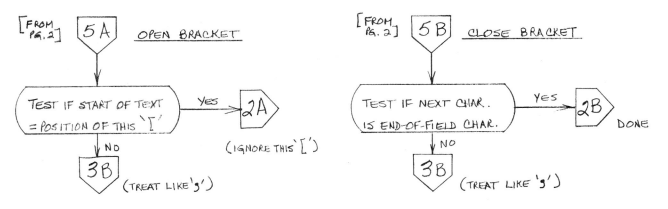

[FROM PG. 2] **5A** OPEN BRACKET

TEST IF START OF TEXT = POSITION OF THIS `[` — YES → **2A**

(IGNORE THIS `[`)

NO → **3B** (TREAT LIKE `s`)

[FROM PG. 2] **5B** CLOSE BRACKET

TEST IF NEXT CHAR. IS END-OF-FIELD CHAR. — YES → **2B** DONE

NO → **3B** (TREAT LIKE `s`)

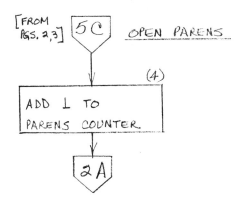

[FROM PGS. 2,3] **5C** OPEN PARENS

(4) ADD 1 TO PARENS COUNTER

→ **2A**

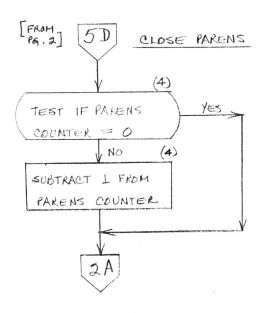

[FROM PG. 2] **5D** CLOSE PARENS

(4) TEST IF PARENS COUNTER = 0 — YES →

NO (4) → SUBTRACT 1 FROM PARENS COUNTER

→ **2A**

APPENDIX G.   DELIMIT IMPRINT STATEMENT ALGORITHM

The Delimit Imprint Statement Algorithm performs the delimiting function
for the Imprint Statement. The one indicator for this field is determined
by Special Tests in Step 3. The complete three-letter tag has been
assigned to this field in Step 2. There are three possible subfields to
the Imprint Statement:

    Subfield 'a' - Place of Publication
    Subfield 'b' - Publisher
    Subfield 'c' - Date of Publication

There are varying patterns of these subfield codes which may occur. However,
the 'c' subfield always occurs at the end, although there may be several
dates in this subfield. For the 'a' and 'b' subfields, each new expression
is given another subfield code. When more than two 'a' subfields occur,
usually the other places of publication are replaced with the term 'etc.',
usually appearing within brackets.

Flowchart Notes

(1)   Since the Imprint subfield codes can be one of several patterns which
       vary in length, a maximum of six characters are set aside.

(2)   Since the date(s) of the 'c' subfield always occur as the last part
       of the Imprint, its extent is determined first. This facilitates the
       processing of the other subfields subsequently.

(3)   Since the 'c' subfield was processed first, the subfield codes must be
       put into their accepted form with the 'c' on the end.

APPENDIX G.   DELIMIT IMPRINT STATEMENT Continued

(4)   Dates may appear several times in this subfield and in various forms; however, the non-numeric qualifiers of the dates precede the dates. It is therefore a straightforward test to determine if more dates exist in this field.

(5)   The 'apostrophe' and 'quotation mark' are ignored in the Imprint.

(6)   A Copyright Date is of the form 'c1968'.

(7)   When no date occurs in the Imprint, by convention the term 'n.d.' is inserted at the end of the Imprint, usually appearing within brackets.

(8)   The actual date of publication is given by convention preceded by the term 'i.e.' when it differs from the one appearing on the Title Page. This date follows the latter date in the Imprint Statement.

(9)   The position is saved of the first non-blank character following the current punctuation (unless the current punctuation is 'open bracket') and the 'potential' start of the next subfield. The text will be analyzed when the next punctuation forward in the text is found; see explanation in (11) below.

(10)   Because of the procedure explained in (11) below, there is no text to analyze here, since the 'open bracket' is either the start of the Imprint text or the start of the 'potential' start of the next subfield.

(11)   When any punctuation is encountered, the text which is analyzed is that between the saved position of the 'potential' start of the next subfield (which by definition precedes the current puntuation in the text) and the position of the current punctuation encountered.

APPENDIX G.   DELIMIT IMPRINT STATEMENT ALGORITHM Continued

(12)   If the text in the area defined in (11) above meets the criteria for
        a new subfield, then the delimiter character can be inserted appropri-
        ately preceding the saved character position of the 'potential' start
        of the next (which is now this) subfield.

(13)   Often following a 'semicolon', either directly or shortly thereafter,
        a 'distribution' phrase will occur which may contain a place of
        publication. This place name should not be considered a new 'a'
        subfield, nor is the 'distribution' phrase to be considered a new 'b'
        subfield.

(14)   Due to the condition described in (13) above, no new 'a' subfields can
        be accepted, and, since new 'b' subfields are only recognized by
        exception following new 'a' subfields, no new 'b' subfields can be
        accepted either. Therefore, no new subfields are further identified
        following the 'distribution' phrase. This can be done with facility
        since the 'c' subfield has already been delimited; this then terminates
        the delimiting of the Imprint Statement.

(15)   Such as Ohio.

(16)   Since multiple initials are of the form: character, period, character,
        period, etc., the first period encountered may not be the end of the word.
        However, for analysis of the initials, the current position must be
        placed at the end of the word.

(17)   When no place of publication occurs in the Imprint, by convention the
        word 'n.p.' is inserted at the beginning of the Imprint, usually
        appearing within brackets.

APPENDIX G.   DELIMIT IMPRINT STATEMENT ALGORITHM Continued

(18)   Multiple word city names may begin with an abbreviated term, such as 'St.', it is ignored until the end of the full place name is encountered. Both the abbreviated place name and the full spelling of the place name will be found in the list of city place names.

(19)   Either the word with the period in it is the first word in the area being tested (meaning that it is a single word abbreviation or multiple initials or a single initial) or it is in one of the words beyond the first word (meaning there are multiple words, the last one of which is an abbreviation or initial(s)).

(20)   It is possible that a state, country, or English County abbreviation may follow a U.S. or foreign city name; when encountered, it is not to be considered a new 'a' subfield.

(21)   The first punctuation encountered will, in general, mark the end of the first 'a' subfield. No validation is made as to the contents of this first 'a' subfield.

(22)   If the previous subfield was 'b', then this is simply a continuation of it and no further processing is necessary, as described in (13) and (14) above. However, if the previous subfield was 'a', then this must be processed as a new 'b' subfield before terminating the processing.

(23)   Usually city place names are not abbreviated, but this test is made here for reasons of contingencies.

(24)   Such as L.A. for Los Angeles, also see (23) above.

APPENDIX G.   DELIMIT IMPRINT STATEMENT ALGORITHM Continued

(25)   The country **name** abbreviation for the United States, 'U.S.' is not
         considered in this list for the 'a' subfield, since it is an often
         found candidate in the 'b' subfield.

(26)   Multiple word country names may begin with an abbreviated term,
         such as 'Gt.', it is ignored until the full place name is
         encountered. Both the abbreviated place name and the full spelling
         of the place name will be found in the list of country place names.

(27)   A single initial is considered to be a 'b' subfield case only.

(28)   **This count is used for testing against the maximum word set in any
         list, just prior to searching the list, for purposes of efficiency;
         however, these tests are implied, rather than stated in the algorithm.**

(29)   The 'tentative 'a' subfield' flag is a mechanism to provide a
         lookahead for clarification in the following case:

                                                    1) city name
                                                    2) state or country name
         ... _____b_____ ; _____?_____ , 3) publisher phrase_____

The questioned new subfield may be either an unrecognized city name,
in which case it may or may not be followed by a qualifying state or
country name; or an additional publisher phrase. Since it is most
likely to be the latter case, no new subfield code is assigned at this
time. The 'tentative 'a' subfield' flag is set in case that the next
phrase is either a city name or a state or country name. If it is,
then the questioned phrase is considered to be a new 'a' subfield and
it is then delimited and assigned a subfield code accordingly. If it
is not, and therefore is a publisher phrase, then no additional
delimiting is necessary and the 'tentative 'a' subfield' flag is reset
to off.

APPENDIX G.   DELIMIT IMPRINT STATEMENT ALGORITHM Continued

(30)   The 'tentative 'b' subfield' flag is a mechanism to provide a
       lookahead for clarification in the following case:

                                         1) city name
                                         2) state or country name
       ... ____a____ , ____?____ , 3) publisher phrase

       The questioned new subfield may be either an unrecognized city name,
       in which case it may or may not be followed by a qualifying state or
       country name; or a publisher phrase. Since it is a new subfield in
       either case, it is delimited and assigned the subfield code for a
       publisher phrase. The 'tentative 'b' subfield' flag is set in case
       that the next phrase is either a city name or state or country name.
       If it is, then the questioned phrase is considered to be a new 'a'
       subfield and the previously-assigned subfield code is changed to an
       'a' code; the text has already been delimited correctly. If it is not,
       and therefore is a publisher phrase, then since the new subfield has
       been delimited and assigned a subfield code correctly, the 'tentative
       'b' subfield' flag is reset to off.

(31)   The 'semicolon' flag is set when a semicolon is encountered in order
       to handle the lookahead case, described in (29) above. It is reset
       after the next phrase has been tested.

(32)   A city name, sometimes followed by a qualifying state or country name,
       may occur in a publisher statement, subfield 'b', and is considered
       part of it unless it follows a 'semicolon', at which time it is
       considered to start a new place statement, subfield 'a'.

(33)   Several city names are often followed by the term 'etc.'. If one of
       these city names is not recognized, it can be found by the identification
       of the term 'etc.', or by the lookahead procedure described in (30) above.

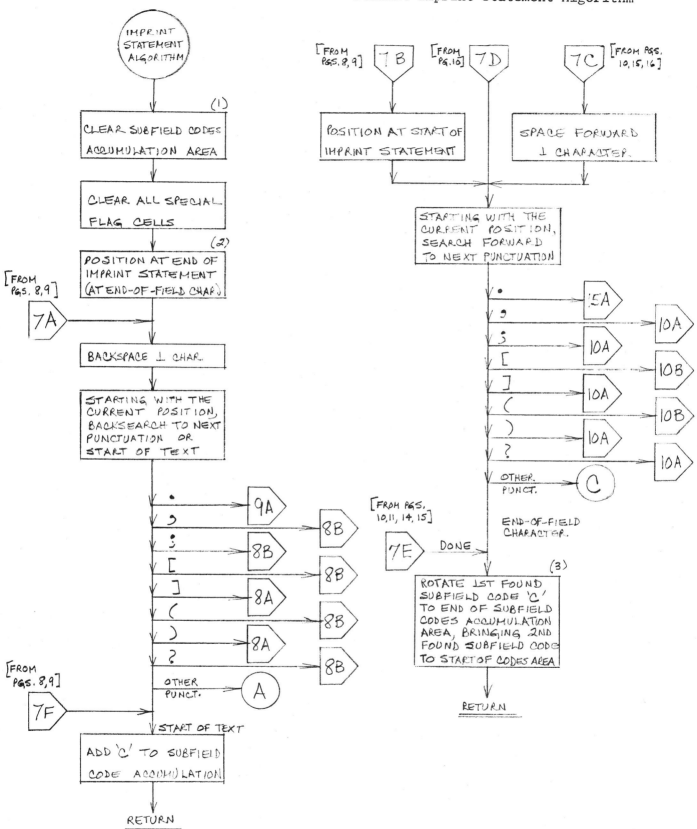

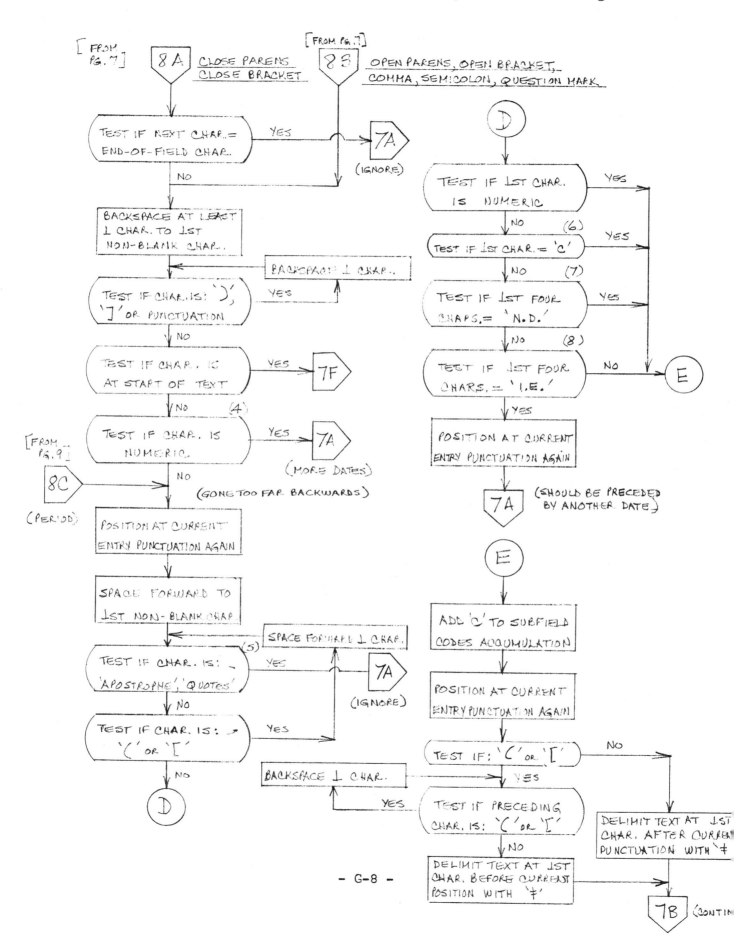

- G-8 -

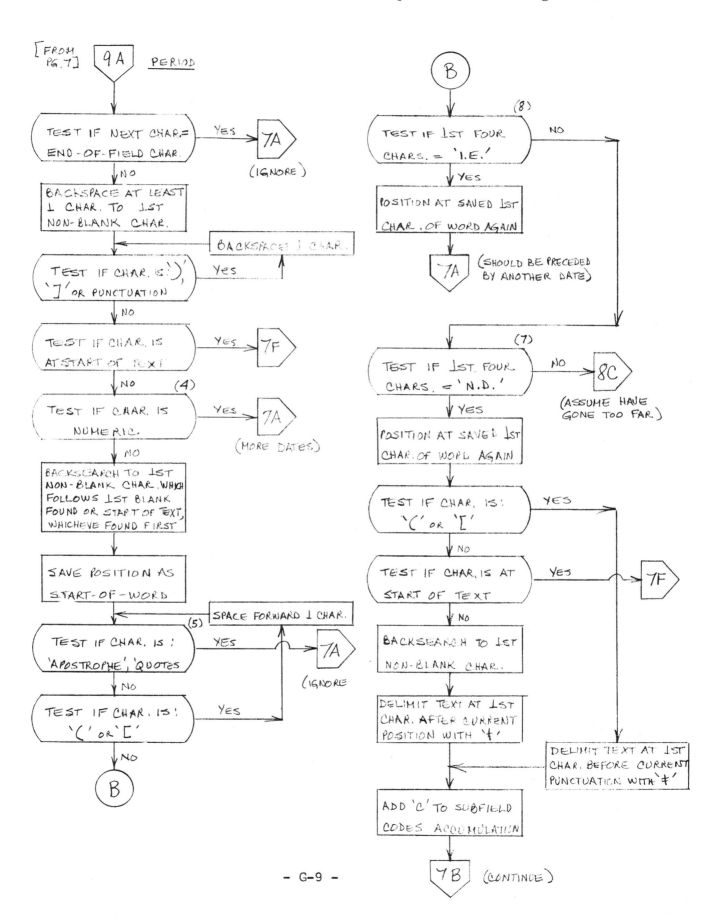

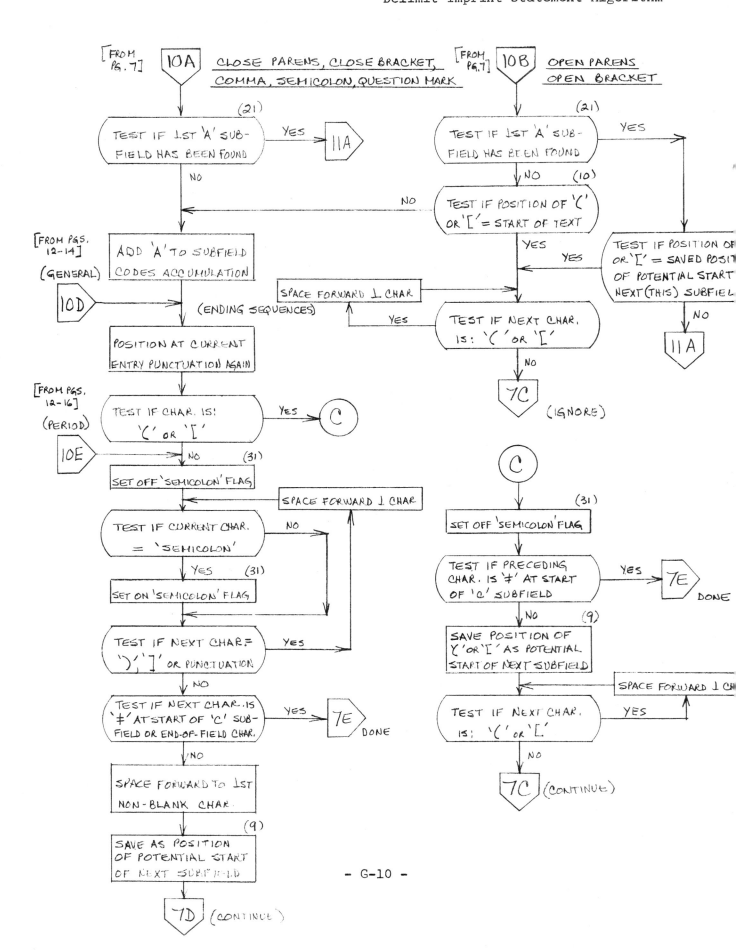

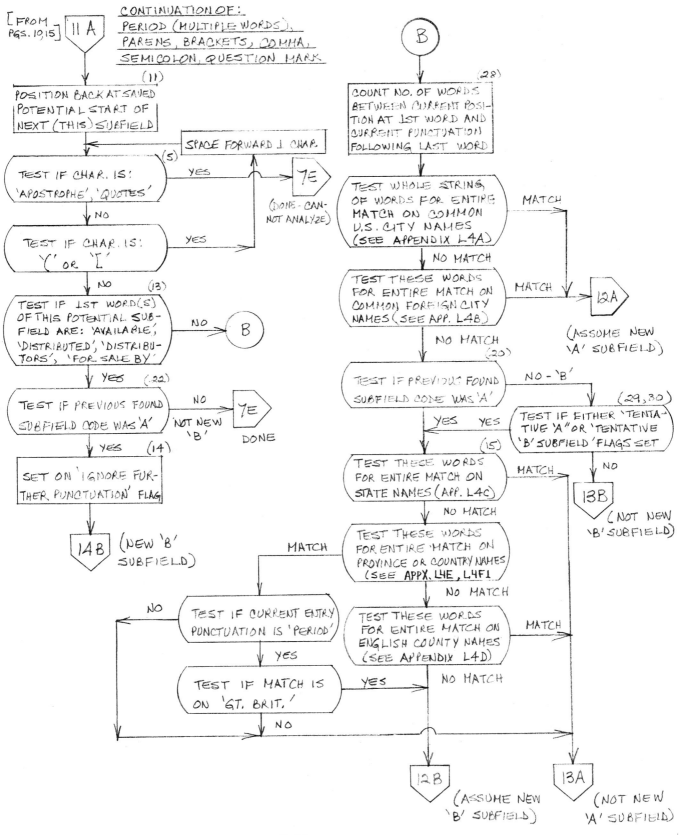

CONTINUATION OF:
PERIOD (MULTIPLE WORDS),
PARENS, BRACKETS, COMMA,
SEMICOLON, QUESTION MARK

[FROM PGS. 10, 15] 11 A

(11)
POSITION BACK AT SAVED POTENTIAL START OF NEXT (THIS) SUBFIELD

SPACE FORWARD 1 CHAR.

(5) TEST IF CHAR. IS: 'APOSTROPHE', 'QUOTES' — yes → 7E (DONE - CANNOT ANALYZE)

NO

TEST IF CHAR. IS: '(' OR '[' — yes →

NO (13)

TEST IF 1ST WORD(S) OF THIS POTENTIAL SUBFIELD ARE: 'AVAILABLE', 'DISTRIBUTED', 'DISTRIBUTORS', 'FOR SALE BY' — NO → B

YES (22)

TEST IF PREVIOUS FOUND SUBFIELD CODE WAS 'A' — NO 'NOT NEW 'B'' → 7E DONE

YES (14)

SET ON 'IGNORE FURTHER PUNCTUATION' FLAG

14B (NEW 'B' SUBFIELD)

B

(28)
COUNT NO. OF WORDS BETWEEN CURRENT POSITION AT 1ST WORD AND CURRENT PUNCTUATION FOLLOWING LAST WORD

TEST WHOLE STRING OF WORDS FOR ENTIRE MATCH ON COMMON U.S. CITY NAMES (SEE APPENDIX L4A) — MATCH →

NO MATCH

TEST THESE WORDS FOR ENTIRE MATCH ON COMMON FOREIGN CITY NAMES (SEE APP. L4B) — MATCH → 12A (ASSUME NEW 'A' SUBFIELD)

NO MATCH (20)

TEST IF PREVIOUS FOUND SUBFIELD CODE WAS 'A' — NO - 'B' → (29, 30) TEST IF EITHER 'TENTATIVE 'A'' OR 'TENTATIVE 'B' SUBFIELD' FLAGS SET — NO → 13B (NOT NEW 'B' SUBFIELD)

YES YES

(15)
TEST THESE WORDS FOR ENTIRE MATCH ON STATE NAMES (APP. L4C) — MATCH →

NO MATCH

TEST THESE WORDS FOR ENTIRE MATCH ON PROVINCE OR COUNTRY NAMES (SEE APPX. L4E, L4F) — MATCH →

NO MATCH

TEST THESE WORDS FOR ENTIRE MATCH ON ENGLISH COUNTY NAMES (SEE APPENDIX L4D) — MATCH →

NO MATCH

TEST IF CURRENT ENTRY PUNCTUATION IS 'PERIOD' — NO →

YES

TEST IF MATCH IS ON 'GT. BRIT.' — YES →

NO

12B (ASSUME NEW 'B' SUBFIELD)

13A (NOT NEW 'A' SUBFIELD)

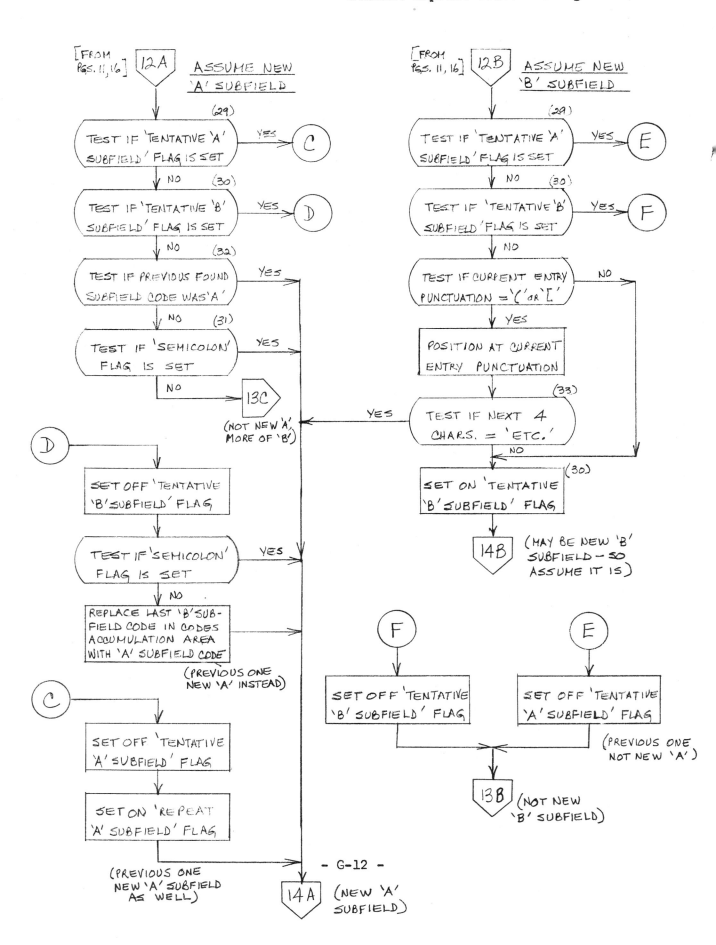

- G-12 -

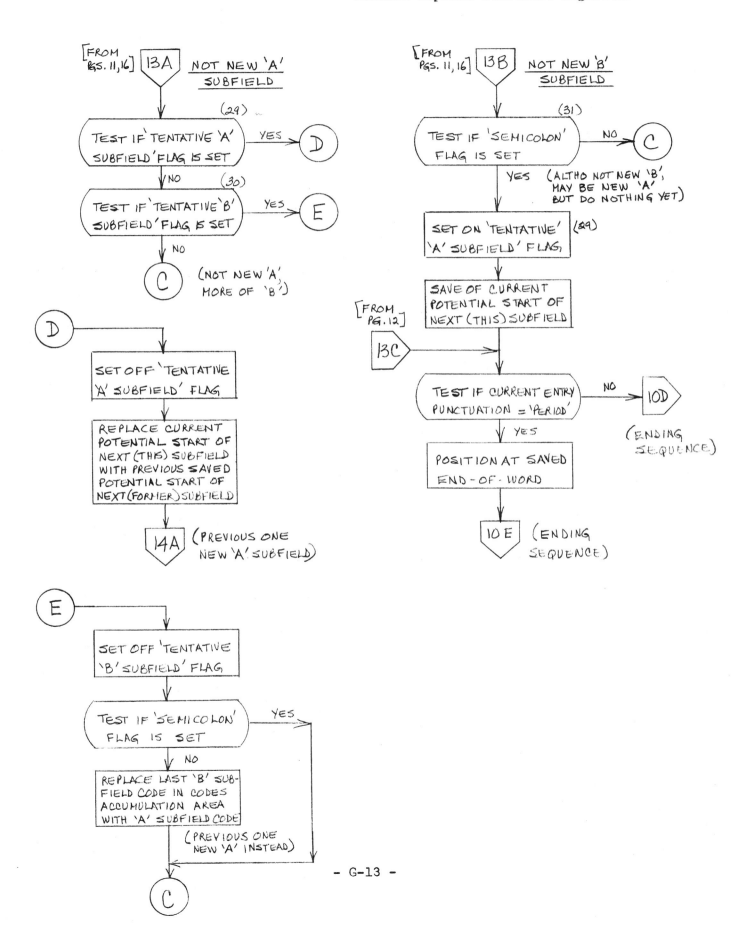

[FROM PGS. 11,16] 13A NOT NEW 'A' SUBFIELD

(29)
TEST IF 'TENTATIVE' 'A' SUBFIELD' FLAG IS SET — YES → D
NO

(30)
TEST IF 'TENTATIVE' 'B' SUBFIELD' FLAG IS SET — YES → E
NO

C (NOT NEW 'A', MORE OF 'B')

D

SET OFF 'TENTATIVE 'A' SUBFIELD' FLAG

REPLACE CURRENT POTENTIAL START OF NEXT (THIS) SUBFIELD WITH PREVIOUS SAVED POTENTIAL START OF NEXT (FORMER) SUBFIELD

14A (PREVIOUS ONE NEW 'A' SUBFIELD)

E

SET OFF 'TENTATIVE 'B' SUBFIELD' FLAG

TEST IF 'SEMICOLON' FLAG IS SET — YES
NO

REPLACE LAST 'B' SUBFIELD CODE IN CODES ACCUMULATION AREA WITH 'A' SUBFIELD CODE

(PREVIOUS ONE NEW 'A' INSTEAD)

C

[FROM PGS. 11,16] 13B NOT NEW 'B' SUBFIELD

(31)
TEST IF 'SEMICOLON' FLAG IS SET — NO → C
YES (ALTHO NOT NEW 'B', MAY BE NEW 'A' BUT DO NOTHING YET)

SET ON 'TENTATIVE' 'A' SUBFIELD' FLAG (29)

SAVE OF CURRENT POTENTIAL START OF NEXT (THIS) SUBFIELD

[FROM PG. 12]
13C

TEST IF CURRENT ENTRY PUNCTUATION = 'PERIOD' — NO → 10D
YES   (ENDING SEQUENCE)

POSITION AT SAVED END-OF-WORD

10E (ENDING SEQUENCE)

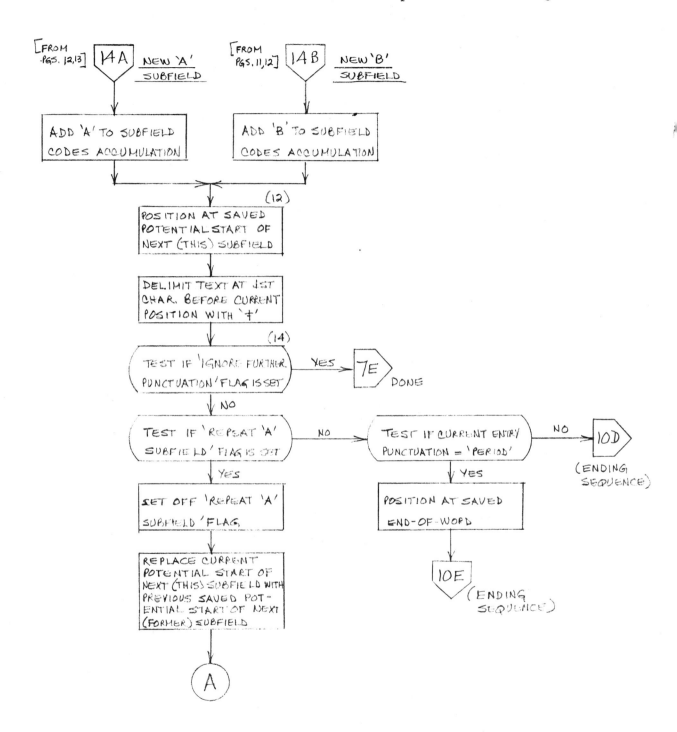

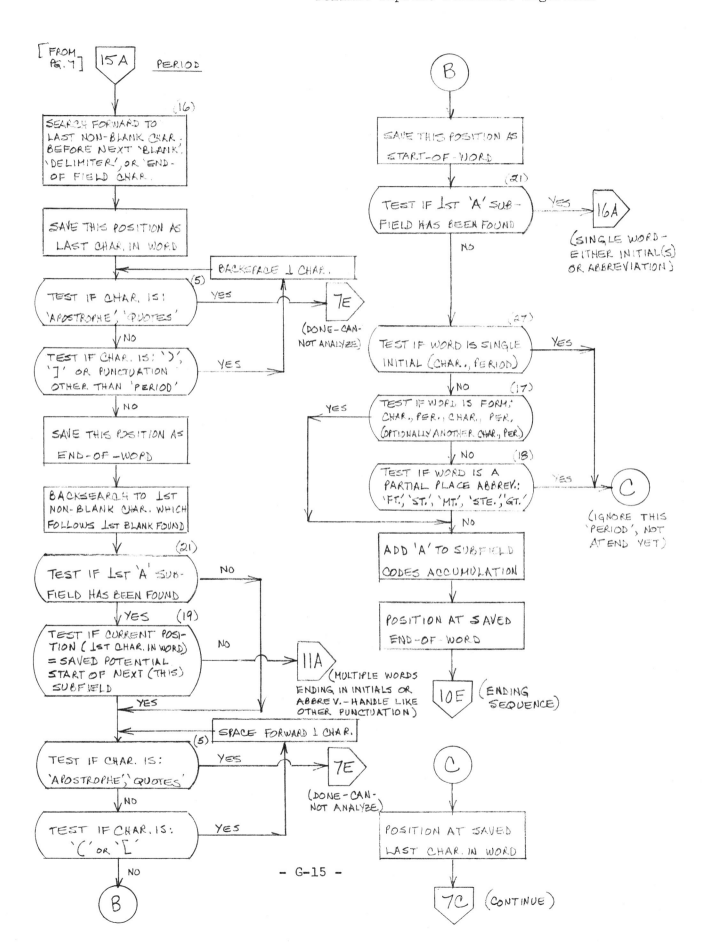

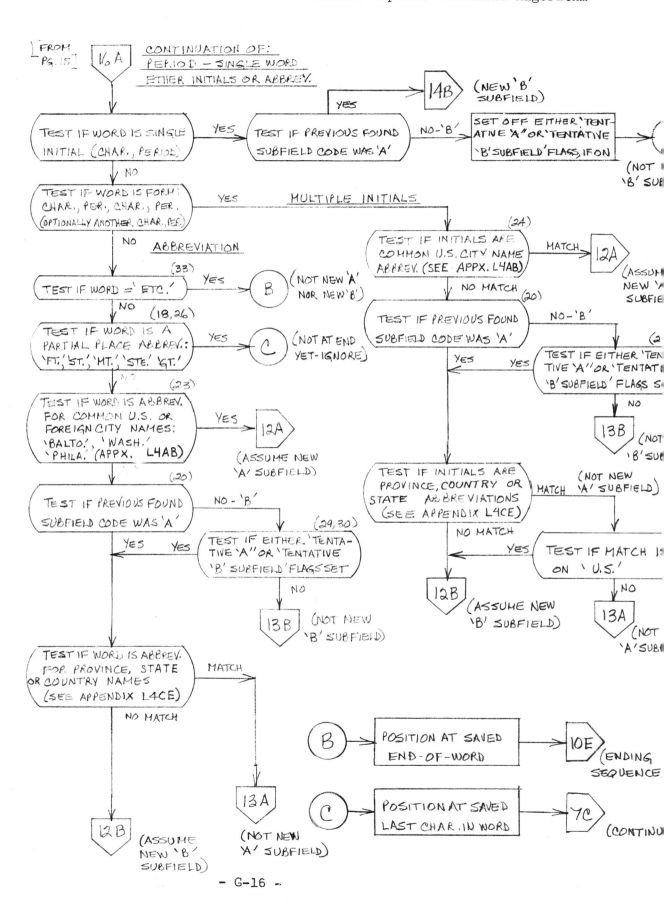

- G-16 -

APPENDIX H.   DELIMIT COLLATION STATEMENT ALGORITHM

The purpose of this algorithm is to delimit a Collation Staement and build
the appropriate string of subfield codes to identify the delimited subfields,
using the notation:

> a = pagination subfield
>
> b = illustrative matter subfield
>
> c = size subfield

The algorithm has been described in the form of a subroutine. It should be
noted that, at any point in searching the field, if an end-of-field condition
is encountered, the routine will return with no further action. This is not
specifically shown in the flowchart due to lack of space and reflects an
error condition which will only occur if the pagination subfield is
unrecognizable or a size subfield (one of which must always be present) is
unrecognizable or missing.

For example: xii, 300 p. illus.

Would be delimited: ‡xii, 300 p.‡illus.

and the subfield codes 'ab' would be accumulated.

APPENDIX H.   DELIMIT COLLATION STATEMENT ALGORITHM, Continued

Flowchart Notes

(1) The algorithm to Determine Roman Numerals is the same as that given in Appendix K. The only difference is that lower-case Roman Numerals must be accomodated.

(2) The Illustration terms are given in List 5C of Appendix L. They are summarized below:

        chart(s)

        coat(s) of arms

        diagr(s).

        facsimile(s), facsim(s).

        forms

        geneal. table(s)

        illus.

        map(s)

        music

        phonocylinder, phonodisc, phonofilm
        phonoroll, phonotape, phonowire

        photo(s).

        plan(s)

        plate(s)

        port(s)., group port(s).

        samples

        table(s)

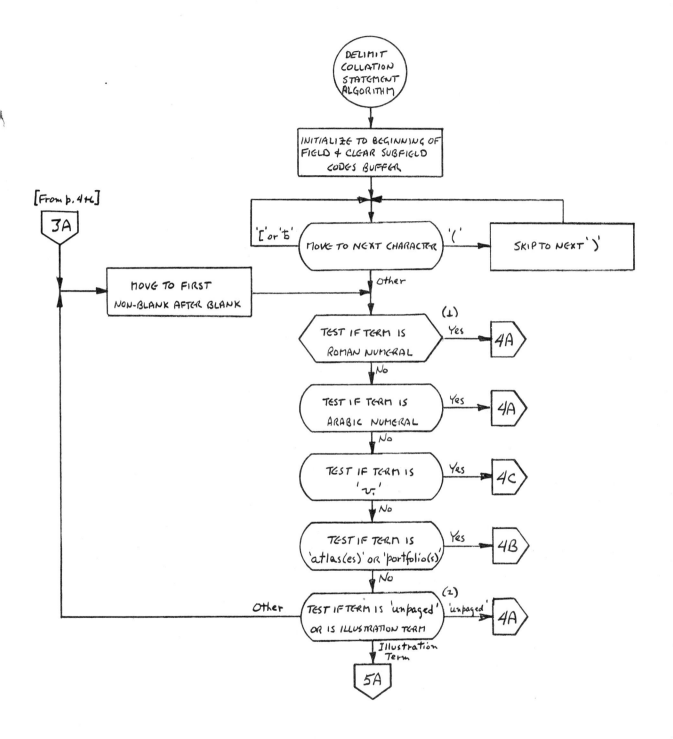

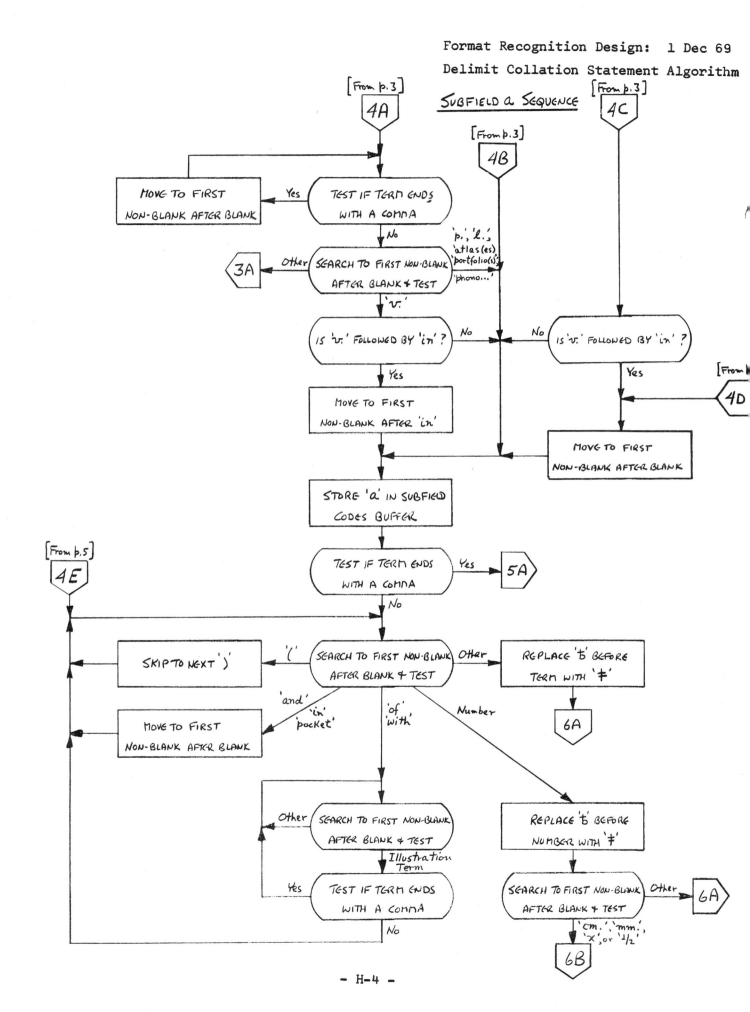

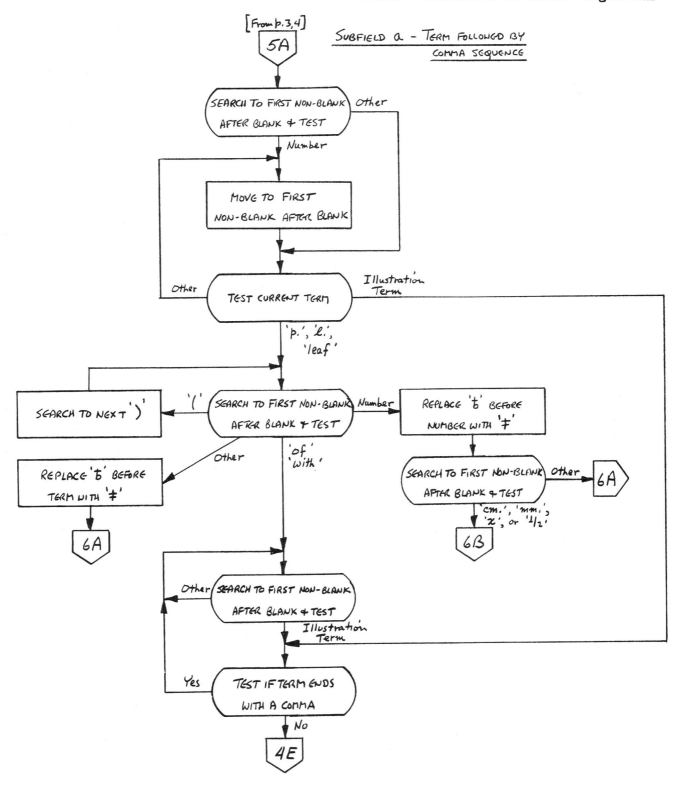

SUBFIELD a - TERM FOLLOWED BY COMMA SEQUENCE

[From p. 3, 4]

5A

SEARCH TO FIRST NON-BLANK AFTER BLANK & TEST — Other

Number

MOVE TO FIRST NON-BLANK AFTER BLANK

Other — TEST CURRENT TERM — Illustration Term

'p.', 'l.', 'leaf'

SEARCH TO NEXT ')' — '(' — SEARCH TO FIRST NON-BLANK AFTER BLANK & TEST — Number — REPLACE 'ƀ' BEFORE NUMBER WITH '≠'

Other

REPLACE 'ƀ' BEFORE TERM WITH '≠'

6A

'of' 'with'

SEARCH TO FIRST NON-BLANK AFTER BLANK & TEST — Other — 6A

'cm.', 'mm.', 'x', or '1/2'

6B

Other — SEARCH TO FIRST NON-BLANK AFTER BLANK & TEST

Illustration Term

Yes — TEST IF TERM ENDS WITH A COMMA

No

4E

- H-5 -

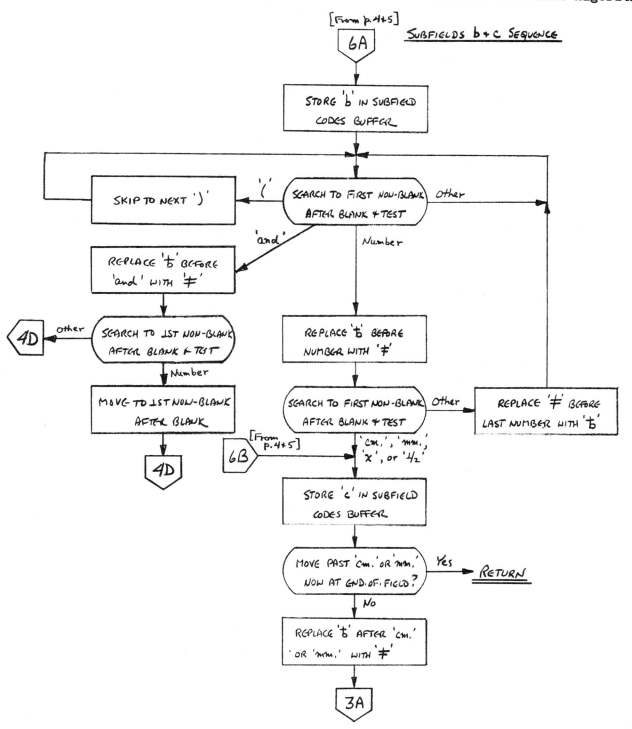

SUBFIELDS b + c SEQUENCE

APPENDIX I.   DELIMIT CALL NUMBER AND COPY STATEMENT ALGORITHM

An LC Call Number is a field made up of letters, numbers, and periods. It
may also be followed by a date, which is expressed as a blank and four digits
(sometimes followed by a lower-case letter). In addition, the term 'LAW' may
appear in place of an LC Call Number.

A Copy Statement may consist simply of copy information proper, preceded
by hyphens; or a Call Number (or 'LAW') followed by the copy information,
separated by hyphens.

The subfield codes accumulated by this algorithm consist of:

   a = Class portion of Call Number

   b = Book portion of Call Number

   c = Copy information

The expected code combinations are:

   a = Class number only
     Call Number = 'LAW'
     Call Number falls in subset of 'KF' numbers

   ab = Call Number

   abc = Call Number plus copy information

   c = Copy information only

The algorithm consists of the following 7-step process:

1. If the field begins with hyphens, go to Step 7.c].

2. If the field begins with the term 'LAW', the subfield code 'a' is
  accumulated. This completes the processing of this algorithm, unless
  'LAW' is followed by hyphens - in which case processing continues at
  Step 7.b].

APPENDIX I.   DELIMIT CALL NUMBER AND COPY STATEMENT ALGORITHM, Continued

3.   a]   If the field consists simply of letter(s) followed by number(s) (possibly including a period), do not delimit it:

      ex: QA37   is not delimited
               HF5415.13   is not delimited

      The subfield code 'a' is accumulated. This completes the processing of this algorithm.

     b]   If this type of number is followed by a date, it is delimited before the blank preceding the date:

      ex: HA12 1967   becomes   HA12‡ 1967
               KF5556 1966   becomes   KF5556‡ 1966

      The subfield codes 'ab' are accumulated. This completes the processing of this algorithm.

4.   If the field begins with 'KF' (possibly followed by another letter), followed by number(s), followed by a period, then:

     a]   If there are $\leq$ 2 following numbers, before the period, do not Delimit:

      ex: KF32.J8 1968   is not delimited
               KF26.L354 1966a   is not delimited

      The subfield code 'a' is accumulated. Go to Step 7.

     b]   If there are $>$ 2 following numbers, before the period, delimit it before the last period in the Call Number:

      ex: KF879.A4A5 1968   becomes   KF879‡.A4A5 1968
               KFN5225.Z9F3   becomes   KFN5225‡.Z9F3

      The subfield codes 'ab' are accumulated. Go to Step 7.

APPENDIX I.   DELIMIT CALL NUMBER AND COPY STATEMENT ALGORITHM, Continued

5.   If the field begins with 'CS71', it is delimited before the blank
     preceding the date:

     ex: CS71.S889 1968   becomes   CS71.S889‡ 1968

     The subfield codes 'ab' are accumulated. Go to Step 7.

6.   In all other cases, delimit the field before the last capital letter
     in the Call Number, except when the last capital letter is immediately
     preceded by a period (or space). In this latter case, delimit before
     this preceding period (or space):

     ex: PS3553.E73W6   becomes   PS3553.E73‡W6
              PZ10.3.U36Sp   becomes   PZ10.3.U36‡Sp
              E595.F6K4 1968   becomes   E595.F6‡K4 1968

              HQ734.S585   becomes   HQ734‡.S585
              E469.8.G3   becomes   E469.8‡.G3
              TX652.5.G63 1968   becomes   TX652.5‡.G63 1968

     The subfield codes 'ab' are accumulated.

7.   Search the field for the existence of hyphens:

     a]   If there are no hyphens in the field, this completes the processing
          of this algorithm.

     b]   If there are hyphens in the field, insert the delimiter before the
          first hyphen.

     c]   Add 'c' to the accumulated subfield codes. This completes the
          processing of the algorithm.

APPENDIX J.   (OTHER) ADDED ENTRY 2ND INDICATOR ALGORITHM

This algorithm assigns the 2nd indicator to an (Other) Added Entry field,
as follows:

                A = Alternative Entry
                S = Secondary Entry
                N = Analytical Entry

The 'additional filing information used with Analytical Entries' subfield,
which may follow the title subfield in an Analytical Added Entry, is also
delimited off, when present, and the code 'u' is added to the Entry's
subfield codes.

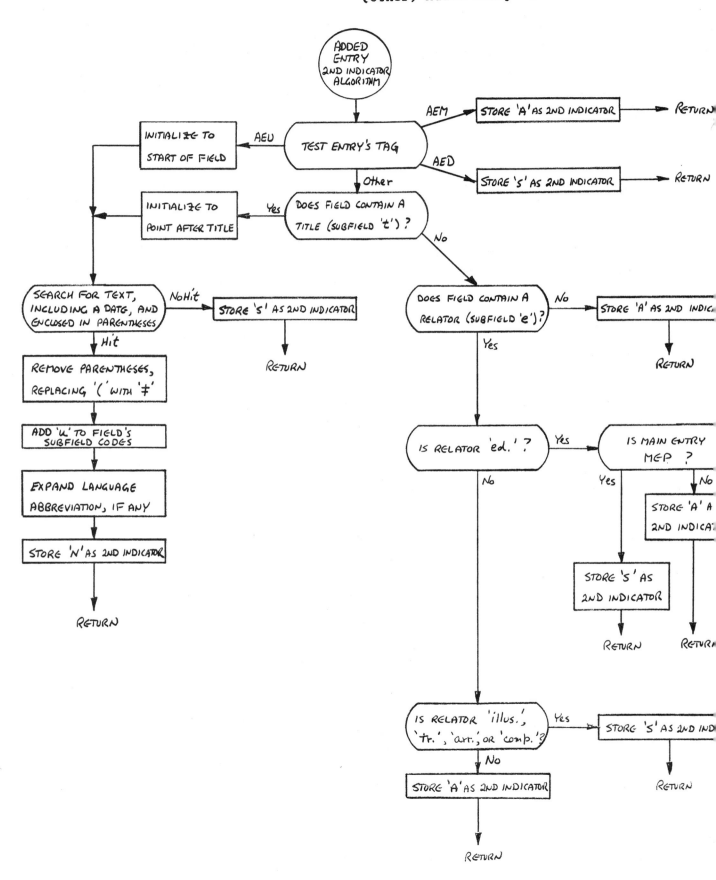

APPENDIX K.   TEST FOR ROMAN NUMERAL ALGORITHM

This algorithm utilizes a precedence matrix, which consists of a column for each valid character (M, D, C, L, X, V, and I) and a set of rows, each of which defines the legal rules of combination at some point in the numeral.

The procedure used by the algorithm is to first initialize to the beginning of the suspected Roman Numeral in the text and to Row 1 of the matrix. Then a repetitive loop is entered which uses the next character in the text to determine a column, with the intersection of that column with the current row giving the number of the row to be used with the next character in the text. This loop continues until one of the following happens:

1)   A hyphen is encountered in the text, in which case the algorithm resets to Row 1 of the matrix and procedes to the next character in the text. (This allows for a range of Roman Numerals, e.g. I-X.)

2)   A blank, punctuation, or end-of-field is encountered in the text, in which case the test has succeeded and the text is a Roman Numeral.

3)   A character other than M, D, C, L, X, V, or I is encountered, in which case the test has failed (e.g. X-ray).

4)   A zero element is encountered at a row/column intersection in the precedence matrix, which is the type of failure resulting from the illegal combination of otherwise valid characters (e.g. VIM).

		M	D	C	L	X	V	I	Text at this point
Row	1	1	2	3	6	7	10	11	Start or ...M
	2	0	0	3	6	7	10	11	D
	3	5	5	4	6	7	10	11	...C, C
	4	0	0	5	6	7	10	11	...C, CC
	5	0	0	0	6	7	10	11	CCC, CD, CM
	6	0	0	0	0	7	10	11	...L, L
	7	0	0	9	9	8	10	11	...X, X
	8	0	0	0	0	9	10	11	...XX, XX
	9	0	0	0	0	0	10	11	...XXX, XXX, XL, XC
	10	0	0	0	0	0	0	11	...V, V
	11	0	0	0	0	13	13	12	...I, I
	12	0	0	0	0	0	0	13	...II, II
	13	0	0	0	0	0	0	0	...III, III, IV, IX

Columns

APPENDIX L. KEYWORD LISTS

This appendix contains the lists of keywords to be used with
the preceding flow charts. The lists are not in their final form--
they will doubtless evolve as the format recognition programs are
debugged and become operational. Some lists will probably shrink,
others will grow and it is quite possible that new lists will be
required to help solve unforseen problems while some of the present
lists may be abolished.

The lists will be in core when the program is operating, at other
times they will be stored on disc. The format recognition program will
include a routine for updating the lists without recompiling the entire program. Changes in the lists will be input on punched cards
containing a special shift character to signal an upper case character.
A similar method will be used to indicate diacritics and special characters,
such as the ∅ in K∅benhavn.

Different ways of matching the keywords are used: 1) Certain parts
of the program require each word in a string of text be matched with each
word on a list, e.g., the meeting keywords; in other cases only the first word
is matched with a list. 2) On some lists ellipses have been used to
indicate that a word must be preceded or followed by other text, e.g.,
"King of ..." on the honorary titles list.

Since some of the tables are used with natural language text, e.g.,
the imprint, the form of a term on a list cannot be assumed to be the
form prescribed by LC practice or the <u>Anglo</u> <u>American</u> <u>Cataloging</u> <u>Rules</u>.
For instance, if "Cal." appears as part of the place in an imprint in a title
page the cataloger will probably transcribe it in the nonstandard form rather than
emend it to "Cal[if.]" Since this is so the form "Cal." if found in Table 4CE
as well as the correct form, "Calif."

CONTENTS

TABLE 1A. CORPORATE NAME KEYWORDS.

NOTE: The presence of another first character upper case word is assumed.
Table 1A also includes names of States and cities from tables
4A and 4C.

Academy	Library
Alliance	ltd.
America	Monarchy
	Museum
Associates	Organization
Association	Party
Bank	Program
Board	Project
Cathedral	Railroad
Center	Service
Church	Society
College	Station
Commission	Union
Committee	United Nations
Company	University
Corporation	
English	
firm	
Foundation	
Gallery	
Hospital	
Inc.	
Institution	
Joint	
Laboratory	

TABLE 1B. CORPORATE NAME FORM SUBHEADINGS.

Articles of confederation.

Articles of religion.

Articles of visitation.

Book of common prayer.

Canons, decretals, etc.

Canons, nomocanons, decrees, etc.

Catechism

Charter.

Constitution.

Court rules.

Courts.

Courts-martial ...

Courts of inquiry ...

Declaration of Independence

Declaration of independence.

Homilies.

Injunction.

Laws, statutes, etc.

Liturgy and ritual.

MSS.

Ordinances, etc.

Ordnances, local laws, etc.

Treaties...

Treaties, etc...

TABLE 1C PARENTHETICAL TERMS WITH DIRECT ORDER CORPORATE NAMES.

NOTE: Table 1C includes names or abbreviations of States, Provinces, Counties and countries from tables 4C, 4D, 4E and 4C-E. Terms for ships, etc. are in the second alphabetic sequence.

(Adventist)

(Apostolic)

(Association)

(Firm)

(Founded...)

(Fraternal order)

(Masonic order)

(Military order)

(New constitution)

(Society)

(Strangites)

(Aircraft carrier)

(Attack aircraft carrier)

(Battleship)

(Boat)

(Corvette)

(Cruiser)

(Destroyer)

(Destroyer-mine-layer)

(Flagship)

(Four-masted bark)

(Frigate)

(Ironclad)

(Man-of-war)

(Nuclear ship)

(Packet)

(Seaplane tender)

(Ship)

(Spanish galleon)

(Steamship)

(Submarine)

(Training launch)

(U.S. aircraft carrier)

TABLE 1D. MEETING KEYWORDS.

Assembly

Colloquium

Conference

Congress

Consultation

Convention

Course

Festival

Forum

International School

Meeting

Olumpic Games

Panel

Round

Seminar/Seminars

Study Group

Symposium

Synod

Tribunal

Workshop

TABLE 2A. FORENAME ENTRIES WITHOUT TITLES OR DATES.

Aesopus

Appolonius Rhodius

Apuleius Madaurensis

Archimedes

Aristoleles

Aristophanes

Democritus

Demosthenes

El Cid Campeador

Epictetus

Epicurus

Euclides

Euripides

Galenus

Gautama Buddha

Hannibal

Herodotus

Hippocrates

Homerus

Isocrates

Jesus Christ

Martinus

Origenes

Pausanias

Petronius Arbiter

Philo Judaeus

Philoctetes

Pindarus

Plato

Plotinus

Plutarchus

Proclus Diadochus

Phythagoras

Quintus Veranius

Sappho

Socrates

Sophocles

Thucydides

Xenophon

TABLE 2B. HONORARY TITLES WITH PERSONAL NAMES.

NOTE: Keywords followed by an asterisk should be transposed so they follow all words starting with a upper case letter, e.g., Sir is moved from before to after forenames.

(Anglo-Norman poet)	Duke	known as
Antipope	Duque	Lady*
apostle	Dr.	Lord*
Baron	Earl (only if pre- ceded by an ordinal number)	Maharaja
Baroness		Marquis
Baronesse	Earl of ..	Marchioness
barrister	Edler	martyr
bart.	Emperor	Metropolitan
(Biblical character)	fra	Mother
Bp.	Freidame	Mrs.*
Brother	Freifrau	Patriarch
called...	Freiherr	Pope
Cardinal	Freiin	Pres...
chef...	Fürst	Prince...
Chief	Graf	Princess...
Chorepiscopus	grafinia	Prinz
Crown Prince of ...	Grand... (duke, vizer, muffi, etc.)	Professo...
Consort...		pseud.
Conte	Hon.*	Queen of
Contesse	Indian chief	Rev.*
Countess	King	Ritter
Dame*	King of...	Saint
	Kniâz	

- L-9 -

TABLE 2B.

Sayed

Shah

Sir*

Sister

Swami

the...(e.g. Stylite,
   Great, etc.)

(Trojan hero)

Venerabilis

Virgin

vicomte

Viscount...

Viscountess

wife of

writer on...

TABLE 2C. RELATOR TERMS.

NOTE: This table includes the legal relators in table 5A. The terms
       here may be followed by "and..." as in ed. and tr.

arr.

comp. (includes comp. and...)

ed. (includes ed. and...)

illus.

joint... (only with added entries)

praeses

supposed...

respondent

tr.

TABLE 2D. PERSONAL NAME FORM SUBHEADINGS.

Appendix Vergiliana (includes same with title following) Subfield t

Legend. (Includes Legend. title) Subfield k

Spurious and doubtful works. Subfield k

TABLE 2E. NON-MULTIPLE NAME PREFIXES.

A	Van
al-	Ver
Am	Von
Aus'm	y
da	z
De	Zum
De la	Zur
Del	
Della	
der	
Des	
Di	
Du	
El	
La	
Le	
Li	
Lo	
Mac	
Ten	
Ter-	

TABLE 3A. TITLE SUBFIELDS KEYWORDS

NOTE: Except when both b and c subfields have been found or when over-
       ridden by a "Title. thru..." tracing a semicolon always terminates a
       subfield.

1. Subfield b is determined by:

    a. The following words immediately after a comma, colon, semicolon
        or bracket (open or close): a, the, an, hearing, report

    b. The following words immediately after a period: A (not followed by
        a period), The, Agreement, An, Hearing, Report

    c. The following additional words immediately after a comma: who, with

    d. The following words immediately after a semicolon: from, or, and,
        poems, essays, proceedings, report, conference, Conference, one, two,
        three (and the spelled out form of other numbers)

2. Subfield c is determined by the following words immediately after any
    punctuation: by, edited, translated, collected, published, prepared,
    compiled, illustrated (This includes these words starting with a capital
    letter)

3. Imbedded c subfield words: Same as 2. above

4. Abbreviations unlikely to terminate a subfield:

Apr.	Dr.	Mrs.	Res.
Aug.	Feb.	no.	Rev.
Capt.	illus.	Nov.	Sgt.
Col.	Illus.	Oct.	St.
Cong.	introd.	photo.	vs.
Dec.	Introd.	photos.	
Dept.	Lt.	Pref.	
doc.	Mar.	pref.	
	Mr.	Pvt.	

TABLE 3B.   EDITION SUBFIELD B.

&c.

etc.

introd.

Jr.

photos.

pref.

with

by

edited

translated

TABLE 4A. U.S. CITIES WITH PLACE OF PUBLICATION CODE.

NOTE: The geopraphic area code (GAC) is machine derivable from the pub. code.

Akron OHU	Cambridge MAU	Duluth MNU
Albany NYU	Carbondale ILU	Durham NCU
Albuquerque NMU	Carson City NVU	East Lansing MIU
Ames IAU	Chapel Hill NCU	Edgartown MAU
Amherst MAU	Charleston WVU	El Paso TXU
Anchorage AKU	Charlotte NCU	Englewood Cliffs NJU
Ann Arbor MIU	Charlottesville VAU	Eugene ORU
Annapolis MDU	Chattanooga TNU	Evanston ILU
Atlanta GAU	Cheyenne WYU	Fargo NDU
Atlantic City NJU	Chicago ILU	Fayetteville ARU
Augusta MEU	Cincinnati OHU	Fort Collins COU
Austin TXU	Clevland OHU	Fort Worth TXU
Baltimore MDU	College AKU	Frankfort KYU
Baton Rouge LAU	College Park MDU	Ft. Collins COU
Berkeley CAU	College Pk. MDU	Ft. Worth TXU
Binghamton NYU	College Station TXU	Gainesville FLU
Birmingham ALU	Columbia MOU	Gary INU
Bismarck NDU	Columbus OHV	Grand Rapids MIU
Bloomington INU	Concord NHU	Greensboro NCU
Boise IDU	Corvallis ORU	Harrisburg PAU
Boston MAU	Dallas TXU	Hartford CTU
Boulder COU	Davis CAU	Helena MTU
Bowling Green OHU	Dayton OHU	Honolulu HIU
Brooklyn NYU	Denver COU	Houston TXU
Brattleboro VTU	Des Moines IAU	Indianapolis INU
Buffalo NYU	Detroit MIU	Iowa City IAU
Burlington VTU	Dover DEU	Ithaca NYU

Irvine CAU	Missoula MTU	Providence RIU
Jackson MSU	Mobile ALU	Provo UTU
Jacksonville FLU	Montgomery ALU	Pullman WAU
Jefferson City MOU	Montpelier VTU	Raleigh NCU
Jersey City NJU	Morgantown WVU	Rapid City SDU
Juneau AKU	n.p. XX	Reno NVU
Kansas City MOU	Nashville TNU	Richmond VAU
Kent OHU	New Haven CTU	Riverside CAU
Kingston RIU	New Orleans LAU	Rochester NYU
Knoxville TNU	New York NYU	Sacramento CAU
Lafayette INU	Newark DEU	Salem ORU
Lansing MIU	Niagara Falls NYU	Saint Augustine FLU
Lawrence KNU	Norfolk VAU	Saint Louis MOU
Lexington KYU	Norman OKU	Saint Paul MNU
Lincoln NBU	Oakland CAU	Salt Lake City UTU
Little Rock ARU	Oklahoma City OKU	San Antonio TXU
Logan UTU	Olympia WAU	San Diego CAU
Long Beach CAU	Omaha NBU	San Francisco CAU
Los Angeles CAU	Orono MEU	San Juan PRU
Louisville KYU	Pasadena CAU	San Jose CAU
Macomb ILU	Philadelphia PAU	Santa Barbara CAU
Madison WIU	Phoenix AZU	Santa Fe NMU
Manhattan KNU	Pierre SDU	Savannah GAU
Memphis TNU	Pittsburgh PAU	Scranton PAU
Miami FLU	Pocatello IDU	Seattle WAU
Milwaukee WIU	Portland ORU	South Bend INU
Minneapolis MNU	Princeton NJU	Spokane WAU

TABLE 4A. (Continued)

Springfield ILU

Williamsburg VAU

St. Augustine FLU

Winston-Salem NCU

St. Louis MOU

Worcester MAU

St. Paul MNU

Wyandotte MIU

Stanford CAU

Yellow Springs OHU

State College PAU

Stillwater OKU

Stony Brook NYU

Storrs CTU

Syracuse NYU

Tacoma WAU

Tallahassee FLU

Tempe AZU

Toledo OHU

Topeka KSU

Trenton NJU

Tulsa OKU

Tucson AZU

University Park PAU

University Pk. PAU

Urbana ILU

Utica NYU

Vermillion SDU

Washington DCU

Wheaton ILU

Wheeling WVU

Wichita KSU

TABLE 4B1.   STANDARD FORM OF FOREIGN CITIES WITH GEOGRAPHIC AREA CODE OR

PLACE OF PUBLICATION CODE.

NOTE: Three character codes are pub. codes for Canada, United Kingdom and

USSR (last character is C, K or R respectively); the GAC is machine

derivable for these.   Both the pub. code and GAC are given for China

and Australia.   In the other cases the GAC is given and the

last two characters constitute the pub. code.

Aachen E-GW	Belgrad E-YU	Canberra U-AT-NE
Addis Ababa F-ET	Bern E-SZ	Cape Town A-SA
Adelaide AT; U-AT-SA	Bogotá S-CK	Caracas S-VE
Aleppo A-SY	Bologna E-IT	Ciudad Trujillo NWDR
Algiers (City) F-AE	Bolzano (City) IT	Cluj E-RM
Amsterdam E-NE	Bombay A-II	Coimbra E-PO
Ankara A-TU	Bonn E-GW	Cologne E-GW
Antwerp E-NE	Bordeaux E-FR	Copenhagen E-DK
Asunción S-PY	Bratislava E-CS	Cremona E-IT
Athens E-GR	Bremen E-GW	Czernowitz UNR
Auckland U-NZ	Brescia E-IT	Damascus A-SY
Augsburg E-GW	Breslau E-PL	Danzig E-PL
Bagdad A-IQ	Brisbane AT; U-AT-QN	Delhi A-II
Baku AIR	Brunn E-CZ	Dresden E-GE
Barcelona E-SP	Brunswick (City) E-GW	Dublin E-IE
Basel E-SZ	Bucharest E-RM	Dusseldorf E-GW
Beirut A-LE	Budapest E-HU	Durazzo E-AA
Belfast E-UK-NI	Buenos Aires S-AG	Edinburgh STK
	Cairo F-US	Erivan AIR
	Calcutta A-II	Essen E-GW
		Florence E-IT

TABLE 4B1. (Continued)

Frankfurt am Main E-GW	Krakow E-PL	Melbourne AT; U-AT-VI
Fredericton NKC	Kyoto A-JA	Mexico (City) N-MX
Freiburg i. B. E-GW	Lahore A-II	Milan E-IT
Geneva E-SZ	Leghorn E-IT	Minsk BWR
Ghent E-BE	Leipzig E-GE	Monte Carlo E-MC
Glasgow STK	Lemberg UNR	Montevideo S-UY
Guatemala (City) NGGT	Leningrad RUR	Montreal QUC
Haarlem E-NE	Lhasa CC; A-CC-TI	Moscow RUR
Hague E-NE	Liége E-BE	Mosul A-IQ
Hamburg E-GW	Lille E-FR	Munich E-GW
Hanover (City) E-GW	Lima S-PE	Nagasaki A-JA
Havana NWCU	Lisbon E-PO	Nancy E-FR
Helsinki E-Fl	Liverpool ENK	Naples E-IT
Istanbul A-TU	London ENK	New Delhi A-II
Jaffa A-IS	Lübeck E-GW	Nice E-FR
Jassy E-RM	Luxemburg (City) E-LU	Nuremberg E-GW
Jerusalem A-IS	Lyons E-FR	Odessa UNR
Johannesburg F-SA	Madras A-II	Osaka A-JA
Kaunas LIR	Madrid E-SP	Oslo E-NO
Kazan RUR	Mainz E-GW	Ottawa ONC
Kharkov UNR	Managua NCNQ	Oxford ENK
Kiel E-GW	Manchester ENK	Padua E-IT
Kishinev MVR	Manila A-PI	Panama (City) NCPN
Koblenz E-GW	Maracaibo S-VE	Paris E-FR
Konigsberg RUR	Marseille E-FR	Peking CC; A-CC-PE

TABLE 4B1 (continued)

Prague E-CS

Pretoria F-SA

Quezon City A-PH

Quito S-EC

Rangoon A-BR

Reims E-FR

Reykjavik E-IC

Riga LVR

Rio de Janeiro S-BL

Rome (City) E-IT

Rotterdam E-NE

Rouen E-FR

San Salvador NCES

Sevastopol UNR

Seville E-SP

Shanghai CC; A-CC-SM

Smyrna A-TU

Sofia E-BU

Stockholm E-SW

Strassburg E-FR

Stuttgart E-GW

Sydney AT; U-AT-NE

Tallinn ERR

Tartu ERR

Tashkend UZR

Tegucigalpa NCHO

Teheran A-IR
The Hague E-NE
Thessalonike E-GR

Tokyo A-JA

Toronto ONC

Toulouse E-FR

Treves E-GW

Tunis (City) F-TI

Turin E-IT

Uppsala E-SW

Utrecht E-NE

Valencia (City) E-SP

Valparaiso (City) S-CL

Venice E-IT

Vienna E-AT

Vilna LIR

Warsaw E-PL

Wiesbaden E-GW

Zagreb E-YU

Zurich E-SW

Zutphen E-NE

TABLE 4B2. LOCAL FORM OF FOREIGN CITIES WITH GEOGRAPHIC AREA CODE OR

PLACE OF PUBLICATION CODE

NOTE: Three character codes are pub. codes for Canada, United Kingdom and
USSR (last character is C, K or R respectively); the GAC is machine
derivable from this. Both the publ. code and the GAC are given for
Chinese and Australian cities. In all other cases the GAC is given
and the last two characters constitute the pub. code.

Agra A-II	Brunswick E-GW	Gent E-BE
Ahmedabad A-II	Brussel E-BE	Gloucester ENK
Aix-la-Chapelle E-GW	Bruxelles E-BE	Haag E-NE
Alger F-AE	Bucuresti E-RM	Halifax NSC
Alipore A-II	Cernăuti UNR	Harmondsworth ENK
Allahabad A-II	Charlottetown PIC	Hawthorn AT: U-AT-VI
Anvers E-NE	Cheltenham ENK	Hyderabad A-II
Antwerpen E-NE	Chester ENK	Iasi E-RM
Aydar A-II	Cuttack A-TH	Karachi A-PK
Baghdad A-IQ	Den Haag E-NE	København E-DK
Bâle E-SZ	Douglas UIK	Köln G-GW
Bangalore A-II	Dulwich ENK	Kuala Lumpur A-MY
Bangkok A-TH	Dundee STK	Lausanne E-SZ
Basle E-SZ	Durrés E-AA	Leicester ENK
Beograd E-YU	Edmonton ABC	Leiden E-NE
Berne E-SZ	Exeter ENK	La Haye E-NE
Bolzano E-IT	Firenze E-IT	Lucknow A-II
Bozen E-IT	Gand E-BE	Lund A-II
Braunschweig E-GW	Gdańsk E-PL	Luxemburg E-LU
Brno E-CZ	Genève E-SZ	Luxembourg E-LU

TABLE 4B2.

Lvov UNR

Lwow UNR

Milano E-IT

München E-GW

Nagpur A-II

Nairobi F-KE

Napoli E-IT

Newcastle-upon-Tyne ENK

Nottingham ENK

Nürnberg E-GW

Prag E-CS

Praga E-CS

Regina SNC

Roma E-IT

's Gravenhage E-NE

Salford ENK

Salisbury ENK

Saskatoon SNC

Simla A-II

St. John's NFC

St. Peter Port UIK

Trier E-GW

Turku E-FI

Vancouver BCC

Varanasi A-II

Venezia E-IT

Warszawa E-PL

Wellington U-NZ

Wien E-AT

Winnipeg MBC

Wroclaw E-PL

TABLE 4AB - CITY NAME ABBREVIATIONS

N-US-MD	Balto.	Baltimore
N-US-IL	Chi.	Chicago
N-US-CA	L.A.	Los Angeles
N-US-NY	N.Y.C	New York City
N-US-CA	S.F.	San Francisco
N-US-DC	Wash.	Washington

TABLE 4C - U.S. STATES

N-US-Al	Alabama		N-US-NC	North Carolina
N-US-AK	Alaska		N-US-ND	North Dakota
N-US-AZ	Arizona		N-US-NH	New Hampshire
N-US-AR	Arkansas		N-US-NJ	New Jersey
N-US-CA	California		N-US-NM	New Mexico
N-US-CO	Colorado		N-US-NY	New York
N-US-CT	Connecticut		N-US-NB	Nebraska
N-US-DC	District of Columbia		N-US-NV	Nevada
N-US-DE	Delaware		N-US-OH	Ohio
N-US-FL	Florida		N-US-OK	Oklahoma
N-US-GA	Georgia		N-US-OR	Oregon
N-US-HI	Hawaii		N-US-PA	Pennsylvania
N-US-IL	Illinois		N-US-RI	Rhode Island
N-US-ID	Idaho		N-US-SC	South Carolina
N-US-IN	Indiana		N-US-SD	South Dakota
N-US-IA	Iowa		N-US-TN	Tennessee
N-US-KS	Kansas		N-US-TX	Texas
N-US-KY	Kentucky		N-US-UT	Utah
N-US-LA	Louisiana		N-US-VT	Vermont
N-US-MA	Massachusetts		N-US-VA	Virginia
N-US-MD	Maryland		N-US-WA	Washington
N-US-ME	Maine		N-US-WV	West Virginia
N-US-MI	Michigan		N-US-WI	Wisconsin
N-US-MN	Minnesota		N-US-WY	Wyomining
N-US-MS	Mississippi			
N-US-MO	Missouri			
N-US-MT	Montana			

TABLE 4D - PROVINCES (Canadian, Australian, etc.) and BRITISH COUNTIES

E-UK-ST	Aberdeen	E-UK-WL	Denbighshire
N-CN-AB	Alberta	E-UK-EN	Derbyshire
E-UK-WL	Anglesey	E-UK-EN	Devonshire
E-UK-ST	Angus	E-UK-EN	Dorsetshire
E-UK-NI	Antrim	E-UK-NI	Down
E-UK-ST	Argyll	E-UK-ST	Dumbarton
E-UK-NI	Armagh	E-UK-ST	Dumfries
E-UK-ST	Ayrshire	E-UK-EN	Durham
E-UK-ST	Banff	E-UK-ST	East Lothian
E-UK-EN	Bedfordshire	E-UK-EN	Ely, Isle of
E-UK-EN	Berkshire	E-UK-EN	Essex
E-UK-ST	Berwick	E-UK-NI	Fermanagh
E-UK-WL	Brecknockshire	E-UK-ST	Fifeshire
N-CN-BC	British Columbia	E-UK-WL	Flintshire
E-UK-EN	Buckinghamshire	E-UK-WL	Glamorganshire
E-UK-ST	Bute	E-UK-EN	Gloucestershire
E-UK-ST	Caithness	E-UK-EN	Hampshire
E-UK-EN	Cambridgeshire	E-UK-EN	Herefordshire
F-SA---	Cape Province	E-UK-EN	Hertfordshire
E-UK-WL	Cardiganshire	E-UK-EN	Huningdonshire
E-UK-WL	Carmarthenshire	E-UK-ST	Inverness
E-UK-WL	Caenarvonshire	E-UK-EN	Isle of Man
E-UK-EN	Channel Islands	E-UK-EN	Isle of Wight
E-UK-EN	Cheshire	E-UK-EN	Kent
E-UK-ST	Clackmannan	E-UK-ST	Kincardine
E-UK-EN	Cornwall	E-UK-ST	Kinross
E-UK-EN	Cumberland	E-UK-ST	Kirkudbrightshire

E-UK-ST	Lanark	N-CN-PI	Prince Edward Island
E-UK-EN	Lancashire	N-CN-QU	Quebec
E-UK-EN	Leicestershire	U-AT-QN	Queensland
E-UK-EN	Lincolnshire	E-UK-WL	Radnorshire
E-UK-NI	Londonderry	E-UK-ST	Renfrew
N-CN-MB	Manitoba	E-UK-ST	Ross and Cromarty
E-UK-WL	Merionethshire	E-UK-ST	Roxburgh
E-UK-EN	Middlesex	E-UK-EN	Rutlandshire
E-UK-ST	Midlothian	E-UK-EN	Salop
E-UK-EN	Monmouthshire	N-CN-SN	Saskatchewan
E-UK-ST	Moray	E-UK-ST	Selkirk
E-UK-ST	Nairn	E-UK-ST	Shetland
N-CN-NK	New Brunswick	E-UK-EN	Shropshire
U-AT-NE	New South Wales	E-UK-EN	Soke of Peterborough
N-CN-NF	Newfoundland	E-UK-EN	Somersetshire
E-UK-EN	Northamptonshire	U-AT-SA	South Australia
U-AT-NO	Northern Territory	E-UK-EN	Staffordshire
E-UK-EN	Northumberland	E-UK-ST	Stirling
N-CN-NT	Northwest Territories	E-UK-ST	Suffolk
E-UK-EN	Nottinghamshire	E-UK-EN	Surrey
N-CN-NS	Nova Scotia	E-UK-EN	Sussex
N-CN-ON	Ontario	E-UK-ST	Sutherland
E-UK-ST	Orkney	U-AT-TA	Tasmania
E-UK-EN	Oxfordshire	E-UK-NI	Tyrone
E-UK-ST	Peebles	U-AT-VI	Victoria
E-UK-ST	Pembrokeshire	E-UK-EN	Warwickshire
E-UK-ST	Perth	E-UK-ST	West Lothian

TABLE 4D, Continued — Provinces and British Counties

U-AT-WE	Western Australia
E-UK-EN	Westmorland
E-UK-ST	Wigtown
E-UK-EN	Wiltshire
E-UK-EN	Worcestershire
E-UK-EN	Yorkshire
E-UK-EN	Yorkshire, East Riding
E-UK-EN	Yorkshire, North Riding
E-UK-EN	Yorkshire, West Riding
N-CN-YK	Yukon
E-UK-ST	Zetland

TABLE 4E - COUNTRY NAMES

A-AF	Afghanistan	A-CY	Cyprus
E-AA	Albania	E-CS	Czechoslovak Republic
F-AE	Algeria	F-DM	Dahomey
F-AO	Angola	E-DK	Denmark
S-AG	Argentine Republic	NWDR	Dominican Republic
U-AT	Australia	A-PK	East Pakistan
E-AU	Austria	S-EC	Ecuador
F-CG	Belgian Congo	F-UA	Egypt
E-BE	Belgium	NCES	El Salvador
F-BY	Biafra	E-UK-EN	England
S-BO	Bolivia	F-ET	Ethiopia
F-BS	Botswana	E-FI	Finland
S-BL	Brazil	E-FR	France
NCBH	British Honduras	S-FG	French Guiana
E-BU	Bulgaria	F-GO	Gabon
A-BR	Burma	F-GM	Gambia
F-BD	Burundi	E-GX	Germany
A-CB	Cambodia	F-GH	Ghana
F-CM	Cameroon	E-UK	Great Britain
N-CN	Canada	E-GR	Greece
F-CX	Central African Republic	NCGT	Guatemala
A-CE	Ceylon	F-GV	Guinea
F-CD	Chad	S-GY	Guyana
S-CL	Chile	NWHT	Haiti
A-CC	China	NCHO	Honduras
S-CK	Columbia	A-HK	Hongkong
NCCR	Costa Rica	E-HU	Hungary
NWCU	Cuba	E-IC	Iceland

A-II	India	F-MR	Morocco
A-IO	Indonesia	F-MZ	Mozambique
A-IR	Iran	E-NE	Netherlands
A-IQ	Iraq	U-NZ	New Zealand
E-IE	Ireland	NCNQ	Nicaragua
A-IS	Israel	F-NG	Niger
E-IT	Italy	F-NR	Nigeria
F-IV	Ivory Coast	E-UK-NI	Northern Ireland
NWJM	Jamaica	E-NO	Norway
A-JA	Japan	A-PK	Pakistan
A-JO	Jordan	A-IS	Palestine
F-KE	Kenya	NCPN	Panama
A-KR	Korea	S-PY	Paraguay
A-LS	Laos	S-PE	Peru
A-LE	Lebanon	A-PH	Phillipine Islands
F-LO	Lesotho	E-PL	Poland
F-LB	Liberia	E-PO	Portugal
F-LY	Libya	F-RH	Rhodesia, Southern
E-LU	Luxemburg	E-RM	Rumania
F-MG	Malagasy Republic	E-UR	Russia
F-MW	Malawi	F-RW	Rwanda
A-MY	Malaysia	A-SU	Saudi Arabia
F-ML	Mali	E-UK-ST	Scotland
E-MM	Malta	F-SG	Senegal
F-MU	Mauritania	F-SL	Sierra Leone
N-MX	Mexico	A-SI	Singapore
A-MP	Mongolia	F-SO	Somalia

F-SA	South Africa		F-ZA	Zambia
F-SX	South-west Africa		F-TZ	Zanzibar
E-SP	Spain			
F-SJ	Sudan			
S-SR	Surinam			
F-SQ	Swaziland			
E-SW	Sweden			
E-SZ	Switzerland			
A-SY	Syria			
F-TZ	Tanganyika			
F-TZ	Tanzania			
A-TH	Thailand			
F-TG	Togo			
F-TI	Tunisia			
A-TU	Turkey			
F-UG	Uganda			
F-UA	United Arab Republic			
N-US	United States			
F-UV	Upper Volta			
S-UY	Uruguay			
E-VC	Vatican			
E-VC	Vatican City			
S-VE	Venezuela			
A-VT	Vietnam			
E-UK-WL	Wales			
A-PK	West Pakistan			
A-YE	Yemen			
E-YU	Yugoslavia			

TABLE 4CE - STATE, PROVINCE, AND COUNTRY ABBREVIATIONS

Code	Abbr.	Name	Code	Abbr.	Name
E-UK-ST	A'deen.	Aberdeen	E-UK-WL	Carn.	Caernarvonshire
N-US-AL	Ala.	Alabama	E-UK-EN	Ches.	Cheshire
N-CN-AB	Alta.	Alberta	E-UK-ST	Cla.	Clackmannan
E-UK-WL	Ang.	Anglesey	E-UK-ST	Clack.	Clackmannan
E-UK-NI	Ant.	Antrim	N-US-CO	Colo.	Colorado
E-UK-ST	Arg.	Argyll	N-US-CT	Conn.	Connecticut
N-US-AZ	Ariz.	Arizona	E-UK-EN	Corn.	Cornwall
N-US-AR	Ark.	Arkansas	E-UK-EN	Cumb.	Cumberland
E-UK-NI	Arm.	Antrim	N-US-DC	D.C.	District of Columbia
E-UK-ST	Ayr.	Ayrshire	N-US-DE	Del.	Delaware
N-CN-BC	B.C.	British Columbia	E-UK-WL	Den.	Denbighshire
E-UK-EN	Beds.	Bedfordshire	E-UK-WL	Denb.	Denbighshire
E-UK-EN	Berks.	Berkshire	E-UK-EN	Derb.	Derbyshire
E-UK-ST	Berw.	Berwick	E-UK-EN	Derbs.	Derbyshire
E-UK-WL	Breck.	Brecknockshire	E-UK-EN	Devon.	Devonshire
E-UK-EN	Bucks.	Buckinghamshire	E-UK-EN	Dors.	Dorsetshire
E-UK-EN	C.I.	Channel Islands*	E-UK-ST	Dumb.	Dumbarton
F-SA---	C.P.	Cape Province	E-UK-ST	Dumf.	Dumfries
E-UK-WL	Caern.	Caerarvonshire	E-UK-EN	Dur.	Durham
E-UK-ST	Caith.	Caithness	E-UK-EN	Eng.	England
N-US-CA	Cal.	California	E-UK-EN	E.R. Yorks	Yorkshire, East Riding
N-US-CA	Calif.	California	E-UK-NI	Ferm.	Fermanagh
E-UK-EN	Cambs.	Cambridgeshire	E-UK-ST	Fife.	Fifeshire
N-CN---	Can.	Canada	N-US-FL	Fla.	Florida
E-UK-WL	Card.	Cardiganshire	E-UK-WL	Flint.	Flintshire
E-UK-WL	Carm.	Carmarthenshire	E-UK-WL	Flints.	Flintshire

TABLE 4CE-STATE, PROVINCE, AND COUNTRY ABBREVIATIONS

N-US-GA	Ga.	Georgia	E-UK-EN	Leics.	Leicestershire
E-GX---	Ger.	Germany	E-UK-EN	Lincs.	Lincolnshire
E-UK-WL	Glam.	Glamorganshire	E-UK-NI	Lond.	Londonderry
E-UK-EN	Glos.	Gloucestershire	N-CN-MB	Man.	Manitoba
E-UK---	Gt. Brit.	Great Britain	N-US-MA	Mass.	Massachusetts
E-UK-EN	Hants.	Hampshire	N-US-MD	Md.	Maryland
E-UK-EN	Herefs.	Herefordshire	N-US-ME	Me.	Maine
E-UK-EN	Herts.	Hertfordshire	E-UK-WL	Merion.	Merionethshire
E-UK-EN	Hunts.	Huntingdonshire	N-US-MI	Mich.	Michigan
E-UK-EN	I.O.M.	Isle of Man*	E-UK-EN	Middx.	Middlesex
E-UK-EN	I.O.W.	Isle of Wight	E-UK-ST	MidL.	Midlothian
N-US-IL	Ill.	Illinois	N-US-MN	Minn.	Minnesota
N-US-IN	Ind.	Indiana	N-US-MS	Miss.	Mississippi
E-UK-ST	I'ness.	Inverness	E-UK-ST	M'loth	Midlothian
E-UK-ST	Inv.	Inverness	N-US-MO	Mo.	Missouri
E-IE---	Ire.	Ireland	E-UK-EN	Mon.	Monmouthshire
N-US-KS	Kan.	Kansas	N-US-MT	Mont.	Montana
E-UK-ST	Kin.	Kinross	E-UK-WL	Montg.	Montgomeryshire
E-UK-ST	Kinc.	Kincardine	N-CN-NK	N.B.	New Brunswick
E-UK-ST	Kirk.	Kirkcudbrightshire	N-US-NC	N.C.	North Carolina
E-UK-ST	Kirkcud.	Kirkcudbrightshire	N-US-ND	N.D.	North Dakota
N-US-KY	Ky.	Kentucky	N-US-NH	N.H.	New Hampshire
N-US-LA	La.	Louisiana	N-US-NJ	N.J.	New Jersey
E-UK-ST	Lanarks.	Lanarkshire	N-US-NM	N.M.	New Mexico
E-UK-EN	Lancs.	Lancashire	E-UK-EN	N.R. Yorks.	Yorkshire, North Riding
E-UK-EN	Leic.	Leicestershire			

Table 4CE, Continued - State, Province, and Country Abbreviations

N-CN-NS	N.S.	Nova Scotia	U-AT-QN	Qnsld.	Queensland
U-AT-NE	N.S.W.	New South Wales	N-US-RI	R.I.	Rhode Island
U-AT-NO	N.T.	Northern Territory	E-UR-RU	R.S.F.S.R.	Russian SFSR
N-CN-NS	N.W.T.	Northwest Territories	E-UK-WL	Rad.	Randorshire
N-US-NY	N.Y.	New York	E-UK-ST	Renf.	Renfrew
U-NZ---	N.Z.	New Zealand	E-UK-ST	Ross	Ross and Cromarty
N-US-NB	Neb.	Nebraska	E-UK-ST	Rox.	Roxburgh
N-US-NV	Nev.	Nevada	E-UK-EN	Rutland.	Rutlandshire
N-CN-NF	Nfld.	Newfoundland	U-AT-SA	S.A.	South Australia
E-UK-EN	Norhants.	Northamptonshire	N-US-SC	S.C.	South Carolina
E-UK-EN	Northants	Northamptonshire	N-US-SD	S.D.	South Dakota
E-UK-EN	Northld.	Northumberland	N-CN-SN	Sask.	Saskatchewan
E-UK-EN	Nthmb.	Northumberland	E-UK-ST	Scot.	Scotland
N-US-OK	Okla.	Oklahoma	E-UK-ST	Selk.	Selkirk
N-CN-ON	Ont.	Ontario	E-UK-EN	Shops.	Shropshire
N-US-OR	Or.	Oregon	E-UK-EN	Soms.	Somersetshire
N-US-OR	Ore.	Oregon	E-UK-EN	Staffs.	Staffordshire
E-UK-ST	Ork.	Orkney	E-UK-ST	Stir.	Stirling
E-UK-EN	Oxon.	Oxfordshire	E-UK-EN	Suss.	Sussex
N-CN-PI	P.E.I.	Prince Edward Island	E-UK-ST	Suth.	Sutherland
NWPR---	P.R.	Puerto Rico	N-US-HI	T.H.	Territory of Hawai
N-US-PA	Pa.	Pennsylvania	U-AT-TM	Tas.	Tasmania
E-UK-ST	Peeb.	Peebles	N-US-TN	Tenn.	Tennessee
E-UK-WL	Pemb.	Pembrokeshire	N-US-TX	Tex.	Texas
N-CN-QU	Que.	Quebec	E-UK-NI	Tyr.	Tyrone
			N-US---	U.S.	United States

E-UR---	U.S.S.R.	Soviet Union
NWVI---	V.I.	Virgin Islands
N-US-VA	Va.	Virginia
U-AT-VI	Vic.	Victoria
N-US-VT	Vt.	Vermont
N-US-WV	W. Va.	West Virginia
U-AT-WE	W.A.	Western Australia
E-UK-EN	W.R. Yorks.	Yorkshire, West Riding
N-US-WV	W. Va.	West Virginia
N-US-WV	W.Va.	West Virginia
E-UK-EN	War.	Warwickshire
E-UK-EN	Warks.	Warwickshire
N-US-WA	Wash.	Washington
E-UK-EN	West.	Westmorland
E-UV-EN	Westmld	Westmorland
E-UK-ST	Wig.	Wigtown
E-UK-EN	Wilts.	Wiltshire
N-US-WI	Wis.	Wisconsin
E-UK-EN	Worcs.	Worcestershire
N-US-WY	Wyo.	Wyoming
E-UK-EN	Yorks.	Yorkshire
N-CN-YK	Yuk.	Yukon.

TABLE 4F1 - OTHER PLACE NAMES - NO COMMA AND NO PARENTHESES

E-UR-GS	Abkhasia	NWBC	Barbuda
E-IT	Abruzzi and Molise	E-SP	Basque Provinces
A-TS	Abū Zaby	LNBM	Bermuda Islands
E-FR	Alsace	E-FR	Berry
POAS	American Samoa	E-UR-MV	Bessarabia
E-AN	Andorra	A-BT	Bhutan
E-FR	Angoumois	E-CS	Bohemia
E-GE	Anhalt	NWCR	Bonaire
E-FR	Anjou	A-BN	Borneo
NWAQ	Antigua	E-YU	Bosnia and Herzogovina
E-IT	Apulia	POSO	Bouganville Island
E-FR	Aquitane	E-FR	Bourbonnais
E-UR-AR	Armenia	I-BI	British Indian Ocean Territory
NWCR	Aruba	A-MY	British North Borneo
LSAI	Ascension Island	E-FR	Brittany
E-FR	Artois	E-GE	Brandenburg
E-FR	Aunis	E-GW	Bremen
E-FR	Auvergne	A-BX	Brunei
E-UR-AJ	Azerbaijan	E-GW	Brunswick
LNAZ	Azores Islands	E-AT	Burgenland
NWBF	Bahamas	E-FR	Burgundy
A-BA	Bahrein	E-IT	Calabria
E-GW	Baden	E-IT	Campania
E-GW	Baden-Württenberg	NCCZ	Canal Zone
PONN	Banks Islands	LNCA	Canary Islands
NWBB	Barbados	POGN	Canton and Enderby Islands

TABLE 4Fl (continued)

F-SA	Cape Province	E-DK	Faroe Islands
LNCV	Cape Verde Islands	POFJ	Fiji Islands
E-AT	Carinthia	E-FR	Flanders
POCI	Caroline Islands	E-FR	Foix
E-SP	Catalonia	A-CH	Formosa
NWCJ	Cayman Islands	E-FR	Franche-Comte
E-FR	Champagne	POFP	French Polynesia
I-CQ	Comoro Islands	E-NE	Friesland
POCW	Cook Islands	E-IT	Friuli-Venezia Giulia
E-FR	Corsica	POGG	Galapagos Islands
E-GR	Crete	E-UR-UN	Galicia
E-YU	Croatia	E-FR	Gascony
NWCO	Curacao	E-NE	Gelderland
E-YU	Daghestan	E-GI	Gibraltar
E-YU	Dalmatia	POGN	Gilbert Islands
E-FR	Dauphine	N-GL	Greenland
NWDQ	Dominica	E-GW	Grenzmark Posen-Westpreussen
E-NE	Drenthe	E-NE	Groningen
A-IO	East Indies	NWGP	Guadalupe Island
POEA	Easter Island	E-FR	Guyenne
POGN	Ellice Islands	A-CC-KN	Hainan Island
E-IT	Emilia	E-GW	Hamburg
POGN	Enderby Islands	I-HM	Heard Island
E-PL	Ermland	E-GW	Hesse
E-UR-ER	Estonia	E-GW	Hesse-Nassau
LSFK	Falkland Islands	NWHI	Hispaniola

TABLE 4F1 (continued)

E-GW	Hohenzollern	E-GW	Lippe
A-CC-SU	Hsin-chieng Wei-wu-êrh tzũ chih ch'ü	E-UR-LI	Lithuania
E-GR	Islands of the Agean	E-FR	Lombardy
E-FR	Ile de France	E-FR	Lorraine
E-YU	Istria	PONL	Loyalty Islands
E-NO	Jan Mayen Island	E-GE	Lubeck
A-IO	Java	E-IT	Lucania
A-IO	Kalimantan Barat	E-GE	Lusatia
E-UR-RU	Kerelia	A-PH	Luzon
E-UR-KZ	Kazakhstan	E-UR-UN	Lvov
POKI	Kermadec Islands	E-FR	Lyonnais
E-UR-KG	Kirghizistan	A-MH	Macao
A-CC-KC	Kuang-hsi Chuang tsu tzǔ chih ch'ü	E-GE	Macedonia
		LNMA	Madeira Islands
A-II	Laccadives	A-IO	Madura
E-FR	Languedoc	E-IT	Magna Grecia
E-IT	Latium	I-XC	Maldive Islands
E-UR-LV	Latvia	E-MM	Malta
NLWI	Leeward Islands	A-CC	Manchuria
A-IO	Lesser Sunda Islands	E-FR	Marche
E-LH	Liechtenstein	E-IT	Marches
E-IT	Liguria	POXD	Mariana Islands
E-BE	Limburg	POFP	Marquesas Islands
E-FR	Limousin	POXE	Marshall Islands
POLN	Line Islands	NWMQ	Martinique
		I-MF	Mauritius

I-HM	McDonald Island	POXH	Niue
E-GE	Mecklenburg	E-FR	Nivernais
POME	Melanesia	U-AT	Norfolk Island
POMI	Micronesia	E-FR	Normandy
POXF	Midway Islands	A-MY	North Borneo
A-PH	Mindanao	E-GW	North Rhine-Westphalia
E-UR-MV	Moldavia	A-OK	Okinwa Island
A-IO	Moluccas	E-GW	Oldenburg
E-MC	Monaco	A-MK	Oman
E-YU	Montenegro	F-SA	Orange Free State
MWMJ	Montserrat	E-FR	Orleanais
E-CS	Moravia	E-NE	Overijssel
A-MK	Muscat	A-PP	Papua
A-MK	Muscat and Oman	A-CC-KN	Paracel Islands
PONU	Nauru	E-GR	Peloponnesus
F-SA	Natal	E-FR	Perche
E-FR	Navarre	E-FR	Picardy
A-NP	Nepal	E-IT	Piedmont
NWNA	Netherlands Antilles	POPC	Pitcairn Island
A-IO	Netherlands East Indies	E-FR	Poitou
PONL	New Caledonia	R,T	Polar regions
N-USN	New England	POPS	Polynesia
A-NW	New Guinea	E-GX	Pomerania
PONN	New Hebrides	E-FR	Provence
A-CC-NN	Ninghsia Hui Autonomous Region	E-GX	Prussia

NWPR	Puerto Rico	E-YU	Slavonia
A-QA	Qatar	E-CS	Slovakia
I-RE	Réunion	E-YU	Slovenia
E-GW	Rhine Province	POFP	Society Islands
E-GW	Rhineland-Palitinate	I-XO	Socotra
E-FR	Rivera	POSN	Solomon Islands
E-FR	Roussillon	LSFK	South Orkney Islands
N-CN-NT	Rupert's Land	E-FR	Southern France
A-JA	Ryukyu Islands	F-SS	Spanish Sahara
E-GW	Saarland	E-GR	Sparta
A-MY	Sabah	E-NO	Spitsbergen
NWSB	Saint-Barthélemy	LSXJ	St. Helena
NWXK	Saint Lucia	NWXM	St. Vincent
E-FR	Saintonge	A-SI	Straits Settlements
A-PH	Samar	E-AT	Styria
POSH	Samoan Islands	A-IO	Sumatra
LSFK	Sandwich Land	E-NO	Svalbard
A-MY	Sarawak	E-GW	Swabia
E-IT	Sardinia	NWSV	Swan Islands
E-FR	Savoy	E-UR-TA	Tajikistan
E-GW	Schaumburg-Lippe	E-GE	Thuringia
E-GW	Schleswig-Holstein	A-CC-TI	Tibet
E-YU	Serbia	NWTR	Tobago
I-SE	Seychelles Islands	POTL	Tokelau Islands
E-IT	Sicily	POTP	Tonga Islands
A-SK	Sikkim	E-FR	Touraine

Table 4F1 (continued)

F-SA	Transvaal	POWK	Wake Island
E-RM	Transylvania	A-IO	West Irian
E-IT	Trieste	E-GW	Westphalia
NWTR	Trinidad	POWS	Western Samoa
NWTR	Trinidad and Tobago	E-UR-BW	White Russia
ISTD	Tristan da Cunha	NWWI	Windward Islands
A-TS	Trucial States	E-GW	Württemberg
POFP	Tuamoto Islands	E-NE	Zealand
E-UR-TK	Turkestan ASSR		
E-UR-TK	Turkmenistan		
NWTC	Turks and Caicos Islands		
E-IT	Tuscany		
E-AT	Tyrol		
E-UR-UN	Ukraine		
E-IT	Umbria		
E-NE	Utrecht		
E-UR-UZ	Uzbekistan		
E-FR	Valois		
E-IT	Veneto		
E-IT	Venezia Giulia		
E-IT	Venezia Tridentina		
NWVI	Virgin Islands of the United States		
E-YU	Voivodina		
E-AT	Vorarlberg		

TABLE 4F2 - OTHER PLACE NAMES - NO COMMA BUT WITH PARENTHESES

A-YS   Aden (Protectorate)

A-CC   China (People's Republic of China, 1949-)

F-CF   Congo (Brazzaville)

F-CG   Congo (Democratic Republic)

POWF   Futana (Island)

E-UR-GS   Georgia (Transcaucasia)

E-GE   Germany (Democratic Republic, 1949-)

E-GW   Germany (Federal Republic, 1949-)

F-EG   Guinea (Region)

E-GW   Hanover (Province)

N-US-HI   Hawaii (Ter.)

E-IE   Ireland (Eire)

POJI   Johnston Island (Atoll)

A-KN   Korea (Democratic People's Republic)

A-KO   Korea (Republic)

A-KU   Kuwait (State)

E-FR   Maine (Fr.)

F-ML   Mali (Republic)

A-CC-IM   Mongolia (Inner)

A-MP   Mongolia (Mongolian People's Republic)

E-NE   Netherlands (Kingdom, 1815-)

A-PP   New Guinea (Ter.)

A-PH   Panay (Island)

E-UR   Russia (1917. Provisional Govt.)

E-UR   Russia (1917- R.S.F.S.R.)

TABLE 4F2 - OTHER PLACE NAMES - NO COMMA BUT WITH PARENTHESES

E-UR   Russia (1923- U.S.S.R.)

E-SM   San Marino (Republic)

F-SF   Sao Thomé Príncipe (Province)

LSFK   South Georgia (Island)

A-VN   Vietnam (Democratic Republic, 1946-)

NWVB   Virgin Islands (Presidency)

TABLE 4F3 - OTHER PLACE NAMES - WITH COMMA BUT NO PARENTHESES

NWLA	Antilles, Lesser		E-GW	Palatinate, Upper
A-YS	Arabia, Southern		A-CH	Pescadores Islands, Formosa
E-AJ	Austria, Lower		F-RH	Rhodesia, Southern
E-AJ	Austria, Upper		F-EG	Rio Muni, Spanish Guinea
E-GW	Bavaria, Lower		E-UR	Russia, Northern
E-GW	Bavaria, Upper		E-UR	Russia, Southern
E-NE	Brabant, North		NWSD	Saba, Netherlands Antilles
N-CN-NT	Canada, Northern		E-GW	Saxony, Lower
A-CCS,			POSC	Santa Cruz Islands, Oceanica
A-CC-SU	China, Northwest		A-CC-SH	Shansi, China
I-XA	Christmas Island, Indian Ocean		A-CC-SP	Shantung, China
E-GX	Germany, Northern		A-CC-SS	Shensi, China
E-GR	Greece, Modern		NWEU	Sint Eustatius, Netherlands Antilles
N-GL	Greenland, South		F-FT	Somaliland, French
NWGD	Grenada, West Indies		NWXI	St. Christopher, Nevis and Anguilla
NWGS	Grenadines, West Indies			
F-PG	Guinea, Portuguese		NWST	St. Martin, Netherlands Antilles
E-NE	Holland, North			
E-NE	Holland, South		F-ML	Sudan, French
F-IF	Ifni, Morocco		A-IO	Sunda Islands, Lesser
A-IO	Irain Barat, Indonesia		A-PT	Timor, Portuguese
A-CC-KA	Kansu, China		E-IT	Trentino-Alto Adige, Italy
A-PH	Negros, Phillipines		POWF	Uea (Island), Oceanica
U-AT-NO	Northern Territory, Australia		E-UK-NI	Ulster, Ire.
			U-AT-VI	Victoria, Australia

TABLE 4F4 - OTHER PLACE NAMES - WITH COMMA AND WITH PARENTHESES

A-CC-AN	Ahnwei, China (Province)
A-BX	Brunei, Borneo (State)
A-CC-CH	Chekiang, China (Province)
A-CC-FU	Fukien, China (Province)
A-CC-HE	Heilungkiand, China (Province)
A-CC-HO	Honan, China (Province)
A-CC-HP	Hopei, China (Province)
A-CC-HU	Hunan, China (Province)
A-CC-HH	Hu-pei, China (Province)
A-CC-KI	Kiangsi, China (Province)
A-CC-KU	Kiangsu, China (Province
A-CC-KR	Kirin, China (Province)
A-CC-KN	Kwantung, China (Province)
A-CC-KW	Kweichow, China (Province)
A-CC-LP	Liaoning, China (Province)
E-GE	Prussia, East (Province)
A-CC-SZ	Szechwan, China (Province)
A-CC-TS	Tsinghai, China (Province)
A-CC-YU	Yünnan, China (Province)

TABLE 4F5 - AREA NAMES - NO COMMA AND NO PARENTHESES

* = 'comma' form exists

F	*Africa	AK	Caspian Sea
EA	Alps	AK	Caspian Sea region
EA	Alps region	U-URK	Caucasus
SA	Amazon River	NC	Central America
AA	Amur River	EC	Central Europe
SN	Andean area	B	Commonwealth of Nations
T	Antarctic regions	FG	Congo River
NW	Antilles	FG	Congo Valley
N-USA	Appalachian area	EO	Danube River
N-USA	Appalachian region	EO	Danube Valley
MA	Arab Countries	A	East
AR	Arabia	ME	Eurasia
AU	Arabian Sea	E	*Europe
R	Arctic Ocean	H	French Union
R	Arctic regions	NL	Great Lakes
A	*Asia	NP	Great Plains
L	Atlantic Ocean	AH	Himalaya Mountains
FA	Atlas Mountains	N-CNH	Hudson Bay
EO	Balkan Peninsula	A-CCY	Hwang-Ho River
EB	Baltic States	A-CCY	Hwang-Ho Valley
E-URL	Bashkiria	EI	Iberian Peninsula
EL	Benelux Countries	I	Indian Ocean
MB	Black Sea	I	Indian Ocean region
MB	Black Sea region	AI	Indochina
CC	Caribbean area	E-URV	Kirov region

TABLE 4F5 (continued)

* = 'comma' form exists

A-CCK	Kulun Mountain region	LN	North Atlantic Ocean
SP	La Plata River	N-USC	North Central States
CL	Latin America	PN	North Pacific Ocean
AW	Latin Orient	R	North Pole
AW	Levant	PO	Oceanica
AM	Malaya	N-USO	Ohio River
F-MG	Madagascar	N-USO	Ohio Valley
N-CNM	Maritime Provinces	E-CS	Oravia region
MM	Mediterranean region	P	Pacific Ocean
MM	Mediterranean Sea	N-USP	Pacific States
AG	Mekong River	AP	Persian Gulf
AG	Mekong Valley	R,T	Polar regions
CM	Middle America	N-CNP	Prairie Provinces
N-USL	Middle States	EP	Pyranees
N-USC	Middle West	EP	Pyranees region
N-USM	Mississippi River	MR	Red Sea
N-USM	Mississippi Valley	MR	Red Sea region
N-USS	Missouri River	ER	Rhine River
N-USS	Missouri Valley	ER	Rhine Valley
AW	Near East	FR	Rift Valley
N-USN	New England	NR	Rocky Mountain region
FI	Niger River	FD	Sahara
FI	Niger Valley	EV	Scandinavia
FL	Nile River	EV	Scania
FL	Nile Valley	E-URS	Siberia
N	North America	S	South America

LS   South Atlantic Ocean

AO   South China Sea

PS   South Pacific Ocean

T   South Pole

N-USU Southern States

E-URO Soviet Central Asia

E-URF Soviet Far East

CC   Spanish Main

E-URR Stavropol'skiy kray

FU   Suez Canal

AT   Thian Shan Mountains

E-URU Ural Mountain region

E-URP Volga River

E-URP Volga Valley

FV   Volta River

FV   Volta Valley

NW   West Indies

A-CCG   Yangtze River

A-CCG Yangtze Valley

E-URO Yakutia

FZ   Zambesi River

TABLE 4F6 - AREA NAMES - NO COMMA BUT WITH PARENTHESES

E-YU	Bačka (Region)
AE	East (Far East)
E-YU	Karst region (Dinaric Alps)
FN	Sudan (Region)

TABLE 4F7 - AREA NAMES - WITH COMMA BUT NO PARENTHESES

   * = 'no comma' form exists

FC   *Africa, Central   FU   Suez, Gulf of

FE   *Africa, East   E-UR-UN   Ukraine, Western

FQ   *Africa, French Equatorial

FH   *Africa, Italian East

FF   *Africa, North

F-SA   *Africa, South

FS   *Africa, Southern

F-SX   *Africa, Southwest

FB   *Africa, Sub-Saharan

FW   *Africa, West

AC   *Asia, Central

AS   *Asia, Southeastern

AB   Bengal, Bay of

E-URC   Central Black Soil Area, RSFSR

E-URL   Central Region, RSFSR

A-CCP   Chihli, Gulf of

ET   *Europe, East Central

EE   *Europe, Eastern

EN   *Europe, Northern

ES   *Europe, Southern

NM   Mexico, Gulf of

E-URN   Russia, Northwestern

AF   Siam, Gulf of

E-URE   Siberia, Eastern

E-URE   Siberia, Northeastern

E-URW   Siberia, Western

TABLE 4F8 - AREA NAMES - WITH COMMA AND WITH PARENTHESES

S-AG   Río Colorado, Argentine Republic (Río Negro)

S-UY   Río Negro, Uruguay (River)

TABLE 4G.   NONPOLITICAL GEOGRAPHIC KEYWORDS

archipelago

... area

bay

,Bay of

... coast

... Coast

Countries

... countries

... desert

... estuary

... glacier

Gulf of

... hemisphere

Island

islands

Islands

(Islands)

Lake

,Mount

mountain

Mountains

mountains

... peak

... peninsula

plateau

point

... provinces

... range

... region

... regions

... sea

Sound

... States

strait

straits

trail

... valley

TABLE 4H.   "COMPASS" TYPE QUALIFIERS

,Asiatic

,Canadian

,Central

,Eastern

(Far East)

,Lower

,Middle

,New

,Northern

,Old

,Pacific

,South

,Southeastern

,Southern

,Upper

,Western

TABLE 41. POSSESSING COUNTRIES.

Afghan A-AF	Danish E-DK	Maltese E-MM
African F	Dominican NWDR	Mexican N-MX
Albanian E-AA	Dutch E-NE	Nigerian F-NR
Algerian F-AE	Egyptian F-UA	Norwegian E-NO
American N-US	English E-UK-EN	Pakistan A-PK
Antarctic F	Estonian E-UR-ER	Persian A-IR
Arab MA	Ethiopian F-ET	Polish E-PI
Argentine S-AG	European E	Portugese E-PO
Armenian E-UR-AR	Finnish E-FI	Roman E-IT
Asian A	French E-FR	Rumanian E-RM
Australian U-AT	German E-GX	Russian E-UR
Austrian E-AU	Greek E-GR	Scandinavian EV
Bolivian S-BO	Indic A-II	Scottish E-UK-ST
Brazilian S-BL	Indochinese AI	South African F-SA
Bulgarian E-BU	Icelandic E-IC	Spanish E-SP
Burmese A-BR	Indonesian A-IO	Swedish E-SW
British B	Irish E-IE	Swiss E-SZ
Cambodian A-CB	Israeli A-IS	Syrian A-SY
Canadain N-CN	Italian E-IT	Thai A-TH
Central American NC	Iranian A-IR	Tibetan A-CC-TI
Ceylonese A-CE	Japanese A-JA	Turkish A-TU
Chinese A-CC	Korean A-KR	Vietnamese A-VT
Costa Rican NCCR	Lao A-LS	Welsh E-UK-WL
Cuban NWCU	Latvian E-UR-LV	Yugoslav E-YU
Cypriote A-CY	Lettish E-UR-LV	
Czech E-CS	Lithuanian E-UR-LI	

TABLE 4J. SUBJECT SUBDIVISIONS IMPLYING GEOGRAPHIC MAIN HEADING.

Antiq.	Navy
Antiquities	Pol. & govt.
Armed forces	Politics and government
Army	Population
Bound.	Soc. condit
Boundaries	Soc. life & cust.
Census	Social conditions
Comm.	Social life and customs
Commerce	Social policy
Disc. & explor.	Statistics, Vital
Discovery and exploration	Statistics, Medical
Descr.	
Description	
Descr. & trav.	
Description and travel	
Econ. condit.	
Economic conditions	
Economic policy	
Emig. & immig	
Emigration and immigration	
For. rel.	
Foreign population	
Foreign relations	
Geneal.	
Genealogy	
Indus.	
Manuf.	
Manufactures	

TABLE 4K.   PARENTHETICAL TERMS USED WITH CORPORATE NAMES ENTERED UNDERED PLACE.

(1917. Provisional Govt.)

(1917- R.S.F.S.R.)

(1923 - U.S.S.R.)

(Abbey)

(Amt)

(Archdiocese)

(Baptistery)

(Basilica)

(Church)

(... Circuit)

(City)

(Civil government of Burgos)

(Convent)

(... County)

(Colony)

(Democratic Republic...)

(Dept.)

(Diocese)

(Diocese...)

(District)

(Dominion)

(Duchy)

(East Berlin)

(Ecclesiastical Province)

(Ecumenical patriarchate)

(Fascist Republic...)

(Federal...)

(Government)

(Grafschaft)

(Jacobite patriarchate)

(Kingdom)

(Kray)

(Landkreis)

(Latin Kingdom,   )

(Orthodox patriarchate)

(Patriarchate)

(Patriarchate...)

(People's Republic...)

(Principality)
(Province)
(Region)

(Republic)

(Roman province)

(State)

(Ter.)

(Territory under...German occupation)

(Transcaucasia)

(Union)

(Union Ter.)

(United States)

(Viceroyalty)

(Voivodeship)

(West Berlin)

TABLE 4L.   NATIONAL BIBLIOGRAPHY SYMBOLS.

NOTE: British is assumed English, Canadian is assumed Ontario and Russian
        is assumed RSFSR.

AU Austria

Aus Australia

B Gt. Brit.

BB Brazil

BBM Brazil

Be Belgium

Bu Bulgaria

C Canada

CG Canada (Govt.)

CP Canada (Provincial)

Cz Czechoslovakia

CzS Czechoslovakia

D Denmark

F France

Fi Finland

GDNB East Germany

GDB West Germany

It Italy

Ja Japan

N Norway

Ne Netherlands

NeB Netherlands

NZ New Zealand

S Sweden

SANL South Africa

SANB South Africa

Sw Switzerland

USSR USSR

Yu Yugoslavia

TABLE 4M. EAST AFRICAN ACQUISITION CODES AND EQUIVALENT PUBLICATION CODE

An   Angola AO

Et   Ethiopia ET

Ke   Kenya KE

Ma   Mauritius MF

MR   Malagasy Republic MG

Mw   Malawi MW

Mz   Mozambique MZ

Sd   Sudan SJ

SR   Somalia SO

Sy   Seychelles SE

TZ   Tanzania TZ

UG   Uganda UG

Za   Zambia ZA

Zz   Zanzibar TZ

TABLE 5A. LEGAL RELATORS.

NOTE: These terms may occur with personal or corporate entries. They may
be plural (followed by "s") and they may also be followed by terms
such as "-appellee/s", "-appellant/s", and "in error".

contestant

defendant

intervener

intervenor

libellant

libellee

petitioner

plaintiff

respondent

TABLE 5B: LANGUAGE CODES FOR ALTERNATIVE CLASSIFICATION NUMBERS FOR FICTION
IN ENGLISH

PA3050-PA5395 GRC	PG5661-PG5698 WEN	PQ1600-PQ3999 FRE
PA5601-PA5665 GRE	PG7001-PG7405 POL	PQ4001-PQ5991 ITA
PA6000-PA6971 LAT	PG8701-PG8772 LIT	PQ6001-PQ8921 SPA
PA8001-PA8595 LAT	PG9000-PG9146 LAV	PQ9001-PQ9991 POR
PB1201-PB1449 IRI	PG9601-PG9648 ALB	PR1401-PR1799 ANG
PB1501-PB1709 GAE	PH300-PH405 FIN	PR1804-PR2165 ENM
PB2501-PB2621 COR	PH360-PH671 EST	PT1-PT1360 GER
PB2801-PB2931 BRE	PH3001-PH3445 HUN	PT1371-PT1374 GOH
PC800-PC872 RUM	PJ5001-PJ5060 HEB	PT1375-PT1695 GMH
PF1501-PF1558 FRI	PJ7501-PJ8518 ARA	PT701-PT4899 GER
PF3985-PF3986 GOH	PK2030-PK2098 HIN	PT5001-PT5980 DUT
PG705 CHU	PK2151-PK2200 URD	PT6000-PT6471 FLE
PG1000-PG1158 BUL	PL240-PL248 TUR	PT6500-PT6590 AFR
PG1400-PG1596 SER	PL700-PL889 JAP	PT7351-PT7550 ICE
PG1600-PG1696 CRO	PL950-PL988 KOR	PT7581-PT7599 FAR
PG1900-PG1998 SLV	PL2250-PL3207 CHI	PT7601-PT8260 DAN
PG2900-PG3560 RUS	PQ1-PQ1297 FRE	PT8301-PT9155 NOR
PG3900-PG3987 UKR	PQ1300-PQ1545 FRO	PT9201-PT9999 SWE
PG5000-PG5090 CZE	PQ1551-PQ1595 FRM	

TABLE 5C.   ILLUSTRATION TERMS AND CODES.

chart = d

charts = d

coat of arms = i

coats of arms = i

diagr. = a

diagrs. = a

diagrs = a

facsim. = h

facsimile = h

facsimiles = h

facsims = h

facsims. = h

forms = k

geneal. table = j

geneal. tables = j

group port. = c

group ports = c

map = b

maps = b

music = g

phonodisc = m

phonodiscs = m

photo. = a

photos = a

photos. = a

plan = e

plans = e

plate = f

plates = f

port. = c

ports = c

ports. = c

samples = l

table = a

tables = a

TABLE 5D. BIBLIOGRAPHY NOTE KEYWORDS

Bibliograph

Includes bibliography ...

References

Sources:

TABLE 5E. DISSERTATION NOTE KEYWORDS.

Akademisk avhandling

Disertasi

Diss.

Dissertation

Inaug. Diss.

Proefschrift

Promotionsarbeit

Rede

Tez

The author's thesis

The authors' thesis

The editor's thesis

These

Thesis

TABLE 5F. FESTSCHRIFT KEYWORDS

anniversary volume

Commemorating

essays for

essays presented to

essays ... ...presented to

festschrift

in honor of

in memory of

in tribute to

Liber amicorum ...

Memorial addresses and eulogies

memorial session

Memorial services held in

... memorial volume

on the occasion of

to honor

Tributes to

Table 5G. LANGUAGE NAMES AND CODES

Language	Code	Language	Code	Language	Code
Acholi	ACH	Aymara	AYM	Cambodian	CAM
Africans	AFR	Azerbaijani	AZE	Canarese	KAN
Afro-Asiatic (Other)	AFA	Azeri	AZE	Carib	CAR
Akkadian	AKK	Baluchi	BAL	Castillian	SPA
Albanian	ALB	Baltic (Other)	BAT	Catalan	CAT
Aleut	ALE	Bamana	BAM	Caucasian	CAU
Algonquin	ALG	Bambara	BAM	Celtic	CEL
Amarinya	AMH	Bantu	NIC	Central American Indian (Other)	CAI
Amharic	AMH	Bashkir	BAK	Chaldean	ARC
Ancient Greek	GRC	Basque	BAQ	Chechen	CHE
Ancient Hebrew	HEB	Beja	BEJ	Cherokee	CHR
Anglo-Saxon	ANG	Belorussian	BEL	Cheyenne	CHY
Anzanite	ELX	Bemba	BEM	Chibcha	CHB
Apache	APA	Bengali	BEN	Chinese	CHI
Arabic	ARA	Berber Group	BER	Chinook	CHN
Aramaic	ARC	Bihari	BIH	Choctaw	CHO
Arapahoe	ARP	Biluchi	BAL	Church Slavic	CHU
Araucanian	ARN	Bishari	BEJ	Chuvash	CHV
Arawak	ARW	Blackfoot	BLA	Classical Greek	GRC
Armenian	ARM	Bohemian	CZE	Coptic	COP
Armoric	BRE	Breton	BRE	Cornish	COR
Assamese	ASM	Bulgarian	BUL	Cree	CRE
Avar	AVA	Burmese	BUR	Creoles and Pidgins	CRP
Avaric	AVA	Bushman	SSA	Croatian	CRO
Avesta	AVE	Caddo	CAD	Cushitic (Other)	CUS

Czech CZE	Fon FON	Hindustani (Arabic URD
Dakota DAK	French FRE	Hindustani (Nagari) HIN
Danish DAN	French (Middle) FRM	Hottentot SSA
Dano-Norwegian NOR	French (Old) FRO	Hungarian HUN
Delaware DEL		
Denca DIN	Frisian FRI	Hupa HUP
Dinka DIN	Ga GAA	Iai MAP
Dravidian (Other) DRA	Gaelic GAE	Icelandic ICE
Duala DUA	Gaelic (Irish) IRI	Ilocano ILO
Dutch DUT	Gaelic (Scots) GAE	Indic (Other) INC
Efik EFI	Galla GAL	Indo-European (Other) INE
Egyptian EGY	Ge'ez ETH	Indonesian IND
Elamite ELX	Georgian GEO	Interlingua INT
English ENG	German GER	Iranian (Other) IRA
English (Middle) ENM	German (Middle High) GMH	Irish IRI
English (Old) ANG	German (Old High) GOH	Iroquois IRO
Erse GAE	Germanic (Other) GEM	Isi-Xosa XHO
Eskimoan ESK	Gondi GON	Italian ITA
Eskimo ESK	Gothic GOT	Japanese JAP
Esperanto ESP	Greek (Classical) GRC	Javanese JAV
Estonian EST	Greek (Modern) GRE	Judaeo-German YID
Ethiopic ETH	Guarani GUA	Judaeo-Spanish LAD
Ewe EWE	Guerze KPE	Kachin KAC
Fang FAN	Gujarati GUJ	Kafir XHO
Faroese FAR	Hausa HAU	Kamba KAM
Farsi PER	Hawaiian HAW	Kanarese KAN
Finnish FIN	Hebrew HEB	Kannada KAN
Finno-Ugrian (Other) FIU	Herero HER	Kanuri KAU
	Hindi HIN	Karakalpak KAA
Flemish FLE		

Karen KAR	Luba LUB	Mongol MON
Kashmiri KAS	Luganda LUG	Mongolian MON
Kazakh KAZ	Luiseño LUI	More MOS
Kechua QUE	Macedonian MAC	Mossi MOS
Kewa PAA	Madagascan MLA	Multilingual MUL
Khmer CAM	Malagasy MLA	Muskogee MUS
Kikuyu KIK	Malay MAY	Nandi SSA
KiMbundu NIC	Malayalam MAL	Navaho NAV
Kinyarwanda KIN	Malayo-Polynesian (Other) MAP	Nepali NEP
Kirghiz KIR	Malayo-Polynesian, Ancient MAX	Newari NEW
Kongo KON	Mandingo MAN	Nguna MAP
Korean KOR	Manobo MNO	Niger-Congo (Other) NIC
Kpelle KPE	Maori MAO	North American Indian (Other) NAI
Kru KRO	Marathi MAR	Norwegian NOR
Kurdish KUR	Masai MAS	Nubian NUB
Kurukh KRU	Mashona SHO	Nyamwezi NYM
Ladino LAD	Mayan MYN	Nyanja NYA
Lahnda LAH	Mbundu NIC	Nyoro NYO
Lamba LAM	Mende MEN	Ojibwa OJI
Landsmaal NOR	Middle English ENM	Old Church Slavonic CHU
Languedoc PRO	Middle French FRM	Old English ANG
Laotian LAO	Middle High German GMH	Old French FRO
Lapp LAP	Middle Persian PAL	Old High German GOH
Latin LAT	Miscellaneous MIS	Old Persian PEO
Latvian LAV	Modern Hebrew HEB	Oriya ORI
Lithuanian LIT	Moldavian MOL	Osage OSA
Lolo LOL	Mole MOS	Osmanli TUR
Lowland Scots ENM	Mongo LOL	Ossetic OSS

Otomi OTO	Rundi RUN	Sorbic WEN
Pahari PAH	Russina RUS	South American Indian (Other) SAI
Pahlavi PAL	Russian (Old) CHU	Spanish SPA
Pali PLI	Samaritan SAM	Sub-Saharan African (Other) SSA
Panjabi PAN	Sandawe SAD	Sudanic NIC
Panjabi (Western) LAH	Sango SAG	Sukuma SUK
Papuan-Australian (Other) PAA	Sanskrit SAN	Sumerian SUX
Pashto PUS	Scots Gaelic GAE	Susu SUS
Pennsylvania German GER	Selkup SEL	Swahili SWA
Persian (Middle) PAL	Semitic (Other) SEM	Swedish SWE
Persian (Modern) PER	Sephardic LAD	Syriac SYR
Persian (Old) PEO	Serbian SER	Tagalog TAG
Polish POL	Serbo-Croatian (Cyrillic) SER	Tai THA
Polyglot MUL	Serbo-Croatian (Roman) CRO	Tajik TAJ
Portuguese POR	Serer SRR	Tamil TAM
Provencal PRO	Shan SHN	Tatar TAR
Punjabi PAN	Shona SHO	Tchetchen CHE
Pushto PUS	Siamese THA	Telugu TEL
Quechua QUE	Sidamo SID	Temne TEM
Rajasthani RAJ	Sindhi SND	Tereno TER
Rhaeto-Romance ROH	Singhalese SNH	Thai THA
Riksmaal NOR	Sino-Tibetan (Other) SIT	Tibetan TIB
Romance (Other) ROA	Slavic (Other) SLA	Tigre TIG
Romansh ROH	Slovak SLO	Tigrinya TIR
Romany ROM	Slovene SLV	Tsimshian TSI
Rumanian RUM	Somali SOM	Tswana TSW
Rumansh ROH	Songhai SON	Turkish TUR

Table 5G. (continued)

Turkmen   TUK

Turko-Tataric (Other)   TUT

Twi   TWI

Uigur   UIG

Ukrainian   UKR

Umbundu   UMB

Urdu   URD

Uzbek   UZB

Vietnamese   VIE

Vote   VOT

Votian   VOT

Votic   VOT

Votish   VOT

Walamo   WAL

Washo   WAS

Welsh   WEL

Wendic   WEN

Wendish   WEN

Wolof   WOL

Xhosa   XHO

Xosa   XHO

Yao   YAO

Yiddish   YID

Yoruba   YOR

Zapotec   ZAP

Zenaga   ZEN

Zulu   ZUL

Zuni   ZUN

TABLE 5H. UNIFORM TITLE KEYWORDS.

Aboth	Concordat of	Liber ...
... agreement	Convention on...	Libro de ...
Aladdin	... Creed.	Little red hen.
Ali Baba.	... cycle.	Little Red Ridding Hood.
American heritage	Dead Sea scrolls.	...Livre
Ancren riwle	... Declaration of	Lord's prayer
Anglo-Saxon chronicle	digest	Mabinogion.
Anthologae	Domesday book	... magazine
Anthologia Graeca. ...	Edda ...	Magna carta
Arabian nights	Everyman.	Maldon (Anglo ...)
...,Author of.	Gawain.	... manuscript
Beauty and the beast.	Gawain ...	Manuscript ...
Beowulf	Gesta Romanorum	Man'yoshu
Better homes...	Gingerbread boy.	Martyrdom ...
Bible	Grail.	Mayflower compact, 1620.
Book of	Horizon	Monde ...
Book of Mormon	Hop o' my thumb.	monthly
... (Chanson de geste)	I ching	Mother Goose
Chanson de Roland.	Imitatio Christi	Mother Hubbard.
Chicken Little.	Jack and the bean-stalk.	... (Motion picture)
Chronicle	Jack and the beanstalk.	Narrationes (Anglo-Norman law text)
Cinderella.	Jack Sprat.	... (Newspaper)
Cock Robin.	Jack the Giant-killer.	Nibelungenlied
Code of	... journal	Orbis ...
...codex	Journal	... pact
Codex...	King ...	Pagany
Commandments,	Koran	

Panegyrici Latini

Playboy

... plays.

... (... poem)

... (Poem)

Protocol

Punch ...

Puss in boots

... (Radio program)

... review

... reviews

Reynard the Fox.

Rhodian sea-law

Robin Hood.

... (Romance)

Rumpelstiltskin.

... saga.

Seven sages

Seven sleepers

Sinbad, the sailor.

Sir ...

Sleeping beauty.

Snow White ...

Sunset.

Talmud.

...(Television program)

Third programme.

Three little pigs.

Three little kittens.

... times

Tom thumb.

Treaty ...

... ,Treaty of

... treaty

... tribune

Tristan.

Vedas

Whittington and his cat.

TABLE 5I. NON-NUMERIC CHRONOLOGICAL SUBJECT SUBDIVISIONS.

NOTE: Those in the second alphabetic sequence are geologic.

Aboriginal and early period	Algonkian	Oligocene
Ancient	Archaean	Ordovician
Civil War	Cambrian	Paleocene
Colonial period	Carboniferous	Paleozoic
Early	Cenozoic	Pennsylvanian
Medieval	Cretaceous	Permian
Messenian Wars	Devonian	Pleistocene
Middle	Eocene	Pliocene
Modern	Huronian	Pre-Cambrian
Modern period	Jurassic	Quaternary
Old	Laurentian	Recent
Post-exilic	Mesozoic	Rhaetic
Primitive	Miocene	Silurian
Restoration	Mississippian	Tertiary
Revolution	Neocene	Triassic
Revolutionary period		
Talmudic period		
To entrance into Canaan